Kicked Out

Kicked Out

Editor: Sassafras Lowrey
General Editor: Jennifer Clare Burke

Homofactus PRESS

Published in 2010 by Homofactus Press L.L.C.

1271 Shirley

Ypsilanti, Michigan, 48198, U.S.A.

homofactuspress.com

Printed in the United States of America

ISBN: 978-0-9785973-6-8

1. Lesbian, Gay, Bisexual, Trangender Youth. 2. Homelessness.

Cover Design © 2010 Sassafras Lowrey and Jay Sennett

Cover Photo © 2010 Sassafras Lowrey

Book Design © 2010 Jay Sennett and Gwyn Hulswit

Hire them, please.

To the runaways, the throwaways and any other queer kids who aren't quite sure where they are sleeping tonight.

To youth reading this book:

Maybe you picked up this book because you've just been kicked out. Maybe you've been on the streets for a while. Maybe you're standing in a library right now, or a bookstore, or maybe a counselor handed it to you. Maybe you are bitter and cynical, and reading a book is the last thing you want to do.

I won't lie to you: this book won't give you answers, but maybe it will give you hope.

There are lots of people whom I hope will read this book: parents, educators, counselors and more. But the most important readers this book will ever have are you. This book is more for you than anyone else.

I want you to know that this is not an annoying self-help book, and it isn't going to preach at you. No one is going to tell you what you should or shouldn't do, or tell you how you are coping is wrong.

Most of all, I'm not going to tell you that everything is going to be okay.

I am going to tell you that you are not alone.

Table of Contents

---

* Crisis story.

---

* Crisis story.

----

* Crisis story.

Publisher's Note

Jay Sennett and Gwyn Hulswit

Kicked Out is an amazing collaborative work that could have only been realized with the passion, hard work and commitment of the authors and editors who were involved in its creation. It is a book of utmost importance and relevance. As Sassafras Lowrey shared with us, "This book is for the hundreds and thousands of youth who are homeless right now and sleeping right outside your and my doors. This book is for every single queer youth who kills themselves because they are terrified that their parents are going to kick them out. This is for every trans youth being told they have to live in a shelter based on their assigned sex at birth, and this is for every single rural queer teenager who doesn't believe there are even other gay people in the world. [The idea of] *Kicked Out* was always more than a book; it is a social movement."

We believe that *Kicked Out* is part of a movement—a movement based on the telling of stories, of shedding light on truths. We commonly use diction and grammar to tell these stories. As publishers, there is always a fine line between authenticity and grammar. To learn and properly execute the fundamentals of American English grammar requires access to a consistently stable home life, the foundation of education in America. Without that stability, learning can become an arduous task of increasing complexity that results in no high school diploma.

Many Lesbian, Gay, Bisexual, Transgender and Questioning (LGBTQ) youth kicked out of their homes find themselves moving from school to school and shuttled back and forth from foster care to shelters to foster care. They leave midway through any grade year and can never quite catch up. The process whereby educators inculcate subject, object, verb and noun gets preempted as more important priorities take over like survival.

How then are these youth expected to tell their coming out stories? If we are honest, we must admit to possessing a kind of grammatical arrogance whereby what someone says—no matter how truthful or compelling—can be dismissed because of faulty diction and grammar.

As publishers, we believe we are obligated to renounce this arrogance and to share with you in *Kicked Out* crisis stories, stories written by youth living in LGBTQ–friendly shelters. We have reprinted these stories with little editing. These stories are denoted by an asterisk next to the title.

A work of this scope could not be completed without the efforts of several talented individuals. We would like to thank Sassafras Lowrey for conceiving and producing such an important anthology, Sarah Kennedy for initial copy editing work, and Jennifer Clare Burke for making it all come together.

Introduction

Sassafras Lowrey

The streets steal stories. Crush the bodies of boys and girls with molars of jagged concrete.

I tried to remember who we wanted to be, where we came from before our names shriveled under the labels of "at risk," "street involved," "runaways," "throwaways" and "trash." We were swallowed by systems incapable of digesting us.

I collected the stories of my friends, repeating their histories like a chant when they moved on or disappeared. I wanted to pin down their lives, wanted their dreams to be remembered: Mark, who climbed out his bedroom window at fourteen; TJ, whipped with a belt after being found with her fist inside her new stepsister before they ran away together; Princess' haunting, bloodshot eyes and wide smile; Ghost's blond-haired, blue-eyed toddler; Krystal's kittens on leashes and dumpster bagels; Sam, who drove all night juiced up on truck-stop coffee the day she escaped her parents; and the four of us crammed into one studio apartment with two cats, a dog, two ferrets and our breath fogging the January windows. These are only a fraction of the kids I considered family. No matter how hard I tried, I never could collect the stories fast enough. The details shifted away like Portland fog.

The stories of the families found and made were the inspiration for what has become *Kicked Out*. When I was kicked out for the final time at seventeen, the first thing I did—after finding somewhere to sleep for a few days—was go to the library. I scanned each spine and in desperation began pulling books off the shelves, running fingers over tables of contents and skimming introductions. This was the first time a library had failed me. I needed a book about how to live through this more than I needed to know I had somewhere to stay, to know I had a way to get to school or to know what I would have for dinner. I needed a book to prove to me that survival was possible. The only books about queer youth I found didn't talk about police reports, restraining orders or backpacks full of clothes. That day, sitting in a back corner of the public library in Gladstone, Oregon, I pledged that if I survived, I would do everything in my power to make sure that never again would a queer kid feel alone after losing family.

Kicked Out is the book that has dominated my dreams for the past seven years. The book you hold is so much more than anything I could have imagined in that dusty library. There has been nothing typical about the process of creating this book. The authors whom you are about to meet are more family than contributing authors. To all of us, this anthology is so much more than paper and bindings. *Kicked Out* is our commitment to making our community safer for homeless LGBTQ (Lesbian, Gay, Bisexual, Transgender, Queer) youth, and our promise to future generations of queer kids that survival is possible. It is also about combatting the shame so many of us have felt when we have "come out, kicked out" in our communities, queer and otherwise.

Contributors range in age from youth living on the streets to individuals who have been out for decades. *Kicked Out* captures the diversity of homelessness and recognizes that it takes many forms from homeless shelters and couch-surfing to forced institutionalization. Forty percent of homeless youth in the United States identify as LGBTQ (please see Nick Ray's essay on page 180). It happens in every community. Queer teen homelessness occurs across lines of race, class, religion, ability, ethnicity, nationality and geographical region. *Kicked Out's* contributors represent the diversity of this epidemic. In addition to the words of current and former homeless LGBTQ youth, *Kicked Out* includes the expertise of leading local, regional and national organizations whose services and missions are as diverse as the youth themselves.

The two years while *Kicked Out* has been in production have seen changes in the LGBTQ rights movement, yet overall the experience of LGBTQ youth hasn't changed much. I have received emails from current and former youth who thought that they were alone—youth who didn't live in New York City or San Francisco and who hadn't been able to make communities with other youth. They emailed and asked me advice about where to go because they thought their parents might kick them out that night, and they didn't live near any shelters. I have received the desperate phone calls from the staff of LGBTQ youth shelters that lost their funding and were faced with the devastating reality of telling youth they must sleep on the streets because there were no beds for them. I've lost sleep when I knew youth whose stories in these pages were forced back to the streets after funding closed the doors of the shelter they called home.

Just days before the call for submissions for *Kicked Out* closed, I heard of the horrific murder of Lawrence King in California. Lawrence was a queer middle-school student who was gunned down in his classroom in February 2008. Beyond the gruesome details of his passing, the thing that struck me the most was the one thing that everyone seemed to overlook: Lawrence spent the last few months of his all-too-short life living in a foster home for abused and neglected children. As I read that article and the dozens that have come after, I prayed I would see people making the connection between this senseless, tragic murder and the epidemic of queer youth homelessness. However, the media, and even the adult LGBTQ community, remained shockingly silent on this aspect of his life.

"We must never let community leaders forget the work that needs to be done for those who are still living," I demanded of the crowd at the Day of Silence rally in Lawrence's honor in NYC. Community leaders must be held accountable for the way they interface with LGBTQ youth issues. It is not enough to have a Gay–Straight Alliance (GSA) in every high school (though that's a good start). We must also do the dirty work, the heartbreaking work: we must listen to what youth are telling us. We can no longer pretend we cannot hear the tears of the youth who have lost their friends, families and homes because of whom they love or how they define their gender.

Kicked Out is my gift to a community who saved me. The dream of this book kept me company on long nights struggling for sleep on strange couches, but *Kicked Out* is more than that. It has truly become a movement of consciousness-raising and action. It is a promise to the community that we will no longer be silenced or quiet about our experiences. It is a demand that community leaders take this epidemic seriously. It is a challenge to all readers to question their perspective of what homelessness looks like and who homeless youth are.

Building a Home: A Mother's Call to Action

Judy Shepard

Nine years ago, my son, Matthew, was left to die after being brutally beaten simply for being gay. Not a day goes by that I don't think about Matt—his spirit, his passion for people, his smile and his wonderful hugs. He was my friend. He was someone who saw the beauty of difference and the best in all people. My husband, Dennis, our son, Logan, and I miss and love him deeply but know that his legacy will continue.

Since Matt's death and the creation of the Matthew Shepard Foundation, I have been traveling, speaking to and meeting young people across the country. Many of these young people—gay and straight—have reached out to me to share their stories about the pain and hurt of being teased, harassed and mistreated by their peers, and sometimes, even their own family members for being who they are. It is critical for them to be reminded that they are valued and that they matter. It is even more important for these young people to be able to live and grow up in communities feeling welcomed, accepted and safe everyday.

Lesbian, gay, bisexual, transgender, queer and questioning (LGBTQQ) youth are being forced to the streets at alarming rates. It is estimated that between twenty and forty percent of all homeless youth identify as LGBTQQ. In some urban areas, the estimates are even higher. One study estimated that half of homeless youth in central Manhattan are lesbian or gay[1], and another estimated that forty percent of homeless youth in Seattle are lesbian or gay.[2] Regardless of the specific number, it is unacceptable for one young person to be forced to the streets for any reason. How can any parents hurt or denigrate their children for any reason—let alone for being who they are? My son was taken from me

1. Please see Nick Ray's essay, "Lesbian, Gay, Bisexual and Transgender Youth: An Epidemic of Homelessness," on page 180 in this book.
2. Seattle Commission on Children and Youth. (1986). *Survey of Street Youth*. Seattle, WA: Orion Center.

because two men learned to hate—I certainly cannot imagine losing him by choice. Our children need and deserve better from us.

At the same time, safe and inclusive direct service providers and homeless shelters are continually strapped for resources, funds and volunteers. Many youth–serving professionals—from New York and Los Angeles to Iowa and Michigan—are helping our young people survive, helping them get off the streets and providing them with a bed, a warm meal, a friendly face and a safe place to belong. They are doing this with very little support from our government—and very little from our own LGBT community. I am not surprised that our current President and his administration (the George W. Bush Administration at the time of this writing) would turn a blind eye to this problem. But I am disappointed that our own LGBT community hasn't stepped up to address this problem. How can we let this neglect continue?

Our community has a responsibility to take action—immediately. I call on all of us to act today. We must support our LGBTQQ youth. We must talk to our friends and family about the reality facing these young people. We must support these organizations and direct service providers with our volunteer time and financial resources. But most importantly, as mothers and fathers, we need to hug our kids and tell them that they are accepted and loved for who they are—every single day.

.

Dumpster Diving, Gay Skinheads, Boredom and Violence: Pestilential Adventures on the Streets of California

Tenzin

The events of a human lifetime that become burned in the psyche and the soul are often a dichotomous mixture of the horrific and the transcendent, the ugly and the sublime, or the strange and the mortifying. My recollections of my time on the streets are among the most vivid, yet disjointed of all the memories ingrained in my neural pathways.

I remember the way the days seemed to run together in a continuum of boredom and hunger, interspersed with harassment and attacks. The friends and enemies of this time seem to take on superhuman epic proportions in retrospect. Although I would never wish to repeat these experiences, I find myself recollecting my time on the streets with a sort of perverse nostalgia. I have never encountered people I understood as well or felt as accepted by as those friends of my youth. I have rarely felt more alive than I did when fighting skinheads, drinking and laughing with friends singing Henry Rollins, Bauhaus or Smiths songs under bridges and in cemeteries.

The dynamics of the relationships among marginalized queer homeless kids were radically different from those of the dominant culture. The bonding was more intense since we shared a similar history of rejection, betrayal and abuse. We literally depended upon each other for survival. We had been cast away as freaks or had fled from dangerous homes only to emerge into an environment where the hostility and danger were merely less personal than at home. The other kids I met on the streets quickly became my family, since knowing someone for a week on the streets can seem like years. We lacked the luxury of an elaborate social façade to hide behind because we were with our chosen family twenty–four hours a day. The intimacy and camaraderie created by our shared hardships and similar life experiences would be difficult to describe to someone who had never lived on the streets. I remember my friends as if they were war buddies. While "normal" kids played with Barbies, we shared accounts of being threatened with murder and botched suicide attempts.

We expressed pain through self–mutilation and suicidal ideation. Some kids cut themselves. One boy tried to overdose on Flintstone vitamins when he was nine, and a girl in juvenile hall drank Ajax when she was supposed to be cleaning the bathrooms. I lay down on the train tracks and imagined my skull being crushed by the train, cut myself and fantasized about blowing my brains out.

We rejected identification with our families of origin by renaming ourselves. The names we chose often echoed the message we learned from our parents—that we were worthless and damaged, that we were things. By naming ourselves after inanimate objects, freaks and monsters, we transmuted our defects and shortcomings into badges of honor that proudly proclaimed our societal and familial unacceptability. We were kids named Trash, Fish, Psycho, Chainsaw, Smelly Tom, Scummy Sean, Spider, Wolf and Lucifer. We donned elaborate disguises designed to repel and intimidate like vibrantly spiky, poisonous caterpillars.

Negotiating the pragmatic and superfluous aspects of life on the streets required creativity and vigilance. Finding food, getting a place to sleep, locating a shower and dyeing our hair unnatural hues were daily challenges/annoyances. The more vital task was to navigate the myriad potential dangers to one's physical and psychological safety posed by the adults who preyed upon discarded adolescents. Other street kids could also be a danger when they "taxed" you for necessary articles of clothing, such as shoes and jackets that were not easily replaced; they were less scary than the adults. Kids were recruited by religious cults, pimps, gangs and drug dealers. Child Protective Services and the police could put us in group homes, foster homes or juvenile hall since it was illegal to be "incorrigible" under the Reagan administration. Suffice it to say that the sanctuary afforded by the foster care system was lacking as evidenced by the elevated rates of sexual and physical abuse and murder of children in state care. Homeless kids were beaten, raped and murdered. I am still haunted by the vicarious attacks and exploitation perpetuated against those with whom I grew up.

Street kids and foster children were considered fair game for sexual predators since we were already perceived as damaged and worthless. Our worthlessness was undoubtedly compounded by being queer/gender–variant. A man combed the Tenderloin district for young runaway boys and street hustlers and would offer them shelter and opportunities for gainful employment if they would fuck him in exchange. He fancied himself as quite the philanthropist. When I stayed in this man's house with a close friend with AIDS, I remember thinking that the place was like a perverse inversion of the Peter Pan story where Wendy was an unscrupulous, self–aggrandizing pedophile, and the lost boys were desperate queer kids. Accepting shelter indoors was often more perilous than sleeping outside, although this was not always the case. Lancy was raped, murdered and discarded under a freeway overpass at fifteen. Daniel was violently sodomized by an AIDS assassin at the age of fourteen in an alley in San Francisco's Tenderloin district and acquired AIDS from the attack. Many others were assaulted. I learned quickly that the last thing one wants to be while homeless is alone.

I was so terrified on my first night sleeping alone outside in Santa Rosa that I put my purple sleeping bag in front of the mall on Fourth Street so that I would be near people in case trouble arose; I thought that it was ironic that this sleeping bag had once accompanied me on more wholesome childhood adventures such as spending the night at grandparents' houses and voluntary camping. Over the next two days, I met other kids, including a boy named Casey, who became my best friend. Casey was gay, and I am an asexual transman. We shared a common history of abuse and betrayal and had both been homeless at other times and places. Both our mothers chose to remain with our abusers while we lived on the streets and in foster care. We lived together on rooftops, in an abandoned fire–damaged house with a charred mattress and a phone melted to the table, in the heater vents of the public library, in a storage shed, on sidewalks, in graveyards and in the shrubbery in front of an ice–skating rink. This lifestyle was dangerous to begin with, but it became infinitely more so after we made enemies of the local neo–Nazi constituent.

Casey and I were part of a gang of mostly queer young males called the Fourth Street Mutants. Deaf Dan and Psych Ike were reformed skinheads and punks; John was clean cut with an innocent, angelic face that enabled him to shoplift anything without arousing suspicion; Scummy Sean was an older punk; and Benjamin was very young and new to the streets. Although we initially eschewed the use of violence, pacifism is sometimes a luxury that only those who don't mind being hacked up and thrown into dumpsters can afford. Casey and I were closest to Deaf Dan, who lived like an exotic, hideous animal in a decrepit shack in someone's yard with a burnt, slashed and mutilated American flag on the wall. We would watch in horror and amusement as he ravenously devoured anchovies, Dinty Moore chili and clam chowder cold and straight from the can. Deaf Dan was like a big brother to us, and we loved him. Allegiances can shift quickly on the streets depending on fluctuating power dynamics and resources, and we felt shocked and betrayed when Deaf Dan and Benjamin defected to the neo–Nazi skinhead gang.

The neo–Nazis ruthlessly recruited angry, young, disenfranchised boys and men into their ranks and provided them with food, intoxicants, safety in numbers and the entertaining opportunity to rape, beat and "tax" people for their shoes and clothing. Casey and I dealt with Deaf Dan's betrayal by antagonizing the skinheads at first. I criticized the spelling errors, improper grammar and logical flaws in their pathetic, vitriolic literature, while Casey had sexual liaisons with several neo–Nazis and bragged about it. We laughed at the hypocrisy of skinheads who spouted homophobic, anti–Semitic and racist sentiments while having gay sex and being members of the ethnic groups they claimed to abhor. One skinhead was Mexican, and another was Jewish. Although Casey and I had fun tormenting the skinheads, our behavior was unwise and had severe repercussions (although it seems likely that the neo–Nazis would have targeted us anyway as they did so many others who never bothered them). By the time the Nazi's reign of terror was over, friends were raped, beaten and in San Quentin prison; I ended up in a mental institution and subsequently left town for safety reasons.

I lived in terror of sexual assault while living on the streets since I had been attacked and abused previously by several different people during childhood and early adolescence. When the skinheads threatened to rape me once they found where I was sleeping, I became frightened. I began changing campsites more frequently than usual particularly when Casey was away, staying with his sister. I had a high threshold for corporeal pain and was a fearless fighter, but the prospect of sexual assault has always been confusing and terrifying. Being a child with a male gender identity, developing breasts and other female gender signifiers were already traumatic. Having my femininity reified by rapists and child molesters who perceived me as a female sex object compounded this trauma. I got a knife to defend myself from the skinheads since I wasn't confident that I could fight off more than two.

One night, when Casey was away staying with his sister, the skinheads found me. Until then, the heater vent at the downtown library had been my favorite place to sleep since it was warm, quiet, remotely sanitary and somewhat difficult to access by others. We would lift off the heavy metal grate and jump down into the rectangular pit, reminiscent of a cozy coffin sans dirt and satin.

I felt paralyzed and disoriented by the sight of the skinheads looming six feet above me through the waffled grate. It was late; the streets were empty, and I was trapped. Our former friend, Deaf Dan, had told the Nazis where to find me, and that betrayal was more difficult to apprehend than the knowledge that I was about to be gang–raped. They called me a dyke, and a skinhead named Jake told me he was going to make me "suck his Aryan cock." I remember laughing nervously and asking him if it had a swastika tattooed on it. I planned to stab him. Luckily, as the skinheads were about to lift the grate off the heater vent, a group of inebriates emerged from a bar across the street. I screamed, and the Nazis made an abrupt departure, but threatened to return.

Strangely, the unconsummated assault seemed to affect me as profoundly as prior assaults, and I became unbalanced and withdrawn. Betrayal by former friends, family and the child welfare system left me with the sense that nothing was reliable if those who were supposed to care for you would not only allow you to suffer irreparable psychic and physical harm, but actively rejoice in it. The preexisting case of post–traumatic stress disorder I derived from being threatened with firearms and violent assaults in foster care and other environments was exacerbated by these incidents. I became suicidal and was involuntarily institutionalized in a mental hospital shortly afterward.

The Nazis raped our friend, Holly, and when the police refused to arrest the perpetrators, a friend attacked the skinheads responsible and ended up in San Quentin Prison under the three strikes law. The violence continued to escalate, and SHARP skins (skinheads against racial prejudice) came up from L.A. to beat up the skinheads. After my release from the mental institution, I left town to do seasonal work while living in a tent in Marin and moved on to San Francisco.

Although many people attempted to rape me after my encounter with the neo–Nazis, I made sure no one ever succeeded again. I bashed a man's head repeatedly into the dashboard of his car until he was unconscious and bloody when he tried to assault me on a road near a farm in Novato. I smashed another man violently against a wall after he ripped my clothing and tried to push me down onto the ground. I became more adept at defending myself and others over the years and began to enjoy fighting.

San Francisco was not an ideal refuge from the skinheads. I felt a sense of profound desolation and alienation that went deeper than the terror of dealing with the Nazis. I missed my friends. I felt disconnected from and often repulsed by people in San Francisco and felt more worthless and disposable. Once, a man and a woman with a gun attempted to force me into a dumpster in San Francisco's Tenderloin district so they could rape me. I informed them they would have to shoot me first if they wanted me to get into the garbage with pathogens and AIDS–tainted hypodermic syringes. While they were pondering this information, I ran away towards Market Street and pretended to call the police from a pay phone. I was sleeping in the empty fountain in San Francisco's Civic Center in an attempt to avoid the chilly wind in January 1991, when Mayor Frank Jordan ordered the police to come and confiscate the blankets of the homeless, disabled Vietnam Veterans as "evidence" for vagrancy. I was completely appalled by this cruelty and approached a young officer. I asked him if his family was proud of him for serving and protecting disabled citizens who fought for their country. The cop got tears in his eyes and left.

I identified with the veterans because they had been similarly disposed of like worthless toilet paper and had varying degrees of post–traumatic stress disorder, not unlike many homeless youth. Another cop informed me that homeless people didn't have rights as citizens since we didn't own property, but I doubt his interpretation of the Bill of Rights would fly with San Franciscans who rented their apartments but were still uppity enough to believe they were entitled to civil liberties. Police beat a friend senseless in an alley for public intoxication. I learned not to rely on police assistance before long and often took matters into my own hands and intervened in street fights and domestic squabbles. I had many violent altercations in San Francisco, most of which I won. Many others weren't as fortunate.

In San Francisco, I slept on doorsteps, in a seismically–damaged office building squat, a broken van on Stanyan Street, Golden Gate Park and the occasional homeless shelter. Although I still often went hungry, food was more plentiful. I ate bread off the ground, volunteered with Food Not Bombs, ate food donated by benevolent pizzerias and Hare Krishnas and availed myself of the vegetarian offerings at some food kitchens. Hygienic concerns were more difficult to navigate in San Francisco since public bathrooms were scarce and unsafe. I washed in the sink of the panhandle bathroom where people got raped and junkies shot up. I was frequently reprimanded for brushing my teeth in the McDonald's bathroom on Haight Street. The combination of lacking sanitation, absent medical care, malnutrition and decreased immunity from exposure to the elements permanently impacted my physical health. Untreated renal infections and a blood–borne staph infection from stepping on a bloody, broken bottle after my shoes were stolen caused permanent damage to my kidneys. I was hospitalized and near death on several occasions.

The insidious nature of early exposure to such volatile environments is that a sense of danger and chaos often persist long after one has left the streets. I have a laundry list of the ghosts who didn't survive embedded in my psyche. My friend, Jason, was brutally shot in Monte Rio years after he left the streets. Many others died from overdose, car crashes, AIDS, suicide and homicide. Yet those who physically survived their ordeals were often less fortunate than the dead. Many survivors went insane, became drug addicted, or transformed into people who inflicted damage on the next generation.

Although I am far luckier than most, the psychic legacy of my time on the streets persists to this day. The impact of these experiences reverberates years later in the form of post–traumatic stress disorder, survivor's guilt, grief and rage. A sense of contamination and alien defectiveness due to my transgendered status and what I experienced growing up has made it difficult to relate to others lacking similar life experiences.

As ordained clergy, I tend to keep this part of my life hidden because I worry what people would think if they knew what happened to me; that I beat people to a pulp or threatened them with murder to protect myself and my friends; and that I spent much of my life prior to having my child and monastic ordination wishing I was dead like my friends. This image of my prior self is antithetical to the happy, shiny, robed, Buddhist, monastic persona I now inhabit, a person who strives to understand and love all sentient beings (even the ignorant, cruel and annoying ones) and wants everyone to be free from suffering.

The intensity of my friendships with other queer (and non–queer) youth established through shared hardships on the streets was unlike anything I have experienced since. Our bonds were strengthened by our time spent on a level of basic survival and danger; we provided each other a sense of belonging and acceptance we never had at home. I never would have survived without the benefit of my chosen family of discarded misfits.

I send my love and gratitude to all those who traveled on this journey with me, especially since I survived with my psyche and corporeal form relatively intact when so many others did not. I send my compassion to the current and future generations of homeless queer youth who suffer from a lack of resources, love and understanding. My hope is that someday we can live in a world where some people are not less valued based on the superficial distinctions of sexual and gender identity.

My New Nuclear Family: Surviving the Fallout

Philip J. Reeves

So much of my past seems like a dream.

I came to New York on what felt like a thunderstorm, and the lightning flashes of memories and consequences haven't stopped yet. I have two dads. Where we came from, employers can fire gay men for being gay. Even in New York, however, people sometimes look apologetically at me when I tell them I have two fathers. They think it must be difficult or embarrassing for me, or that I may be unbalanced because I lack a strong female role model. To the later, I once jokingly replied, "That's not true. Hillary Clinton is my role model."

What makes my family special is that I have a family of choice. I came into Steve and Sam's lives when I was nineteen. People may want to think that sexual minorities cannot make good parents, but I have had heterosexual parents and homosexual parents: let me say, I didn't know what a real father was until I had experienced two of them. Steve and Sam have shown me more of what a family should be than I learned in the first part of my life, and they had to work harder than most heterosexuals to get where they are today. When Sam and Steve decided to be a committed couple in 1982, both sets of their parents pushed them out of their families. They started their lives together alone and poor. When they saw me twenty three years later without a home, they stepped in and took a damaged nineteen–year–old into their lives. Before my new dads, everything seemed like a bad dream in a long string of nightmares.

Night terrors plagued my sleep as a child. The worst monsters I faced in my dreams, however, were the same ones I faced everyday when I woke up. As conservative, evangelical Christians, my birth parents did exactly what they thought the Bible told them to do, no matter whom it hurt. "Spare the rod, spoil the child" was only one of the many rules my siblings and I lived under. That rule meant we children met a leather belt in a dark bedroom regularly.

Our parents controlled everything in our lives from our appearance to our friends and activities; they even forbade us from dating until we were ready for marriage, which meant we couldn't be alone with the opposite sex.

My church encouraged these rules, and my mother read our diaries, our mail, and listened to our phone calls to make sure we followed every one. If they thought we broke any of them, we received another severe beating with a leather belt. Life was difficult for all my siblings, but things were different for me.

I was the youngest boy and didn't fit in with my brothers or my sister. My older brothers paired off, and my younger sister had her dolls and her own friends. We all suffered because of our parents' physical and verbal abuse, and we passed more onto each other. When we hurt each other physically and emotionally, it was usually done in the same fashion our parents did it to us. We did try to protect each other, but it usually took the form of defending our parents' actions. We told ourselves that we deserved everything that happened to us. Because our parents' actions were guided by the Bible, it was easier to follow the rules than to challenge our God and our parents.

Most of my childhood, I lived waiting for something extraordinary to happen. I remember seeing my friends with their parents, and some of them obviously really loved each other. I cried myself to sleep one night after spending time at a friend's house because his parents were so nice to me. I knew that coveting was against the Ten Commandments. I didn't know if it was a sin to covet love. The biggest demon in my life, however—far worse than the fear of discipline— was the burning secret that turned my troubled childhood into the nightmare it became. When I was a junior in high school, my secret terrors and my grim reality collided spectacularly.

My parents discovered my secret by accident. They learned I had unchristian taste in art when they found some pornography I had hidden. That wasn't so shocking. They had learned the same about my brothers years earlier. Mine, however, was a big deal because I had pictures of men.

My parents were horrified by me and told me I had to change. I sought reparative therapy at my church. The goal of this therapy was to cure me of my homosexuality. My parents wanted me fixed, and I didn't want to let them down. I tried everything the church leaders told me. I memorized Bible verses. I prayed all the time. I tried not even to think about men. I also participated in a form of physical touch therapy. They thought that positive, nonsexual, physical contact with another male would help in the healing process. The pastor held me in his arms and encouraged me to cry. His wife had to be in the room to make sure nothing inappropriate happened. I was humiliated, and I did cry. I bawled in that man's arms, not because the process of changing my sexuality was so painful, but because I hated myself.

The church taught, "Love the sinner, hate the sin." I did not try to sin, and I couldn't stop my thoughts; nonetheless, I was told I sinned. My sin was part of who I was. So instead of learning to hate the sin, I learned to hate myself. I thought I would be alone the rest of my life. I would never be able to fulfill a woman, and I was a disgrace to my family. My church did not know what to do with me, and I felt completely afraid, alone and confused. I thought my options were to fight my feelings or to go to hell. With only those choices, I kept on fighting my desires, slowly killing myself.

I didn't realize I had other options until college. I was not allowed to move out. My parents wanted to maintain the strictest control possible over me at home, but at school, I met a boy. He was the first gay guy I had really gotten a chance to know. As I learned more about him, I realized that gay people are not depraved human beings. He was no different from me, except he tried to love himself. I realized that if my parents' God punished people for loving other people, He was not my God. I began believing in a loving God. I asked my friend to be my boyfriend, and I was willing to face whatever consequences I might receive.

Four days after starting my relationship, I couldn't keep it a secret any longer. I didn't know what my parents might do when I told them, so I told my boyfriend and a couple other friends that I planned to tell my parents the truth. One of the friends I told, Mike, knew about my parents enough to be worried. He told me that if I didn't call him when it was over, he would either come to my house himself or call the police. The plans were set, and all I had to do was take the daunting step.

I got home, and my parents beat me to the punch. They wanted to have a talk. "Phil, we feel that you've been hiding something from us," started my mother. I decided to ease into the discussion with my minor crimes. "I've asked someone out," I said calmly seeing the angry looks in my parents' eyes, and I hurried on to explain. "We believe the same things. We respect each other, and we want to save sex until we are married."

"It doesn't matter. You know the rules: no dating until you are ready for marriage," huffed my mom.

"What's this girl's name?" asked my dad.

"Well…" I paused to swallow and to take a deep breath. I could tell this was the end of the life I knew. "His name is John."

I listened as the ground shook, and the earth threatened to swallow me whole: "You're full of shit." "We thought you had fixed this." "You're going to get AIDS!" "How can you do this to us!" The earthquake ended five hours later, and I stood trembling, but still firm. Until one am, we yelled, argued, cried and read the Bible. The argument ended with them giving me an ultimatum: if I wanted to keep my family, I would have to break up with John, drop several classes and give up my car. I would only be allowed to leave the house under the supervision of one of my brothers or parents and only to attend classes or church services. If I did not agree to these terms, I would have to leave the house and the family, without any support.

My parents gave me until the end of the week to decide. In their eyes, I changed from being a good son who did bad things to being a bad son, and I knew it. I had to get away, but I knew they wouldn't just let me leave peacefully. At 1:30 am, when my parents went to bed, I called Mike and told him what had happened and that I needed a ride. He said he would bring a friend and come pick me up. Then I started throwing my clothes and school books into a couple of clothes baskets and my backpack.

When Mike got to my block, he called my house. I heard the phone ring and picked it up, but my parents answered first. Mike told them he had the wrong number and hung up. I ran out into the winter night to the end of the driveway where Mike and our friend, Eric, were in the getaway car, a pale, old Buick glowing in a mixture of yellow and blue from the streetlight and the moon. I dropped my first clothes basket near the car for Mike, who was the passenger, to collect. I told him I would be right back and ran back inside for the rest of my essentials. The rocks and ice cut into my bare feet, and the frigid air frosted my breath; they were only an afterthought to the pounding in my chest.

As I got back inside, I saw the light turn on in my parents' room. They heard the door close, and the car running outside. Their last chance for control was slipping away. My room was in the basement at the end of a hallway, and my parents lived upstairs on the ground floor. When I came back out of my room with my backpack and my other clothes basket, both my parents were in the hallway blocking my path.

They looked wild. I didn't know what else to do, but repeat the same thing over and over in as soothing a voice as I could muster. "I have to go. You have to let me go." I was terrified.

As if we hadn't had the entire previous discussion they replied, "What's going on? You can't leave." They wouldn't move, so I just started walking into them, continuing to repeat my plea. The rhythm of my words and my pounding heart melded with their now repeated complaints into a moment now burned into my mind. My dad began pushing me back down the hallway, and I returned his gesture, pushing him into a wall. I panicked, dropped the clothes basket and ran up the stairs; my dad jumped at me and grabbed my legs. I kicked myself free from his grip and headed for the front door.

Mike saw me burst out of the house, followed closely by my mom, and then my dad still only in his underwear. Mike jumped into the car and yelled for me to get in. I jumped in, and Eric hit the gas just as my dad dove in front of the car. Eric swerved away from him, and we sped toward the highway. Afraid they might follow us, we headed in the opposite direction from our final destination.

Looking back through the rear window of that old Buick, I saw my life falling apart. I had finally escaped—but without a coat, without shoes and without a family. After we felt sure we weren't being followed, and the adrenaline started to fade, reality came tearing its way into my mind. I made the leap I knew I had to make, but I felt as though I were falling through emptiness and chaos. The strength I held during the escape left me, and the emotional shell I had worn for my whole life came crumbling down to reveal a terrified, wounded, six–foot–four little boy. "I don't think I have a family anymore," burst from my lips. I could see Eric's eyes on me through the mirror; Mike turned around, and they both reached a hand back to comfort me.

"We're your family now." That's all they had to say. After years of being told if I ran away no one would take me in, those two straight men opened their hearts to a person they hadn't even known for a year. At that moment, I knew I still had brothers, and that everything would work itself out. After nineteen years of abuse—of dreaming of getting away—I was finally free.

I stayed with my boyfriend, John, for a while until I finally got an emergency dorm room at school. When summer came, I had nowhere to live. Steve, the director of my college choir, and Sam, his partner, let me stay in their house. Our deal was that if I helped them with remodeling their house and the household chores, they would give me room and board. I planned to move back into the dorms in the fall. I had no idea how much they would change my life. I thought I was damaged goods, but they saw something good in me. They remembered how hard it had been to be kicked out of their parents' homes and to live on their own early in their lives. They refused to let that happen to another young man. Before I knew it, I was thinking of them as dads, and they thought of me as a son. I was truly an unexpected child.

My birth parents harassed us when they discovered where I was, but my new fathers held strong and protected me. When I knew my birth parents could find me, the night terrors from my childhood began again. I feared that they would kidnap me, or that—since they loved hunting, and we lived in a conservative place—my birth parents might do worse to Steve and Sam. I had nightmares about my birth parents coming to our house, killing my dads and hauling me away in a van.

One night I woke up screaming in the darkness. I was terrified, but I could feel two pairs of hands holding both of mine. My fathers were there whispering, "It's okay. You're safe now." I realized that my dads kneeling next to my bed holding my hands were more of a family to me than my birth parents ever could be. They loved me just the way I was, and I loved them. They gave me the fatherly love I had coveted as a child. I felt safe, and, for once, I felt like a normal, lovable human being. After that, the night terrors stopped.

The transition into Steve and Sam's family was difficult because the conservative community in which we lived was outraged when they found out two gay men had accepted a good, Christian boy into a life of sin. They even forced one of my dads into retirement after intolerable harassment at his work. We made the news and the top ten scandals list for the city newspaper at the year's end. People knew our faces, and some even mumbled, "Faggots," while passing us in grocery stores. The only people who understood were the people who knew my old family. They had guessed what went on within the walls of my birth family's house, and one of them even apologized for not doing anything for my siblings or me earlier. I guess my old church was right when they taught me to fight my sexuality, or go to hell; they just didn't make clear that they were the ones who would make the hell for me. Their torment couldn't stop us though. Those were just the birthing pains for the beginning of a beautiful, loving family.

I've changed my name to my dads' name, and we now live in New York. As far as I know, my birth parents do not even know our address—at least, I hope they don't. I finally know what it feels like to have parents who love me. They always wanted a child, and I always wanted real parents. Finally, I have a life I can enjoy living.

Sylvia's Place Resident

Samantha Box

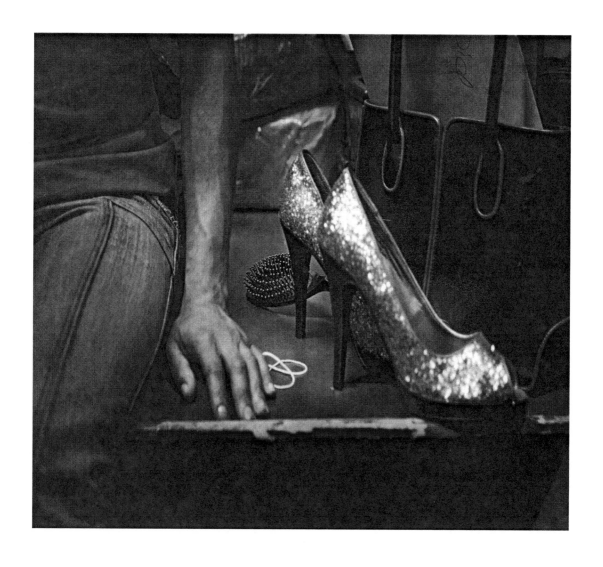

Stories From the Streets*

Cupid & Dija

Editor's note: Over the two years I actively worked on Kicked Out, I met some of the most incredibly resilient, talented, strong people. Among them are Cupid and Dija. On a cold, rainy night in early December, they sat with me for an abbreviated writing workshop in the corner of the shelter they call home. Near the Christmas tree filled with rainbow ornaments, we sat at a small table, sticky with Kool–Aid spills. Around us was a chaotic mix of youth, dancing, talking and fighting in a small room lined with towers of canned food donations.

Given all the distractions around us, the girls did their best to focus on my writing prompts, which was no easy feat even for veteran writers, let alone two teenagers in extreme conditions. I gave mostly very open–ended prompts, such as: "No one has ever told me…" and "I believe…." With their understandable inability to focus and to write for more than a few minutes, I did a series of what I call "rapid–fire writing prompts." I gave a new prompt as soon as their attention waned so that they could focus again on a new stimulus.

The resulting patchwork of writing reflects their similarly patchworked lives and an existence of awkward starts and uncertain directions. The fragmentary writing stands in stark contrast to Dija's and Cupid's clear sense of themselves, evident even in the rushed writing workshop results below.

◊ ◊ ◊ ◊ ◊ ◊

Cupid: All I remember was my birth mother spazzin' out because she caught me in bed with my first girl. She's Muslim, and my aunt is Roman Catholic. So you know I became a disgrace.

Dija: "By the time you read this"...a typical opening sentence of the runaway letter, right? Do you, dear reader, remember scribbling these words your very self?

Cupid: As much stuff I've been experienced, I should've been shot, poisoned, or had a heart attack so only the great lord or whatever has the answer to that. All I know is I live to go forward. To be someone. To become a lawyer. By the time this book is published, I'd be graduated from college with an associates degree in paralegal studies. I'd be an intern at a law firm and preparing to attend another college for my bachelor's in the law field. I'll be aiming to have an entry–level position as a paralegal.

Dija: The saddest part of this, my dear reader, is that if you are reading this book, searching for a method to help someone or if you are yourself a person in search of advice, then it saddens me to say to you that there is no advice. You ran away. Why did you run away? I don't know, but your reasons can't be too different than the rest of the youth of America. But I will say this: if you ran away because you were thrashed too badly and abused, then keep running. Make your way to the nearest police station or church. These places do not have people in them who can help you, but they can put you into contact with people who can. If your abuse is sexual, then do the same thing. If you ran away after some verbal abuse, then go home. Chances are you have a family that loves you. Being alone and homeless is not cool. Do not ever think it is. Life is <u>not</u> a videogame; please learn to separate fantasy from real life before it is too late.

Cupid: My family was never there, but they showed no remorse in throwing me out broke in the rain at the age of sixteen.

Dija: I learned on my own that not everyone related to a person by blood, is family. But no one ever told me that not everyone who is your friend, is your family. With most difficulties I was to face, I learned to appreciate something that I had lost. What I say here is serious. Every big decision a person deliberates will set a significant element in the rest of their lives. In fact, after making so many of these "mistakes," I am alive because of charity alone.

Cupid: If you got kicked out, guess what? "You're on your own."

Dija: Graphic, explicit and rude, is the shock of lifestyle and cultural metamorphosis. The realization of how few of your compatriots turn out to truly be your friend at all. The realization of how many of your companions swiftly become your enemy, or finally reveal that they always were.

Cupid: I am writing this because society wants to be blind over the LGBTQ homeless youth epidemic and the lack of resources that we have to get out of this situation.

Dija: What I remember most about leaving home was falling into the inorganic nooks and crannies of the steel saw known to many as "the system." Being there, a helpless minor, chewed on by…uncaring employees…

Cupid: No one ever told me that being strong is by starting from nowhere and having nothing.

Framing Federal Policy to Benefit LGBTQ Homeless Youth

Richard Hooks Wayman

Senior Youth Policy Analyst

Introduction

Lesbian, gay, bisexual, transgender and queer youth remain overrepresented in youth living on the streets, sleeping in shelters or doubled up in precarious housing circumstances. The crisis of youth homelessness among LGBTQ youth includes hundreds of thousands of youth who experience short–term homelessness and tens of thousands who sleep on the streets each year. Research indicates that this population experiences greater physical and sexual exploitation while homeless than their heterosexual peers.[1]

Yet mainstream culture and even the LGBTQ adult community rarely invest substantial resources to address this tragedy. It is not an exaggeration that queer and transgender youth are attacked, sexually exploited and die on our streets each year. Tragically, most remain hidden or ignored. The National Alliance to End Homelessness is working to highlight the needs of LGBTQ homeless youth and to advance public and private investment in shelter, housing and services to end the exploitation and homelessness of LGBTQ youth.

History of the National Alliance to End Homelessness

The National Alliance to End Homelessness ("the Alliance") is a nonpartisan, mission–driven organization committed to preventing and ending homelessness in the United States (endhomelessness.org). We work collaboratively with the public, private and nonprofit sectors to build state and local capacity, leading to stronger programs and policies that help communities achieve their goal of

---

1. There are over twenty research studies offering findings on LGBTQ homeless youth. To learn more, please see the National Alliance to End Homelessness' research brief, "Incidence and Vulnerability of LGBTQ Homeless Youth" at http://www.endhomelessness.org/content/article/detail/2141.

ending homelessness. We provide data and research to policymakers to inform policy debates and to educate the public and opinion leaders nationwide.

In 1983, a group of concerned leaders founded the National Citizens Committee for Food and Shelter to help meet the emergency needs of a growing population of homeless people across the country. By 1987, the organization changed its focus from emergency and crisis–intervention services to efforts to end homelessness. At that time, the organization became known as the National Alliance to End Homelessness. The Alliance grew from a federation of more than 2,000 providers and public agencies to a current network of over 7,000 partners, making the Alliance the largest partnership dedicated to ending homelessness.

From 2003 to 2007, the Alliance expanded its organizational capacity considerably in the areas of policy, capacity building, education and research. In 2003, the organization broadened its program and policy focus to include health issues that affect homeless people. In 2004, the Alliance launched the Center for Capacity Building, focused at that time primarily on assisting communities to develop plans to end homelessness. In 2006, the Alliance launched the Homelessness Research Institute, the research and education arm of the organization. Finally, first in 2004 and then in 2006, the Alliance expanded its program and policy expertise in the area of youth homelessness.

Combatting the Homelessness of LGBTQ Youth

In 2007, the Alliance founded the National Advisory Council on LGBTQ Homeless Youth, a national coalition of experts and field advocates who possessed the expertise and focus to design a national policy agenda for ending homelessness among LGBTQ youth. Specific accomplishments include:

- Establishing the National Advisory Committee on Homelessness among LGBTQ Youth that meets in person and communicates frequently to identify needed policy and practice reforms.

- Publishing a national research bibliography on homeless youth studies, including LGBTQ youth.

- Organizing workshops on LGBTQ homeless youth at the National Conference to End Homelessness (summer, 2007) and presenting those findings and recommendations throughout 2008 and 2009 to several national child welfare conferences for Black Administrators in Child Welfare, Pathways, Coalition for Juvenile Justice, and Runaway and Homeless Youth Training and Technical Assistance Center.

- Creating and circulating a research brief focused on studies of LGBTQ Homeless Youth titled, "Incidence and Vulnerability of LGBTQ Homeless Youth."[2]

- Identifying community programs exhibiting the best practice standards and methodology in serving LGBTQ homeless youth.

- Making a policy platform about ending homelessness among LGBTQ youth and sharing this platform with communities who focus on developing ten–year plans through the Alliance's newsletter, its national conference and its technical assistance[3] to nonprofit partners in implementing research–informed services.

- Publishing the National Recommended Best Practices in Serving LGBTQ Homeless Youth.[4]

While not all policy recommendations may be adopted in Congress, the ability to speak from a broader coalition of organizations enabled advocates to have a stronger voice. Additionally, the Alliance's actions in mobilizing advocacy geared toward LGBTQ homeless youth represented an important first step toward articulating a role for the federal government in addressing the needs of this special population.

The Alliance now focuses on two primary areas of reform: (1) encouraging homeless youth services to become champions for LGBTQ homeless youth; and (2) expanding our national capacity to offer access to housing for LGBTQ homeless youth. First, the National Advisory Council on LGBTQ Homeless Youth will assist field program experts to improve the level of services offered to LGBTQ homeless youth by establishing a guide to promising program practices and policies in nonprofit sector shelters, drop–in centers, outreach services and youth housing programs. The Alliance wishes to end discrimination

2. Please visit this link for more information: http://www.endhomelessness.org/content/article/detail/2141.

3. "Technical assistance" is one–to–one support of nonprofit systems to help them implement policies, programs and service methodologies that meet the needs of homeless youth, as informed by research.

4. Please see http://www.endhomelessness.org/content/article/detail/2239.

and incompetence in the professional services rendered to LGBTQ homeless youth within in the homeless youth service system. Second, Alliance staff and Council members will organize federal advocacy efforts to increase the level of federal appropriations to youth services and housing through the Runaway and Homeless Youth Act programs and the Department of Housing and Urban Development's (HUD) homeless assistance projects.

The Alliance focuses on developing the means to ensure an adequate supply of shelter, housing and supportive services to end youth homelessness. Currently, federal funding to homeless youth services is wholly inadequate to prevent the exploitation of LGBTQ youth in street environments. The federal government appropriates over $115 million each year for the Runaway and Homeless Youth Act. Under this federal program, street outreach programs make over 740,000 street contacts annually. However, fewer than 43,000 youth find access to a shelter bed, and the United States houses fewer than 3,600 youth annually through transitional housing programs. Most communities and cities have no to very few resources (e.g., shelter or housing) because there is little, if any, local, state and federal investment in youth services.

The Alliance and the National Advisory Council on LGBTQ Homeless Youth work with local and national partners to expand federal investment and appropriations to runaway and homeless youth services. Individuals, organizations and businesses wishing to assist us may contact us directly. The Alliance needs support, such as:

- allies willing to communicate with their representatives and senators regarding the need for attention and funding for LGBTQ homeless youth;

- local LGBTQ adults or community centers willing to identify local gaps for LGBTQ homeless youth and to seek local funding to expand services;

- businesses willing to contribute volunteer personnel and resources to support our national advocacy efforts in areas of marketing, training support and advocacy; and

- community– and faith–based organizations willing to build direct relationships with LGBTQ homeless youth as housing providers, mentors and youth advocates.

Beyond the Dollar Signs: Building Lives

While the lack of federal and state dedicated funds for critical shelter, services and housing for homeless youth must be addressed, the social crisis of LGBT youth homelessness will not be solved by increased funding alone. *Relationships* transform people. Change happens when caring adults give their time to build safe relationships with homeless youth and offer a chance for youth to believe in themselves and to lead lives with greater self–determination. Ending youth homelessness requires community–based volunteers, committed businesses and community resources to be in an active relationship with youth.

There is a role for the LGBTQ community to play in ending youth homelessness —a role for advocacy, a role for sustained giving to youth services and a role in reaching out and building relationships with vulnerable queer youth. LGBTQ adults can ensure that vulnerable, homeless youth are not assaulted in street environments and not recruited into the commercial sex industry through strip clubs and prostitution. LGBTQ adults have the opportunity to reflect on their own behaviors and consumption patterns by not supporting businesses or venues that encourage the sexual exploitation of youth through erotic dancing, escort services or prostitution.

Furthermore, private philanthropy and public systems must offer funding to increase community capacity to support and house LGBTQ homeless youth. The Alliance believes broader LGBTQ adult community recognition and support for LGBTQ homeless youth could offer meaningful investment and solutions. A concerted community intervention and public investment could end youth homelessness in the 21st century.

The Circus Project: Getting Youth Off the Ground

Jenn Cohen

Artistic Director, Executive Director & Founder

My first love affair was at thirteen. The object of my adoration: neither female nor male, but element. A lighthouse on a dark, stormy night, it beckoned me. Standing tall and strong in all its majesty rose the foundation of freedom: the flying trapeze. Bodies flew though the air in perfect rhythm. They danced upon the treetops, rejoiced under the sun, flirted with breezes.

One taste and I was hooked. Awkwardness made way for grace, frailty for strength. Boundaries receded as the realm I'd once considered possibility expanded exponentially. Circus became my salvation. It enabled me to survive a tumultuous adolescence and offered the opportunity to embody roles and identities I'd once thought impossible.

For fifteen years, I worked as a professional circus artist and coach. My passion for performing satiated my longing for the spiritual as well as the physical. Flying through the air was the closest I felt to God, the embodiment of spirit in human form. However, the life of a professional athlete allowed little space to attend to either emotions or physical ailments. Circus instilled in me the ability to persist through pain. While crucial in enabling me to survive my youth, the tendency to marginalize suffering became somewhat of a hindrance as I blossomed into adulthood. When the curtains closed and the audience dispersed, I was left with a persistent feeling of emptiness that lurked beneath my well–worn cloak of self–assuredness.

Through a number of synchronistic events, I stumbled upon Arnold Mindell's Process Oriented Psychology, a therapeutic modality rooted in Jungian psychology, Taoism and quantum physics. The connection was immediate. Process Work integrated various philosophies to which I subscribed, bridging the worlds of psychology with social activism, spirituality and artistry. Not only did Process Work offer personal healing, it set forth the momentum for a new passion to emerge: the integration of circus and Process Oriented Psychology for those youth most in need. Thus was born my vision for The Circus Project, an innovative nonprofit that serves homeless and at–risk youth in Portland, Oregon.

The mission of The Circus Project is to enable homeless and at–risk youth to develop their physical and emotional integrity by providing intensive skill training in circus and performing arts; we emphasize empowerment, personal development and relationship building. We strive to expand the definition of "art" beyond that of the various disciplines to encompass a way of looking at the world, appreciating diversity and approaching conflict. Our efforts are based on the belief that art is a powerful vehicle for transformation: it cuts across social barriers to inspire new perspectives and creative solutions to conflict. Given the tools to express themselves and a safe space in which to experiment, marginalized youth evince profound insight and genuine ability while contributing significantly through their artistic work. Training informs the identity of participants on stage, how they relate to others and how they contribute to the society in which they live. We encourage youth participants to create and direct their personal stories in innovative and artistic ways that offer an opportunity to reach the community through the production of original, theatrical performances.

Classes meet three times per week and focus on artistic, skill and personal development. Circus, theater, dance, music and creativity are integrated with life skills such as communication, teamwork, responsibility and respect. Issues that arise in group discussions are used to inform choreography. Improvisation serves as a springboard for personal sharing. While instructors provide the skill base, the material with which they work comes from the youth themselves: the struggles they face, their dreams, their relationships. The core program culminates in annual performances to engage the Portland community.

In addition, we provide internships and career opportunities in performance and coaching. Those youth who complete the initial training period have the opportunity to continue with The Circus Project as interns and later as paid faculty responsible for recruiting and mentoring other street, at–risk and community youth. Youth interested in continued performance also have the opportunity to join our resident performing company.

We recognize that in order to engage in the physical and emotional demands of training, basic needs must be addressed. Thus, youth participants receive healthy food, exercise clothing, bus passes and memberships to the Friendly House Community Center, which offers a daily respite from the hardships of street life in addition to a gym, a shower and internet access. We encourage youth to connect with other nonprofits serving similar demographics, and we provide referrals to night shelters. The Circus Project will expand over the course of its development without sacrificing the quality of the training or the safety of participants. The program is unique in that it first targets those youth most in need and only later expands to include youth whose families might be better able to subsidize their involvement.

While The Circus Project serves youth regardless of their sexual orientation or gender identification, the majority of youth who have graced our program since its inception have been queer–identified. No doubt, these numbers reflect the ratio of LGBTQ youth living on the streets. In addition, it is my experience that circus possesses a decisive lure for those of us identified as queer.

Throughout history, the circus has held the role of the freak show, a place where marginalized people are celebrated for their strange eccentricities and special talents. Thus, circus provides a vehicle for LGBTQ and other youth to celebrate their diversity and to reclaim their unique abilities. The circus ring has long been viewed as a metaphor for the social systems we inhabit. Indeed, all roles have a place under the big top.

Circus provides a unique opportunity to explore our unique personae and the contexts in which they thrive. Circus offers the opportunity to see the "other" in oneself. It provides insight into the mysterious, often disavowed aspects of the self, and engages us on the mythical level. Homeless youth have often deemed the mainstream culture unacceptable, and in turn, the mainstream culture has deemed them unacceptable. Circus prides itself in defying the accepted limits of humanity and offers a place of prayer for those who share its belief in stretching the boundaries of possibility; thus, circus acts as what Sam Keen refers to as "the church of impossible possibilities."

The Circus Project offers a unique approach to working with homeless youth without the pretense of pathology and not under the auspices of "personal growth." While the work is deeply personal, the driving force is not an abstract notion of self–development. Instead, the perceived objective is the presentation of a highly developed piece of theater, the creation of which is dependent upon the mastery of certain types of awareness and life skills. Art must be taught artistically. If our teachers and administrators cannot muster the creativity to inspire and to empower children and young adults in all their uniqueness and varied abilities, they have done little but reinforce the dominant paradigm that created disenfranchised youth in the first place.

Success in circus cannot be attained by simply rebelling against the laws of gravity. On the contrary, the acquisition of flight requires enormous discipline, commitment, awareness and self–care, all of which many street and at–risk youth lack. Developing these qualities for the sake of appealing to, or integrating into, the mainstream holds little appeal for most of these youth. Developing such qualities to fly, however, offers a much more compelling incentive. The Circus Project's use of Process Oriented Psychology brings into the debate the value of both experiential and theoretical learning while highlighting the importance of personal development in education. We shift the dominant educational paradigm that fails to engage a significant portion of youth to one that embraces the varied styles in which we learn.

The Circus Project contributes to the lives of its participants in a variety of ways. Company members encounter many milestones, challenges and resolutions over the course of their tenure, both personal and interpersonal. They acquire strength, flexibility and agility both emotionally and physically. Participants are driven by their own ambition and challenged to bring their personal stories into the creative process. They learn to deal with mistakes and failure as opportunities for transformation rather than obstacles to success. While the work is deeply personal, it encourages participants to work harmoniously with peers and coaches. Circus is by its nature collaborative; company members need to trust one another to work on techniques such as partner acrobatics, pyramids, double trapeze and ensemble work. An additional benefit of circus training for homeless and at–risk youth is learning to negotiate boundaries and to give and receive safe touch.

Early in the program, I noticed I seemed to be much more injury–prone than usual. I attributed my new vulnerability to aging, until the day I introduced the troupe to back handsprings. After carefully explaining the protocol of jumping from one's feet backwards onto one's hands, one of my students quite literally threw himself backwards into my arms. As a coach, it is my responsibility to catch them, to break their falls and to help them land softly, often using my own body as a cushion. I asked him about his thought process midair, and he responded, "I just felt safe and knew you'd catch me no matter what I did." Others nodded in agreement. Apparently, this phenomenon had been happening for some time. Holding the balance between helping participants to feel held and encouraging them to carry their own and others' weight is a constant negotiation, both on stage and in life.

Perhaps no one is better suited to describe The Circus Project's contributions to the youth it serves than the youth themselves:

> *As a result of being involved with The Circus Project, I now consider myself an athlete, something which I never imagined would be possible. I have become a more complete human being. I have grown to value true athleticism, and I have come to know my own strength. Being involved in The Circus Project has been one of the most challenging, at times discouraging, and ultimately empowering, feminist acts I have ever done.* —N

> *This is my second little family....It's like I found my little spot in the world—that one spot that makes sense, especially when I'm upside down—that's when the world makes sense.* —A

Youth engaged in The Circus Project come away from the experience with the technical skills to pursue continued performance, career opportunities in coaching, and the emotional tools to make better choices in their day–to–day lives. Students learn how to *receive* care and training as part of the program, as well as how to *give* care and training, thus enabling them to come full circle.

For more information on The Circus Project, please visit our website: thecircusproject.org.

Rewind

KJP

The memory is clear, even though by all rights I shouldn't be able to remember a May afternoon from my fifth year. It's a warm, sunny day, and my mother looks like a black–and–white blimp. She is wearing a homemade maternity dress of black and white cloth printed with tiny checkers. The huge collar, popular in Moscow in 1991, and the long, tie–up bow make her look like cross between an unbalanced clown and a poodle. I love her—she is my mama.

We are walking along the Yauza River in the botanical gardens, and the riverbank is overgrown with dandelions. Clumps of old yellowed and rotten grass are being overwhelmed by the new growth. My mother is talking about something, maybe the concrete horses in the playground, but I am not listening. Instead I concentrate on the feel of her hand in mine, and the occasional pat she bestows on my head. I am hoarding these touches. I know that once my little brother comes, I will not have them.

When they sat me down on the living room sofa that winter and told me I would have a baby brother, I asked why they wanted another boy. Wouldn't a girl be better? I remember my mother laughing and saying that they already had a girl. Where is this girl? All I know is that I am not a good enough boy, and mama will soon have another boy, a better boy. What will happen to me?

I'm scared. My parents are fighting. Plates are crashing in the kitchen. I take my almost–two–year–old brother, and we climb into the middle section of a book–style folding table. "She is your daughter! You deal with her!" screams my mother. I hear footsteps, and I'm yanked out of my hiding place by the arm. My shoulder screams with pain. "How many times did I tell you not to piss your pants!?" She did, and I tried. When I am awake, I remember that I have to sit down to pee. The girls in my classes told me how girls sit on the toilet the first day of school, and I never miss the bowl now. At night, when I am half awake, instinct takes over, and I try to straddle the bowl…I am seven years old.

It is my eighth birthday, and I am sitting by the well in my auntie's backyard. Auntie is my papa's older sister, and she has three children. My cousins are one boy and two girls; I like the boy. The girls are younger and don't ever want to do anything fun, like climb the fence or chase the neighbor's dogs. Instead, they help auntie in the kitchen and clean the house.

I have never fit in with my father's family. Every summer we go to Sri Lanka, and I have to leave my friends. Instead of going to sleep–away camp, I get bounced around between my father's siblings, spending a week here and a month there. It's like a three–month long game of Snakes and Ladders. Visit all the aunties and uncles and try to stay out of the war zones in the process. I am on display the entire time—the exotic half–white cousin. Papa tells me that I should be a good girl, like my cousins, but I can't do anything right inside the house. I cannot cook over an open flame and have no interest in learning how to sew. I am too impatient with the sweeping to do it properly. The house is large with cream–colored stone walls and open windows everywhere. Sitting on the living room sofa with my girl cousins, I feel myself suffocating.

I do better helping grandma in the fields. She tells me that to be a boy, I should work like a boy, and so I do. There are no questions or demands. I am confused by it, but grandma smells nice, and sometimes she pets my head. Papa doesn't like it. When he catches me in the rice paddies, fishing for frogs with my dress tied up around my knickers, he beats me with a sharp stick, saying things like "strumpet" and "shameful little whore." I know "shameful." What do the rest of the words mean?

That morning, all the cousins and aunties and uncles came and brought presents. I got dresses, one pink with white polka dots and an ugly satin sash. Mama made me wear it even though I wanted to wear shorts. I hate being a girl. I am not supposed to be a girl. Mama made me give away the cool pedal car I got to my boy cousin because it is not a proper toy for a girl.

I look into the well. It must be very deep—there are fishes swimming in it. The fish are not tasty, but grandma says they keep the water clean. I decide I don't believe in god: if he were really up there, would this have happened to me? I look down into the well again. If I throw myself in, one way or another it will be over. It is bad karma to kill oneself, but eventually I'll get back to human state, and then I'll have suffered enough to be born right. All I have to do is lift the mesh cover. It squeaks.

Grandma is looking at me from the kitchen with a knowing look on her face. I will not jump into the well in front of her, not after she told me about a boy from her home village who became a girl, had children even. If he could do it his way, there must be a way for me to do it too. It is only ten years before I turn eighteen. I get up, adjust the hateful sash and go inside to play with my six–month old baby sister. Maybe she'll throw up on the dress, and I can take it off.

It is winter, and my mother is pulling a peeling red toboggan with my siblings. I trail behind, ready to upright the sled if the kids spill over into a snow bank. We are late, and my mother is screaming at me, "You don't appreciate anything! Any other mother wouldn't be taking you to your Georgian dance lessons in this cold. Why do I even bother going through all this trouble of making you into a proper lady? You don't do well in school; you're lazy; you won't get picked to perform again! Why do I bother? You'll end up a prostitute anyway!"

As I follow along, I wonder what's so bad about getting four out of five in math. And I never wanted to dance anyway. She only stuck me in this stupid class after I got kicked out of figure–skating for playing hockey with the boys.

A year later I would deliberately injure myself and would never be able to figure skate again. I was eleven.

It is very early in the morning, well before five. We are sitting in the living room. There are boxes and suitcases everywhere. I'm sleepy, but I'm rocking my sister to sleep. If she wakes up again, we will never leave, says my mother's mother. We sit down for a minute for good luck, as is the Russian custom, and then I am in a backseat of a taxi, already carsick and trying to capture as many details of our communal yard in my mind as I can. I know I will never be back, and like a thief, I secret away the details.

Years later, no more than the memory of the smell of that morning and the peeling green paint chips will remain, only to be pulled out in absolute privacy and shared with no one.

Then we are at customs, and I'm not nervous at all. The date is August 4, 1997, and we are going to America. I turned twelve a month ago, and it's only six years until I turn eighteen.

As we go through the glass doors, I look back. That is the last time I see my grandmother.

There is a TV show on with women who used to be men, and I get to watch a little bit before my mother clicks it off and slaps me for watching such filth. I knew it was possible!

My parents are fighting. My father is screaming about me being friends with a boy. I will be a whore, and no one will marry me. I scream back that I don't want to marry anyway, and Erick is gay. My father's fist comes at my face, and suddenly there is blood dripping down my chin. I brain him with a frying pan. The pan is made of cheap aluminum with the plastic handle attached by two screws. There are stars in front of my eyelids, and I swing blindly until my hands are suddenly lighter, and there is a deafening crash of glass.

There is shouting, and someone is pulling at my long braid. I break away and lock myself in the bathroom. I'm numb, and my ears are ringing. My face is on fire, and I can't quite comprehend what it is I did. I sit on the side of the low bathtub and try to breathe. Every lungful gets stuck halfway down, and I am disgusted at my tears. It's only a bloody nose.

I realize that the apartment has gone silent and creep out to catch a glimpse of a blue police uniform and my mother locking the front door.

When my father comes back from the precinct, we are both silent. The silence lasts for six years.

It is the summer before high school, and I have a list of books to read. One of them is by a guy named David Pelzer. As I read *A Child Called It*, I start to cry. The room smells strongly of formaldehyde. There are about thirty of us crammed into six lab stations, each with a dead frog. There is a blonde girl with glasses sharing my table, and as we slice down the pickled frog's sternum, I meet my best friend.

I decided on New Year's to give being a girl a serious shot. I buy makeup and feminine clothing with the money I save from my weekend job. I buy long skirts with slits to my hips and high–heeled shoes; tight tops that show off my growing cleavage and make me feel like a sausage on the grill when men look at me; embroidered bell–bottom jeans that are too pretty to play footie in. It's fun, kind of like dress–up, and my mother doesn't scream at me as often. She starts taking me along to church, showing off what a good girl I am. I feel like a fake. I try praying to god to make this go away. After four months, I have sex with my boyfriend because that's what girls do.

Two weeks before my sixteenth birthday, I find out I'm pregnant. All of my savings and most of my friend Marina's are spent on the abortion. As I drift under the general anesthesia, I tell myself that I made the choice between my sanity and manhood and my only chance of having a biological child. My regret is that I will have to start saving for top surgery all over again. I tell my mother none of this and stop buying clothing altogether.

When the planes crash into the twin towers outside my physics class windows, I walk home. When I walk in, covered in soot and ash, my mother hits me for…I don't know what. I later find my hideaway place under the mattress devoid of the hundred dollars I did not have time to deposit into the savings account that a friend's mom opened for me.

In December, I get enough courage to type "transgender+teenager" into the search engine. I take care to clean the cache.

My friend, Tanya, is turning seventeen, and we are all going to see Phantom of the Opera. The musical lets out late, and her father drives us to their home to spend the night. I call my mother and let her know where I am. She seems to approve. The next day is Sunday, and it takes me three hours to make it home on the subway. My mother is okay. On Monday morning at the breakfast table after my siblings have left for school, she asks me who else was at the party, and I mention Tanya's girlfriend. Suddenly there is a hand in my hair, and I am being dragged to the bathroom. There is screaming, and my face connects painfully with the mirror. I am bleeding. I am terrified. I grab my book bag and run to the nearest subway station at breakneck speed.

At my guidance counselor's office, it turns out that there is a chunk of flesh missing from my scalp. The Nigerian foster care worker takes one look at my age and tells me to repent, find god and go straight. An hour after she leaves, I receive a message on my cell phone from my mother. If I return home, she will butcher me.

My guidance counselor gives me and my best friend a pass to leave the school, and we sneak into my home, hoping all the while that my mother does not come back. My best friend holds the carving knife at the ready as she watches the door while I frantically throw together my green card, social security card, birth certificate, asthma meds and necessary clothing. I store the lot at her house and get to work that evening. I spend the next few days couch–surfing among my guidance counselor's friends and listening to increasingly dire voicemails from my mother, telling me that I had better cure myself from this sickness, or die. Thankfully the battery runs out in three days, and in my haste, I did not pack the charger.

By the week before Thanksgiving, I am in an overnight shelter in the basement of the Metropolitan Community Church of New York. A guy named Bill tells me that I'm not the first, nor the last. In fact, the shelter itself is named after a murdered homeless gay youth. I make it a point not to end up dead.

Full of equal parts fear and anger, I send out college applications. The return address is my school. I will not be a statistic. I refuse to be a statistic. I did not choose not to die on my own terms by the well back in Sri Lanka only to have my mother make the choice for me. I will survive, and I will make it, if only as a "Fuck you!" to her.

My routine is school, work, shelter—lather, rinse, repeat. I feel free, powerful and safe. I am with my own kind. I am at my best friend's place all the time and almost feel adopted. She makes sure I don't go nuts with the freedom in my head. At the family court hearing, I am able to testify that I cannot, and will not, jeopardize my life in my mother's hands.

The day before Christmas, I arrive at an all-gay group home. A lady named Leslie greets me. I am seventeen years old, and I am free. Every step, every choice I make from now on is mine alone. I am scared shitless.

I'm in college, and I can't wrap my mind around it. I am living in what is known as a SILP, a Supervised Independent Living Apartment. I am working and saving money. I research Gender Identity Disorder and start seeing a shrink. Some days I can't make it out of my bed because my body does not feel like my own.

When my interview for citizenship comes, I show up with my breasts bound and somehow can't utter my chosen name so it can be permanently changed. Instead I shorten my given female name. It isn't my great grandmother's fault I am a man. Leslie makes me put my money into a savings account as a condition of staying in the SILP.

Leslie can't come with me to San Francisco for the surgery. It was hard enough getting Administration for Children's Services (ACS) to grant permission for me to go, even though I am not spending a penny of their money. My best friend Linda's mother is footing the plane tickets, and I am covering everything else. Another friend comes to see me through the surgery and the first two days.

When I am fully cognizant for the first time post-surgery and try walking around, Jake has to stop me from pitching over. Ten pounds are off my chest. I am twenty years old.

We walk the same way, my father and I. It's a strutting, open-stanced gait, which makes us look bigger than we are. We are about the same height, and the Sicilian butcher compliments my father on how his son looks like him. My father mumbles something that sounds like gratitude and scurries to the checkout. As he stands there, I am struck by just how old he looks: thinning salt-and-pepper hair, a well pronounced beer belly and rounded shoulders. Old and tired and defeated by the country he thought would be his chance to be something.

It is all about chances and choices. The risks taken, the effort put in and sheer blind luck.

Later, as I write out the checks for the bills, he asks me if there could have been another way. I think about it for a minute, and frame after frame flashes through my mind. I look him in the face, say "No," and sign the cable bill.

Things have come full circle. I am twenty–two.

Sanctuary at The Attic

Stephanie Mannis

The Attic Youth Center, founded in 1993, is Philadelphia's only agency specializing in the support and personal development of gay, lesbian, bisexual, transgender and questioning youth. I'm fortunate to serve as a board member and a volunteer for this vital organization and to witness firsthand the life–changing effects it has had for hundreds of youth. Many of them have been kicked out of their homes due to their sexual orientation or gender identity. They come to The Attic seeking a safe haven, a place where they'll be heard and understood. These are some of their stories collected through personal interviews conducted at The Attic.

Daniel's Story

Eighteen–year–old Daniel first knew he was gay at thirteen but didn't come out to his family until three years later. The youngest of three brothers and five sisters, Daniel came from a deeply religious Christian family who did not take the news of his sexuality well. When he brought his boyfriend to a family event, his parents staged an intervention.

"I came home from school one day, and [my parents] were sitting on the couch. I was like, 'Hey,' and they said, 'Sit down.' And the whole thing was about how I had to either be straight, or I had to go. Or they were gonna put me on lockdown, and I could just stay in my room and be gay but not act on it." Unable to accept their demands and to reject his sexuality, Daniel was forced to move out of the family home amid threats of a beating from his brother.

After spending many weeks resourcefully rotating among the homes of his boyfriend and several friends, Daniel eventually moved in with one of his sisters. Daniel is mature for his age and fortunate to have a close–knit group of caring friends. During this entire process, his friends banded together to ensure that he stayed in school.

"I was still in school at the time," he recalls, "and [my friends] wanted to make sure that I was still going. Everybody talked to their parents and set up things like, 'Okay, he can stay here for this amount of time and then go there...'" Yet even with this support, he found it difficult to attend classes and to concentrate on his studies due to the distraction and turmoil caused by his living situation.

Drawing on the strong support network provided by his friends and channeling the closeness of his family prior to his coming out, Daniel continued to reach out to his family in hopes of rebuilding his relationship with them. "I just got fed up with it. So I went back down to [their] house and had a conversation with them about how I felt about the situation. They were surprised. My mom actually broke down and was crying."

Now, thanks to his efforts and their eventual willingness to meet him halfway, the family ties are again strengthened. Some awkwardness remains, but it appears they are back on track. Through the support of both his biological and chosen families, Daniel has defied the odds and has reached a good place in his life.

Tony's Story

Tony has faced a far rockier road than many, and his outlook on life reflects this reality. "I was just a troubled kid," he says. "Because of my past, I'm very quick–tempered. My anger gets me into a lot of trouble."

Given up by his biological family at the age of six, he was shuffled among group and foster homes for almost a decade. While in these homes, he was often the target of bullying and harassment due to his sexuality. This treatment made him angry enough, on occasion, to fight back—sometimes resulting in strict disciplinary measures.

"[The staff in the group homes] have to restrain you to calm you down," Tony recalls. "I used to hate being restrained. It's scary, especially when you're a little kid, to have these grown adults with all their body weight on top of you."

When he eventually was adopted by a gay man at the age of fifteen, it seemed like a perfect match. That adoption, however, did not work out as planned. His adoptive father went so far as to out Tony to his biological family before he gave him up, and Tony found himself back in the system before being adopted for a second time by another gay man.

The second adoption was not without its problems either. Though gay himself, Tony's adoptive father was not fully accepting of his new son's sexuality, especially his choice of partners. When Tony, then eighteen, finally brought home the man he'd been dating for a year and a half, his father kicked him out. He lived for a time with his boyfriend and the boyfriend's mother before being allowed to return home. That stay was short–lived, however, and he was kicked out again in a matter of months.

"I said to my dad, 'Nobody seems to really care about me. People say they care, but it just doesn't seem like they do. In the end, I'm always left alone by myself.' And he said to me, 'I'm in the middle of my computer game right now. Talk to me later.' And all he was doing was playing solitaire on the computer. Playing solitaire was more important than me coming to talk to him."

This constant state of flux and repeated rejection has beaten Tony down. He wears his resignation like a heavy cloak, as if unaware of the great inner strength he possesses—a strength that has helped him through trying times. He claims to have major trust issues and what he refers to as a "24/7 defense mechanism" in place, which is understandable, given the obstacles he has overcome.

Despite his rocky youth, Tony had big plans including college and a career. However, getting kicked out forced him to drop out of school, putting his ambitious life plans on hold until he found the stability he sought. The stress and tumult of being kicked out have also contributed directly to his problems in maintaining steady employment and to his increased marijuana use. The drug became a regular part of life due to his constant need to be high, which he has described as a relief and an escape from the problems plaguing him.

Though only twenty years old, Tony sometimes displays the world–weariness of someone twice his age. When asked what kind of support network he has, he replies simply, "None." But he is at The Attic now, and support is just steps away.

Kat's Story

Kat, now fifteen, knew she was a lesbian by the age of twelve. At fourteen, she was outed to her mother by the administration at her school following a fight. (Kat fought back when another girl harassed her at school for being gay; she subsequently was suspended, though the other girl was not.) When her mother returned from a conference at the school, she kicked Kat out of the house. For three weeks, Kat slept at friends' houses or on a park bench, riding the train during the day to stay warm. "I just rode the train back and forth for a while," she says. "They kind of kick you off eventually. Well, it stops running, and then you can't get on buses, so…" she trails off.

The park was riddled with drug users and violence. "There's some weirdos out there," she says. It was a relief when she was allowed back home. However, she was doomed to repeat the experience as she would be kicked out three more times in the following year. Her older sister, a nineteen–year–old cocaine addict who previously identified as gay, was also kicked out of their family home on numerous occasions.

Kat has some experience with drugs as well, though she's not an addict. She has admitted that her sexuality and her living situation have contributed to her drug use, and her ex–girlfriend was an HIV–positive heroin addict. Kat performed a moving spoken word tribute to the girl, who later died as a result of her addiction. This relationship was the catalyst for another incident in which Kat's mother kicked her out of the house. "My ex contracted HIV," she recalls, "and [my mom] found out and got very upset...so she kicked me out for that, too."

The most recent jettisoning occurred, tragically, after Kat was raped, and her mother accused her of lying about it. "I was raped," Kat says, "so that's why I didn't go to school for a week, and that's why I wasn't at home...and I went to school one day, and they called the cops, and they called my mom. She thought I was lying and thought I was looking for attention. She was like, 'Fuck you, get out of my house.' Then I didn't have anywhere to live."

Her life on the run caused Kat to miss her classes, and she was subsequently kicked out of school. "They said, 'There's nothing else we can do for you.'" In search of a support network, she turned to three friends who were all either kicked out or who had run away. "I don't know what I would've done without them," Kat says. Her friends are her family, and the shared experience has brought them closer together.

Though she's now living at home again, at least temporarily, there's a constant threat of the Department of Human Services (DHS) removing Kat from her family. "DHS started coming to the house," she admits. "They left a note, but I ripped it up, so my mom never saw it." The word on the street—and among her peers at The Attic—is that group homes and foster care are not always safe for gay kids because of the harassment and bullying they face. Concerned for her own safety, Kat has promised to run away before letting herself be put in the system and left vulnerable to the rampant homophobia experienced by many youth. However, she concedes that living in the local group home for LGBT youth might be a better alternative to her current situation.

"I can't keep going through this shit," she says.

Bobby's Story

Bobby grew up in a foster home with four brothers and four sisters. "I never really came out to my family," he says, "because of the [attitude] they'd give me, as far as 'Why are you gay?' and 'I don't want any faggots in my house,' things like that. One of my siblings told my family."

On his seventeenth birthday, one of his brothers told their foster mother that Bobby was gay. He recalls, "[My mom] was talking to some of my relatives, and just before I went to blow out the candles on my birthday cake, she told me to leave. I asked her why, and she just said, 'Get the hell out.'"

Bobby now lives in a group home and has no contact with his foster family. His brothers and sisters were upset that he was gay but also angry that he was kicked out. Prior to his ejection from the house, Bobby had had a good relationship with both of his foster parents (his foster father died in 2004) and his siblings. Now, his family consists of a network of friends, primarily those he met at The Attic. "They actually helped me open up, realize who I am and be comfortable [with that]," he says. "When someone asks me, I can say, 'I'm gay.'"

Part of the transition from his foster home to the group home involved changing schools, a daunting proposition for any teen but especially for someone whose whole life has just been upended. Now a junior in high school, Bobby is determined to stay in school and plans to attend nursing school after graduation. His goal is to become a registered nurse. Ever mindful of that goal, he has resisted drugs and alcohol and regularly takes advantage of The Attic's programs to assist its youth with independent living, money management, job searches and preparedness. Despite the odds, Bobby's story is one of success.

Jesquelle's Story

Jesquelle knew she was special even as a child. "I knew that I was just a lot more comfortable with certain issues than other people were," she says. "But I didn't really think much of it." Eventually she determined that she identified as "hybrid" or genderqueer. Though she's attracted to—and has relationships with—women, she doesn't consider herself a lesbian. Perhaps it is this open–mindedness and refusal to conform to gender and sexual norms that led to her clashes with her mother and grandparents, with whom she lived. Though they were accepting and loving toward her gay uncle, Jesquelle's orientation was too much for them. "As you can see, I'm not your stereotypical African–American female," she points out. "I'm weird to them. I'm strange to them. They don't like me the way I am."

Over the years, her family threatened repeatedly to kick Jesquelle out of the house. When they finally told her to leave—"They all ganged up on me," she recalls—it came as no surprise. Her father's abusive nature had caused Jesquelle's mother to leave him thirteen years earlier, so living with him was not an option. Jesquelle almost ended up in a homeless shelter but instead found a home with two friends who were also queer. Unfortunately, she was forced to quit her part–time job and sole means of support due to sexual harassment based on her gender identity.

Though enrolled in community college as an art major, Jesquelle stopped going to her classes when she was kicked out. "I knew I couldn't support myself and go to college at the same time," she says. Between the turmoil of being displaced and not having reliable access to transportation, she admits that she's not really feeling inspired anymore. However, she has become more involved in The Attic, which gives her a sense of purpose, despite her mother's resistance to Jesquelle's involvement. Her mother feels Jesquelle is becoming closer to her chosen family than her biological one, a transition that's understandable given that she was kicked out by her blood relatives.

Nonetheless, Jesquelle insists that she loves her mother, despite her actions, and feels closer to her now that they're not uncomfortably sharing the same living space. She also calls her grandparents on a regular basis to check on them since their health has begun to decline as their age advances. "I try to check on them to see how they're doing," she says, adding: "I love my mom; I really do. We're just different." Though getting kicked out was a bad experience, Jesquelle seems determined to make the best of the situation, demonstrating a maturity beyond her years.

Building a Future

From relatively hopeful stories such as Daniel's and Bobby's to the harsher realities faced by Kat and Tony, the experience of getting kicked out runs the gamut. One thing is constant, though—the need for support as one comes into one's own as an adult, particularly a queer adult who will likely face challenges that those in the heterosexual community do not. Support can come from the biological family (if any contact persists), the chosen family or social services agencies like The Attic. All of the youth who shared their stories spoke passionately about the positive effects The Attic has had on their lives, with some saying they would be lost without it.

Tony spoke of the amazing feeling he had when he first came to The Attic. It was the first time he was truly able to relate to people. Getting kicked out affected every aspect of his life by diminishing his sense of self and making him feel uncomfortable in his own skin. He says, "Coming here, I met so many people and did so many things...It was just a wonderful atmosphere." The support services and camaraderie at The Attic helped him to rebuild his life and to regain his self–confidence.

The staff at The Attic helped Kat find a place to stay at a time when her only other option was to be homeless or to allow a government agency to determine her fate. They also provided a support system in the form of a counselor and a case manager who helped her sort through her situation and plan for her future. In addition, she found friends who understood her and accepted her. Bobby too found new friends at The Attic and speaks about the support groups in glowing terms, citing them as a primary reason he's been able to stay positive and well–adjusted throughout trying times. Daniel, a fixture at The Attic for more than three years, says the staff and youth at the center helped him to feel more comfortable with himself both in and out of school. He appreciates having a forum to talk to sympathetic adults who have helped him to make good decisions in his life.

Jesquelle calls The Attic her "home away from home." A regular at The Attic for more than two years, she now volunteers there and even does some maintenance and housekeeping work to help with facility upkeep. She's also quick to lend an ear when any of her peers need to talk, anxious to be a good listener and a positive influence. "I try to help out around here wherever I can," she says. Surprisingly, Jesquelle professes to feel unworthy around the youth at the center, claiming that many have gone through far worse ordeals than she. Beyond The Attic, Jesquelle is active in the larger LGBT community, drawing on her experience to relate to others and to help them when she can. Being kicked out, she says, gave her a new perspective on the importance of community.

Kat agrees, noting that coping with being kicked out made her a stronger person and instilled in her a sense of pride about her sexuality and her individuality. Though she's been through some tough times, she is still proud that she is able to take a stand for herself and for what she believes in without backing down in the face of adversity. Being kicked out made her appreciate much more in life, including The Attic.

For Bobby, his experiences after being kicked out helped him come to terms with who he is as a person and as a gay man. He's now more comfortable and able to open up to those around him in a way he couldn't before. He's happy to be out and proud of who he is, where he's been and where he's going. Daniel is treading this same path, albeit more slowly. He has only recently begun to be more involved in the LGBT community; after hiding his sexuality at home for so long, he was initially uncomfortable with the level of openness he experienced in the larger gay community. Being kicked out thrust him into the community in such a way that he was forced to come out of his shell; he soon became comfortable interacting with people of different sexual preferences and gender identities. Their stories have helped him come to terms with his own experience.

Though these teens and young adults have had vastly different experiences, the common thread running through all their stories is one of perseverance and hope, despite the obstacles they have faced. Given the proper resources and the resiliency of youth, they can emerge from rejection by their families, forge their own paths in life and even serve as an inspiration to others. However, the tools for survival and opportunities for success must be made available and accessible when these youth are faced with hardship. Otherwise, they may easily fall prey to the dangers of life on the street with potentially disastrous consequences. This is why it is imperative that governments and social services agencies provide programming that focuses on the unique needs of LGBT youth, as well as a safe haven for those who have been kicked out of their homes or simply need a place where they can be themselves. By giving these often overlooked members of society the tools they need to survive and flourish, society as a whole benefits.

To contact The Attic, please visit atticyouthcenter.org.

Running to Stand Still

Sabine Tigerlily Vasco

My parents were contradictions—dichotomous rulers of their reason, theories and motives; slaves to their deceit, blunders and nefarious lives. Their cocky hearts were deaf to their Catholic mothers' voices. Brashly, my mother renounced her family—the lineage of sweat, labor and love that all great-grandparents build into their progeny's immigrant blood. (Step)dad rejected his aristocratic roots—tired of the pressures and privileges of being part of the elite, the upper crust of political and socialite families overseas. Together they pumped U2, The Smiths and their middle fingers into the air as their farewell to all that inhibited them.

I was their experiment.
Their toy.
Their tag-along.
Their witness.

They told me that it was impossible to live an entire life without telling a lie—then challenged me to prove them wrong. They whisked me to coffee shops to discuss politics, religion and the world, and to tell me that the bible was a history book that people used to catalyze pain. They transferred me from public school, to Catholic school, to an uppity private school where women served us roast beef and mashed potatoes tableside from silver platters.

They told me I needed to experience how differently knowledge was taught, depending on where I stood. They took me to meet my new (step) grandparents, our ranch, my sheep, my streams, my mountains, my air. They gave me the space to roam, run and skip rocks. I built model rockets and dreams and launched them into the sky. They stood me before a cliff side on one of our many thousands of acres of forest and mountainside and told me to climb.

When I cried and confessed my fear of scaling the crag, they told me I was bold. They told me they had never known a person less afraid in their lives.

I was their experiment.

I spent half of each year in the transnational mess of one continent and the other in the idyllic mountain ranges of another. I climbed. I laughed. I chased sheep. I wailed, "Sunday, Bloody Sunday," and marched through my childhood, a precocious cosmonaut exploring strange worlds—searching for home.

The memories that flood my head begin flashing onto the dark, sleepless lecture hall of my mind like Kodachrome slides making their way around the carousel projector at the back of the room, each image a peephole into one seedy room after the other.

First slide.

There I was, bathed in the red hue of neon beer signs at my parents' friend's house, carousing with the big boys—swigging sips of backwash from nearly empty bottles of beer and sifting through the haze of thick smoke. They would prop me up on kitchen tables to sing my toddler versions of classic mariachi standards and my own renditions of Joan Jett and Hall & Oates jams. This is how we lived. An endless party that served as an alibi to so many things I didn't understand. Dance, monkey, dance.

In the early years, they were fun and vivacious, carefree and glorious.

I was their toy.

Slide.

Eventually, the parties and the music became too thin of a veil and a façade for whatever truths they were attempting to mask in revelry. At the age of seven, we heaved belongings into trash bags, and hurled them into a U-Haul— unexpected, unplanned. Reasons remained unexplained, and my fear ensured that I would keep any curiosities in lockdown. Although there were so many fragments I couldn't seem to make fit or understand, this crack in their surface revealed a piercing shard of their reality that I could grasp, even as a child: they were not happy-go-lucky souls, but creatures entrenched in the muck of a trap greater than they, a fuzzy and undulating crusade.

We landed in a dingy duplex until my parents found a new home base. I was specifically told to never enter the rooms at the top of the stairs. I was bored. I was mischievous. I was dared. Sneaking into the rooms, I was confronted with things I did not understand, and many reasons to shut the door and shut my mouth.

I was their witness.

Next slide.

The solitary walls of my bedroom are covered with ridiculous, pink-framed pictures of dolls and teddy bears. My bed is covered in a sea-foam green comforter with a hideous floral pattern that assaults the eyes—decor my mother has overlooked consulting me on.

I had outgrown tag-along and had become old enough to know, to understand that my parents weren't like the others—the tedious front and lonely path of secrecy became home.

My parents pretended to be "normal." The crippling unspoken convinced them that never having guests, relatives or friends enter our home was entirely natural. I was taught that answering the telephone was a very dangerous endeavor for children. It was also conventional practice for (step)dad never to leave his bedroom, let alone the house. Daily rituals included scrutinizing every conversation I had throughout the school day, particularly with teachers.
What had they asked?
What did I say?

Their privacy was their greatest treasure, agoraphobics trapped in their self-made prison.

Everything is fine.
Everything is great.
My script.

Eventually, they would doubt my loyalty to their fables and sentence me to twenty-four-hour confinement. They called it homeschooling. But that would come later.

Slide, next slide, please.

I spent a lot of time alone; inviting schoolmates to play was unthinkable. Going outside to find a comrade within the ranks of the neighborhood children—not a viable option.

I spent a lot of time in my room, specifically in my closet, hashing out my inner-workings and my greatest frustration. Safe in my space, amid my Tonka trucks, my Micro-Machines and my whispers, I tried to tackle bigger mysteries than my parents' odd behavior.

I played out scenarios where I was "David" or "Nathan," and the wisps of air around me were sculpted into characters, mostly of imaginary girlfriends named "Stacey" and "Danielle." Had I been born a boy, I would have been free of my utter confusion and my absolute frustration as to why the hell I was a girl.

I asked my mother questions like, "Did you ever think I was going to be a boy?"
"No."
"Why not? You never even considered it?"
"No. Everyone else thought you were going to be a boy, but I knew you would be a girl."
"Well, did you even have a back-up name ready…just in case?"
"Yes. Clark."
"Clark?! Why?"

It was hard for me to fathom how my mother could be capable of naming me anything but something spectacular and unique. She had managed to give me a stellar name with a romantic back story. This is how it went. When my mother was a little girl, my great-grandfather introduced her to a cinematic account of an ancient Italian tribe known as the Sabines. She vowed her first daughter would inherit the name.

"Why Clark?"
"Superman's name is Clark Kent. I would have named you after Superman."

I was her blank slate.

Slide.

My first love was my best friend, Hillary. We were in kindergarten. My second love was Brittany. I fell in love with her the first day of second grade. She was my Kelly Kapowski. I was the man who would fight for her honor. She remains the only girl I have ever duked it out for. Nobody steals my girl's cookies and gets away with it.

Her unrequited love hurt more than the punches.

> un·re·quit·ed (*adjective*)
> 1. not requited
> 2. not reciprocated or returned in kind <*unrequited* love>
> 3. a recurring frame in the carousel slideshow of my life.

I was aware that the girls whom I was head over heels for did not feel the intense yearning that kept me up at night. Their stomachs did not turn with every glance caught or smile exchanged. I also knew that little girls around me liked little boys, and that I was supposed to like little boys, too. I played along, becoming quite the heartbreaker—leaving boys in the dust with empty promises. I'll always remember how indignant I felt when I received a note with the words, "You don't even know the meaning of going steady!" from the boy I had dumped for the second time.

I came to accept my feelings for my female friends as part of the Big Mistake. I reasoned that "had I been born a boy, (fill in the blank) would be my girlfriend." I swallowed any hope for reciprocation and focused on breaking as many boy-hearts as possible.

The carousel revolves.

There are moments that stand out that were meant to prepare me for my mother's response; she knew. Mothers always know.

My mother informed me that if she ever found out I was gay, she would disown me, and that she did not believe in unconditional love. I was twelve. I had been smuggling my emotions deep in my underbelly since I could recollect. Holding their content captive, I ignored their screams and forfeited their revelations. To survive, we must deal with the tangible threats before us, the imminent dangers that could skirt or squelch the one driving force keeping us pushing forth. Resilience demands we duck, dive, twist and bend for the ultimate moment of freedom.

When my mother set the tone of the game, declaring her stance on my intuited transgressive sexuality, she was betting that my deepest and most desperate desire to one day be her daughter would subjugate all else. She was sure this Achilles' heel would be her green light to keep me under her manipulative push-pull. She understood my obstinate loyalty to her. She could feel my perpetual forgiveness emanating towards her. She recognized the fury that shot from my eyes when he hit her, demeaned her and made her his property. But my protectiveness did not console her; it reminded her of the turning points in her life that had led her to this place. She loathed it. She did not like to face the reality that her husband had stripped her of her vitality and the life she had built. That his bullishness had ripped apart the glory of a woman who had once owned her own business, her home and had hosted her own television show. Now a hostage to her marital "bliss," she saw me as a relic of her former self—a reminder of her life before the coup. A direct representation of what she wanted to ignore. An enemy truth within the ranks.

When she assured me she would disown me if I were ever gay, I didn't react. There was no shock or fear. I was a twelve-year-old whose experience had taught her that some things are inevitable and must be. By this point in life, I was sure that I would be booted from hers one day. Ejected from the *potential* to have her be my mother. Because the things that qualify the archetypal mother— nurturer, caregiver and protector—did not exist. Her threat was not "loss of *mother*," so much as "loss of the *possibility* of mother." Even at twelve, that possibility seemed far-fetched and couldn't topple the undeniable nature of my attraction for other girls, and more importantly, the fierce desire to *possibly* be myself one day.

Next frame, please.

(Step)dad was routinely my confidant. My mother and I were perpetually on shaky ground. She wished I'd be more feminine, more like her. I wished she'd quit reminding me how she had let me live with her instead of with my "dysfunctional (biological)father and his uneducated family." This rhetoric first made its appearance after her and (step)dad had conceived a child of their own. It amplified as she became more neurotic and as the tumors in her thyroid sent excesses of hormones to her brain. These hormones in turn produced demon chemicals that inspired her synapses to fire words like, "I wish I would have had an abortion with you," from her mouth.

I was her whipping boy—a scapegoat to her fractured life. My mother was never one for apologies or regrets. Deep down, I suspect that the part of her that had sacrificed her independence to serve her husband grew jagged. As she became more alienated from her former self and her family, the explosions she was juggling became louder. I trained myself to soldier crawl. Coming to my mother for advice was not what I did. (Step)dad was our go-between. The Switzerland. The U.N. peacekeeper assigned to mediate and translate.

Montage.

When I was fifteen, my mother confessed that the man we all believed to be (biological)father, the man she spent my entire life bad-mouthing and comparing me to, was most likely not (actual)father.

Rather, I was most likely the love child conceived with an older, quasi-famous actor. Probably. She couldn't be sure. As I grew older, she began to recognize uncanny similarities between the actor and me. This haunted her. She had to get it off her chest.

The same year, (step)dad was given an ultimatum by his father, a high government official who caught wind of his son's less-than-noble lifestyle. His father could not continue to serve as a public officer with a good family reputation. He offered (step)dad a financial incentive to make some changes.

A few months later, we moved, again, to what felt like the heart of conservatism, an ironic and strange land from where we had come. (Step)dad was going back to school to be a psychologist.

At sixteen, I campaigned to be allowed to return to school. I was ready to see new faces and to escape the twenty-four-hour lockdown with my crazy mother and (step)dad, whose budding advances blurred the line between Father and Daughter.

Turn, Kodachrome, turn.

I set foot in a traditional school for the first time in four years. We met. Her crush was hot and cold—ambivalent and painful. My parents loathed and distrusted her. I was convinced she was the ONLY other lesbian on Earth, and that everything hinged on working things out with her. Exhausted and emotionally spent, my Sisyphean love provoked me to spill the turmoiled contents of my heart to (step)dad. My trust in him was running on fumes, but so was I. His first reaction…"Don't tell your mother."

The train wreck that the Only Other Lesbian on Earth and I had become crashed into a cold November night. At roughly 11 pm (curfew), we screamed our melodrama into the streets. My mom, meanwhile, watched our antics through parted mini-blinds. The next morning, she was livid. She was sick with the flu, sitting upright in bed, her eyes seething with hatred. When she really got worked up, she gritted her teeth together and spit her words out. She reminded me of a rabid dog. My inquisition began, as she demanded to know what the hell was going on. I was bold with truth and no longer afraid.

"I'M GAY, MOM!"
"You're going to hell." Her first words have always been laughable.
"WHY?"
"Because the Bible says so."

I was her mirror. My truth, a reflection of expectations unrealized.

Her blatant hypocrisy fueled me. Emboldened me.

My mother's stubbornness would learn to break me. Over the next few months, I would learn that she would rather I be a prostitute than be gay because, after all, being gay meant I would undoubtedly get AIDS. I found out that washing my clothes with the rest of the family's would contaminate them with "gay cooties." I came to know that I was no longer welcome to the communal stash of food and would be responsible for purchasing my own provisions.

The level of absurdity that these new household norms created made my logic stutter. Gravely, I discovered the excruciating pain of having a tube shoved down my throat in a ritual called "stomach pumping." I ascertained that county-appointed psychiatrists are likely to ask people who have just had the contents of their stomachs emptied and bandages wrapped around their wrists if they have enjoyed a history of playing with their own excrement. (*No, I just want my mother to love me.*)

Most significantly, I confirmed that my mother's heart was dead.

Slip. Slide.

Two days back from the hospital, I was unceremoniously ordered to pack my essential belongings and to leave her household. I felt victorious that I managed to sneak my favorite childhood mug into my pack. There was no time to think. It was as if a fire had sparked and was swiftly ravishing ~~my hope~~ my home. What do you grab? What do you rescue from the flames? Your clothes? A photograph? Your favorite sippy-cup? A simple thread to connect the suddenly scrambled dots of the picture.

I will begin again.

The legendary Sabine women of the ancient Sabine tribe, as oral history accounts, got so fed up with war, they threw their bodies between the Roman and Sabine armies to end their fighting. Sacrificing their safety, to be free of the bloody brawl and relief from the clash, the Sabine women are remembered as fearless warriors whose actions brought about a much longed-for peace.

We will begin again.

Slide.

Thirteen years to refresh the page, to forget and stumble far from the dizzying past. Thirteen years to realize that recapitulating dysfunction is the most dangerous of the habits I fed after the storm. Thirteen years to conquer self-destruction. Thirteen years to realize that exile equals escape.

Thirteen years to forge a new empire—an urban tribe of fierce warriors whose love and support have grown big enough to eclipse the darkness at my heels. We live valiantly, reclaiming our innocence. Declaring toilet paper wars on each other's homes. Founding notorious gangs with adult-sized Big Wheels as our getaways. Wielding laughter to tether our splintered selves.

We load the fresh Kodachrome into restored bodies and push the shutter. Catalyzing serendipitous images of buoyant bliss and saturated bonds of spirit and loyalty. I am home. Within my ship, I am home, navigating my way to the quiet stillness far from my genesis.

Some frames unlock memories that remain untainted.

I miss her cooking the most. And I miss her laughter—lucid and graceful.

Pride and Joy: Finding Safe, Affirming Families for Youth

Family Builders

The needs of LGBTQ youth are vast and urgent. Queer youth remain at higher risk for substance abuse, suicide and homelessness, as the literature has documented repeatedly. Many of these runaway youth identify as LGBTQ and are overrepresented in the foster care system. They may end up in care due to being displaced from their homes because of their sexual orientation and/or gender identity or for parental abuse and neglect.

Many queer youth do not feel safe with their biological families, and they may or may not feel safe in foster or group homes, depending on whether homophobic or transphobic behavior is tolerated (e.g., being called names, bullying and physical abuse). Ultimately some queer youth prefer to live on the streets and to encounter the dangers there than to remain in unsupportive families or foster or group homes. Youth on the street navigate drugs, prostitution and adults who prey on children, among many other dangers.

Given this grim backdrop, Family Builders established the program, Pride and Joy, in 2007 to provide safe and affirming homes for LGBTQ youth in California. Its services are directed at finding families for these youth and maintaining these placements. Family Builders' Pride and Joy program recruits for families—gay or straight—to step up to provide safe, stable care in an accepting, welcoming family environment for LGBTQ youth. We strive to educate the community about the needs of children waiting in foster care, to advocate on their behalf and to place children with permanent, secure families through adoption and other forms of permanence.

Family Builders is not satisfied with providing traditional foster homes for youth. Pride and Joy is innovative in that the program's intent is to find permanent families for queer youth if they cannot return home. After several decades of experience working with children in foster care, we have learned that providing temporary caregivers and homes is not enough to nurture a child into adulthood and beyond. We need only to look at the rates of homelessness and incarceration among former foster youth to understand the limitations of the current child welfare system. Foster care was designed to provide for the basic needs of children, but children also need lifelong connections with caring adults to sustain them throughout their lives. Pride and Joy attempts to find these connections for queer youth, which we believe gives them the best chance for happiness and hope in their futures.

We believe that all young people need the love, nurturing, stability, commitment and unconditional acceptance offered by family. Thus, Pride and Joy's mission is to work with the biological families of queer youth to determine if their relationships can be strengthened and families can become safe and affirming enough for the youth to return home in cases where sexual orientation and/ or gender identity issues are the apparent cause of the youth not being in the family home. Often families become more supportive of their LGBTQ family members over time as myths are dispelled; as stereotypes and prejudices are challenged; and as they cope with issues around loss and change (i.e., the feelings of loss around *possibly* not having grandchildren, learning to accept same–sex partners, etcetera).

For more information, please visit: familybuilders.org.

Sylvia's Place Residents

Samantha Box

the hayop ka! chronicles: a queer pin@y OUTcasted & in the streets

kay ulanday barrett

Editor's note: "pin@y" is a cultural term to show queerness/non–gender conformity in Filipino/a culture. It is similar to "Chican@." Using "Filipin(o)" demonstrates the masculine, and "Filipin(a)" demonstrates the feminine. By using @ instead of "Pinay" or "Pinoy," both can be claimed or can refer to a new gender for people of Philippine ancestry.

it is said that when a child comes
out as gay, a parent suffers a death
when other teenage daughters were
riding out late in the cars of their
boyfriends, she pushed numbers on clocks
12, 1, 2 in the am, snuck
woman hips on notebook lines and
no warning or curfew could stop
this.

a therapist scribbled, made
what she loved—paper and ink and women
a disease.

to fix daughter, mother
rushed green lights, canceled a

usual appointment. sacrifices are
made by mother animals and if their
young aren't following the protocol
fate and fed,
they are killed, eaten alive.

is it because you aren't with a father figure?
is it because you were raped?
when did you start wearing caps, short hair,
wearing pants, speaking up?

hungry mother and therapist
shook questions like branches.
not a syllable filling
and they go on empty–bellied.
girlfriends weren't allowed to
sleep over.

on the lips of an 11th grader
clitoris, hand on thigh, dyke,
are not acceptable vocabulary.
the body gives to
switched pronouns on r&b
love songs.

    say "he" "his" and "him,"
so that you aren't
publicly outcast, beaten to

the point of throat scratch,
made a lesson to other girlboys
by flocking righteous men
who prove
straightness
by touching not caring about
your screaming or disconnection.

this is payment. this is your failing.

be born of volcano blood,
i love you in each language
mouthing letters like
body occupation /
stopping yourself
when you are fiery and aching the most.
be too small of a blue spark
crossing hearts, pumping fingers
confused with your
heat.

–excerpt from my poem, "hayop ka!"

my best shoes; journals from 1995; ripped out diagrams of anatomical daydreaming—breasts, arms, lips (i attempted to draw what romantic experiences i would eventually have, though i can't really draw at all); photo albums. my ma made a concerted effort to fling every inch of me out from our small basement one bedroom. this was our family's house. her aunt bought the house in the 70s stacked high with homeland missing and very little money. a family from pangasinan, philippines, carefully ushered one family member, then the next, sponsored a house full of opportunity for everyone.

i was the pride AND the glitch in the household, a single–handed hope, the first to go to an amerikan university. however, my cookie–cutter, biologically male/asian/best buy–managing boyfriend broke up with me, and all the sudden, it didn't matter what school i attended or even if i was happy. my ascendance into the straight immigrant amerikan dream was under close watch. my ma threw a sneaker at my head as i bounded for a slowly stopping car to scoop me up from this mess i caused. it had to be my fault, of course.

she cursed in tagalog, english and pangasinense and crashed books at my head as i ran out the door—emily dickinson, sarah waters, audre lorde. these queer clues were evident, but distinctly amerikan. whether i reveled in their prose didn't matter; they were fodder for my ma's anger at the time, not literary bravado. she couldn't have cared less; she just needed something in her hands to throw, to purge the loss of me she experienced. the neighbors were gawking by now, and i had tried entirely too hard to maintain the façade of a dignified straight girl, only to have a front row of school kids, grandmas, men watering their lawns, stop in mid–breath. my whole cover undone, for people to pick and prod and talk about. i was getting dizzy from it all.

"you! puneta ka! hayop ka! don't ever set foot here again, kay, unless you get your boyfriend back!" her voice thrown in the air in part prayer and part declaration. "don't you bring her back until she knows she's wrong!"

i blocked them, all her hits, every one, my forearm hot and seething from her fingernails. she could damn well swing all she wanted, but she couldn't touch my face. little did i notice then but it was a crucial exercise in power–shifting. it was reminder that you can't beat the queer outta of me, even if i or school or my own mother wanted it out, even if i sat there slumped as though the air had been let out of me.

fast forward:
i would spend years in secret thirst for her forgiveness. i would come by sharing every detail of heartbreak, testimonies of being done wrong by my lovers and eventually, hold out my mistakes as though a showing of sacrifice. eventually, she would always take my side. she would see that my pain was real on some human level. still, she would brace herself in

pronouns until she didn't have to be corrected. we would grow distant,
my ma and i, unable to maintain or map our hopes for one another. she
would kindly and politely turn down my invitations for her company
at PRIDE parades or performances i featured in that were for queer
audiences as though she was declining a meeting among coworkers due
to stormy weather or a public transportation disaster. as if it were outta
her hands with no other choice. we would mourn our slow distillation,
and i would try to find someone to love whom my ma would smile at,
would think deserving of me.

turns out, i was worse than a whore or a troubled student, no report card praise or celibacy could prevent this exodus. her face shrugged, her body shrinking as we drove further away from albany park. i cringed in the front seat of my escape car. what was i supposed to do? meg, goddess bless her liberal and lily white soul, she spoke mandarin chinese, studied tae kwon do, spoke conversational korean and just began understanding tagalog. later i would grow to abhor her colonial multiculturalism, but at the time, in the car, she and her car were pretty helpful. besides, it was the least she could have done what with all that culture stealing.

at 17, i didn't have a language or poem for this. i had been writing and purging my words by way of burning or burying or storing them in a lockbox. i could disguise my hurt better than giving it air to be said aloud. how could i become this? it's the trick of not getting caught, and i started to get too sloppy, slipping kisses too close to the house, writing gutsy stanzas that made a note of being very, very *descriptive*. i fell for someone, someone who wrote sweaty–palmed verses and made me a melty mess. in class, this girl and i would pass a journal, write updates of our lust in bold cursive. sure, the poetry wasn't that hot, but we felt it anyway. we allowed ourselves space to give off heat as we chose. i could hardly breathe being wrapped up, being frightened to get caught and so nervous for a girl.

i loved my ma. she had raised me a tiny seedling, a carbon copy of her image, stuck in middle amerika michigan among cattails, trailer homes and frankfurter bbqs. we escaped the small rural town we both were trapped in, the only people of color outside of first nations/native american people, and came to chicago where there were bigger buildings, better schools and most important our remaining family members living in the u.s. we called july 4th, 1989, our independence day. i remember leaving late into the night, being awoken from bed and watching the fireworks spit and evaporate along the highway as i sat eating cheetos on a greyhound bus. we thought we were invincible together. she hit me many times after that as puberty set in, as she stumbled upon my queerness by opening high school letters, monitoring friends, reading journal entries.

   i know what you are thinking. domestic violence is domestic violence. but when immigrants of color land here, are forced out here in the u.s., we have to re–invent ourselves. my ma remembered and wept, contained and contained, nothing was fair—the rent, the racism, my family's quiet lull after telling stories about back home, my own bruises. anyway, she was working late–night shifts into the morning; i was the one opening books, which isn't a sacrifice in comparison, right? she pushed out her happiness to live in this country, and i, i had to do the same. besides this is the american dream we are taught: be anything but who you are, and the rewards will come. i could allow this guilt. i could sing the assimilation song. i could feel shrunken as much as my own ma felt depleted day after day. it became a labor i was used to, a skilled task to accept like doing chores or submitting math homework. i accepted my inheritance of never feeling like i deserved my dreams, and let the colonization live within me.

> *rewind:*
> *once, i remember a school teacher gazing at my bruises during some pop quiz. that same spring during recess as i rolled up my sleeves, he then whispered as if in a code, "you know you can hit them back. once you hit them, they shut up. it's what i did to my old man."*
>
> *he said this like we were blood brothers in the same exclusive club. he had forgotten or ignored the fact that straight girls and boys are taught differently. girls don't hit: it's no sign of conventional womanhood. surely, white people can duke it out on one another too, all epic poem and heroic bombast. this is the disrespectful amerikan who can do anything. i was brown and didn't think this measure would have the same effect. he could do that, brawl fist to fist with his father. he would make it ritual as a manly man in a white world. i couldn't possibly, a girl hitting her mother! my heart skipped. hit her back? i froze. i stepped on his toes from*

the shock and clumsily skipped back to my friends, putting the idea away.
it never occurred to me, not once, to do such a thing. hit her back.

this time around, for hope or for disaster, i was the one who escaped, albeit without the necessary plans in order, but my ma made it very clear—i couldn't show face until i touted a boyfriend, any seemingly straight boy, around. i didn't tell my friends at church, in school, at my martial arts school. there was nowhere to go. it was early summer, and i had crumpled up a few dollar bills. no one at all in my life would understand how i fucked up my life or did *this* to my mom.

i had slept on and off the el' train for awhile. what day was it? my cell phone broke; it had crumbled when i fell as my mom chased me. i walked about melting in the sun, slept in parks, arranged food by jumping into people's backyard gardens and stealing a tomato here, a cucumber there. the daily enclave of anarchists and homeless hovering the parks couldn't be the same as me, could they? i thought i was going to be able to come home with my tail between my legs, reeking of humility, clenching promises of hetero boredom i wouldn't be able to keep for very long. i could maintain this unrealistic contract, fake it or morph myself temporarily until i gained trust back, couldn't i? my ma was the eminent matriarch: not one family member could challenge her decisions, and besides, she wouldn't want to tell other family members what i had *chosen* and what a disappointment i had become.

maybe my auntie would roll her car windows down with inventive pity and spot me on some corner where i fell asleep only to bring me rellenong talong and kanin. delighted, while i shoveled the food into my mouth, she would continue by saying how she thought it unjustifiable to kick me out of the house, and that my ma would get a stern talking to, and i would cry from the decadence of both her food and her courage. damn, i miss home food. maybe my ma would cry rivers of sympathy for her girlboi son and crave my distinct sense of humor when she was most sad or, at the very least, needing help operating her new dvd player. any excuse she could find to get me back home.

i'd accept an offer without apology. wouldn't i? maybe she'd call another family friend whose daughter i made out with during one of the cotillions or filipino banquets she feverishly attended, only to discover her friend has accepted her femme lesbian daughter and is attending pflag. *would you like to come with*, she'd insist over the receiver. now, that would be awesome. that would be divine intervention! that would be the promise of a home all closeted and out kids wanna brandish. that's better than having home, a physical place to land, 'cause i wouldn't feel the hate shoot under my skin.

      i wanted to say that ma recognized me in a crowded street and apologized, kissing all the dirt off my face and arms, that she'd embrace the homegrown pin@y i'd become and tell stories of other family members who rubbed junk with other creative queers. we'd chit chat and rejoice about my gay lineage and even how she kissed girls as a curious youngster in a school uniform. she'd smirk and place steaming bowls of rice at the table as though she were giving each one a piece of what she felt, suspended in nostalgia.

      if you saw me in passing, say during your lunch break or if you walked excitedly just as the school bell rang, my muscles were aching from sleeping on the ground. i sank into the sidewalk every time i waited for my ma or my aunties to find me. sank as i waited for this silent heartbreak, made it steep into my hopes until it just settled in, rancid and painful. you probably couldn't see it on my face, but i planned to wait until it became something impossible.

      this wasn't my fucking fault, this hella punishment. melissa and ryan, two shelterheads, sat with me outside sometimes. we poked fun at the kids who had it perfect.
      "there has to be something up with those guerros," melissa
chuckled.
      "it can't all be betty crocker."

      melissa had a bikini kill patch stitched on her coat and spat *the last poets* with finesse. she kicked a cop who wanted a blowjob once and cackled, or so i heard. she had righteous ways, and sometimes we talked about kissing, but really we took turns grabbing food from corner stores and actually sharing the goods. both our moms had hard catholic sticks up their asses and had no choice but to work for other people. both of us missed our moms, but instead talked about the possibility of them being secret lovers.

"my mom's name is cecilia. but for the sake of this, call her cece." i said confidently.

"mi madre, her name's letty. eh…let's keep letty!" she laughed to herself in satisfaction.

we spun our breaths together when the frost got to our eyelashes. we squealed and threw fits of laughter, had our own street side sleepovers. we conjured stories of how they would be of comfort to one another, how they would unfurl their bodies in bed and kiss, how they danced in a kitchen taking turns on spinning and dipping. better than all that, we spelled out how they'd be happy.

"cece's muscles would ache, ay dios! she'd complain about whose house she cleaned or which white bratty kid slobbered on her again. letty would be quick to take off her coat, make her tea, rub her fe——"

"ew! her feet?! that's nasty. her shoulders, girl. her shoulders," i'd say swiftly interrupting melissa's glossy–eyed vision.

"fine. shoulders then."

it was a game that resulted in hunger pangs, melissa scavenging for a cigarette butt, as we talked deep fantasies of being older brown queers with love and spine. we would be enchanted by our long sighs, the possible future we painted by alleyways and park benches. we glowed as these stories catalogued what could be. it wasn't really about our moms; it was about this faggotry and dykery having an ending we could love for ourselves.

it wasn't always about distraction. it was about a payback for our shitty queerdom. ryan always sat and listened, her quiet resulted in sobbing. we usually walked our way to humboldt park, ran behind houses in construction. we usually let ryan fall asleep only to wake us up from nightmares. maybe this vision was too far off for her. we were all just trying to be fed, and we suffered from some form of starvation one way or another.

for days i chewed on stale muffins at midnight, sat sunken in alleys and looked for coins everywhere i walked. i washed up twice in park sprinklers when the younger kids hit boredom and got to usher their summer sweaty bodies to a home and eventually dinner on the table. the dumpsters well after closing had our mark: first was the anarchist bike kids who had made bizarre spokes and seats spin like pinwheels, who climbed their bikes in peaks almost to fall over with bread under both arms. next were the homeless brown kids whose parents were wondering *what they could possibly be doing?* they were eating day–old cookies wrapped faultlessly in garbage bags. they were discussing cops chasing them as they leaned over one another kissing in moonlight, their jeans torn at the knees, trying to keep warm as their backs pressed against concrete.

we played swords with baguettes and passed around old pastries to other youth mingling idle or anyone who held up signs for food. we filled up milk crates, redistributed the wealth others discarded after a few sips of a latte and a conscientious no–carb diet. bandanas over our faces, we kissed through cloth and stuffed our pockets with old tortillas.

being broke never mattered as long as we zig–zagged dawn by the faint arms of streetlights. being poor, we ate the veggies left over from markets' garbage cans. sometimes we were stuck eating quietly, our stomachs churning hymns for something, anything to eat. we screamed punk rock or rock en español by night and closed our eyes tear–filled to juan gabriel on some stranger's porch as soon as the blueline train turned a curve. we stole in places to dance, places where of color kids could shake this hurt off, and it didn't matter where we lived, 'cause we could juke and pop and kiss for free. we ran into the streets high from so much shit and laughed with people we loved, people in the streets who did shit i never could imagine only until then. we gave each other poems at the earlobe in youth drop–ins; we promised to be there for you as you got tested, crossed our fingers to take the free bags of chips from the wait–in area. we built our own solace because our own bloodlines were clearly not enough to make a home.

met up with some kids who smoked and talked on and on about the punk life. got bored of this shit. got tired. walked around halsted street all night and all weekend, watched the old gays peruse their bars, and it's like they don't even see us anymore. have all of them had perfect, pristine stories with loving white parents, true democrats, who wear rainbow flags? i learned to cut my eyes at them as the cops ushered us in like cattle. i couldn't even walk a block with my girl without a loudspeaker that reminded me how different i was than the aforementioned affluent white gays. we didn't have the money to pump into alcohol fountains; therefore, we didn't deserve the leisure of being undisturbed during the weekend. me? i wanted to hit cops back, spit at them as their badges gleamed in my face, grab hold of their loudspeakers and declare:

breeders are NASTY and everybody knows it!

something held me still instead, and I just started to headnod, scraping for the least violent situation. everyone talked about gayness in homogenous terms, talked about some "movement." the only movement i've heard of that's queer are white people talking more about white people talking more about their interests, or better even, white people talking about how exotic it'd be to sleep with a [*enter your mistaken stereotyped ethnicity here*]. clearly, there's a big difference between condo-owning white gay men and me and my friends. gay or not, they got more property than any of my family (blood or chosen) members could taste.

we were all invisible somehow but blessed with different ways to cope. some had luxurious homes to hide behind; others had timeshares; and others just fought to see themselves reflected in the world without getting our asses kicked or our bodies dead.

see, i'm in the last group. i ached for some kind of leisure. i had to work with kissing girls, my brown face, had to fight and scratch for decency without the coveted esteem of money or speaking only english. gotta do this all at once and find food and believe i deserved to breathe. this exhaustion is always. this exhaustion expands into hopelessness. this exhaustion means there's a warrior in me, but i didn't comprehend that just yet. it was out of my league to understand this ease, this nonchalant queerness packaged in liberal gayness. some of us weren't just vagabonds 'cause of our romantic relationships with another person(s), but born outlaws and boundary-breakers at every angle you can find.

i've always been some problem to fix. shit, there were so many of us, so the cops cussed, called us *faggots*, told us to go somewhere, to go *home*. it's as though it's some sort of obvious joke, and we all dispersed sitting on storefront stoops, strewn along the sidewalks smoking, talking and fucking just far enough from streetlamps. this is when some cop wasn't bustin' on some fabulously decked queen or some kid for the slightest look. this is when the nightsticks were somewhat avoidable. this was a story during the hot months, during summer heat when it got so sweaty, that we begged for night to come cool us down. we nudged up against each other to keep from passing out or found someone to kiss to live outside of what made us numb. we thought if we could make it from the streets, we could escape and outlive anything. there was always some song to sing, some kid willing to share a handful of food, some glint of hope that would let the spark in you be. most of us were youth of color, with nowhere to go, but wherever we end up, maybe we'll get there with each other.

i admit, when i was hungry, i'd miss home. when i had too many hours of nothing and got lonely, i'd wonder what it would be like if the world operated in reverse. if arroz y gandules or pancit were the standard, if me and my wonderful partner (also filipina) only heard our homeland tongues on the radio, in gay bars, in conversations of good investments and well–educated propriety. i'd wanna giggle as white kids and rich folks feel upset after being shunned away as "you people." i'd love that. i'd wanna hear only kundimans on the radio station gracing me and my future partner's bed. i'd make the concerns of a brown tranny's lament to be catchy and powerful and priceless. it is—i know it is. this is what kept me awake at night. not the bugs or growling stomach as loud as a stray animal. if i had nightmares, the idea of this got me more smitten than kissing a girl or 300 girls. it was worth to waking up to.

Why?

L. Wolf

Her footsteps on the stairs made my body tremble. I could feel the anger vibrating around her and resonating soundly in every inch of the house. It settled deep in the pit of my stomach, stirring up a primordial fear in me that I didn't know existed until that day. Instead of making a stand, instead of raising my voice, I cowered on the floor.

My home was lost the moment her flesh connected with mine. The home that I knew was filled with a dysfunctional, verbally abusive but loving family in their own strange way. For fourteen years, I had lived with my aunt and uncle. Now, I was being beaten.

Each blow, whether it was by fists or an object, made me feel less and less valuable as a human being. Her words were just as harsh, so harsh in fact that I never repeated what she said to anyone. I closed my eyes as I felt hands on my body, hands that shouldn't have been there, disrespecting me. Each piece of clothing that I wore was forcefully removed. She stormed upstairs while my uncle slept, ignoring the sound of soft cries and an angry voice. I was left at the bottom of the stairs, my hands trembling, my body exposed. I sat there in my underwear, time ticking on slowly, left inside my own head.

My obvious discomfort with my body made her take her time, made her reach into the dirty clothes pile and throw down something for me to wear. After all, I didn't deserve such luxuries like clean clothes. That was exactly how I felt in that moment. It was as though I was the scum of the earth, and for what?

As the night continued, her screams were drowned out by closed windows. It made the living room humid and almost unbearable. It was the middle of the summer and the heat in the room was almost tangible by the time she stormed upstairs again. I cringed as she paused on the steps, ready for another blow.

"And don't you dare fall asleep! If I can't sleep, neither can you, bitch." Her words had caused my uncle to stir, and in a moment of false hope, I thought he was coming to save me. Instead, he offered her a cigarette. I wanted to scream at him. He was a kind, caring person who was manipulated by his sister over and over. I wanted to tell him how he should grow some balls and listen to his own heart for once. I couldn't believe he wasn't taking a stand against my aunt.

I found myself curled up on the couch, staring into the home that I was raised in. It looked so pleasant and lived in, with stuffed animals on the couches and trophies on the mantle. But I knew the outward appearance of the house was merely a façade. A supportive, loving family no longer lived beneath this roof. I never felt quite at home here. I felt like an intruder, someone just existing in the same space as the rest of the household. My aunt made sure that I felt ostracized. She would constantly remind me that we weren't blood relatives, that I was my father's child. I was exactly like him, my aunt told me. If anything, I wanted to be like my mother.

The strong fluorescent lamp a few feet away from me illuminated a picture of my mother, her features so delicate and gorgeous. I wondered, selfishly, why she had left me with this woman. In a moment of frustration, I focused my eyes towards the ceiling, hoping that she could hear my thoughts. I was screaming inside my head, my words harsh and trite.

Why? Why did you leave? Why the fuck am I sitting here getting beaten? What did I do wrong? Would you have done this to me, too? All because I have a girlfriend?

I wanted to stand—run—and leave. Instead, I stayed curled up in a ball on my couch, in a house that was no longer mine. I no longer felt welcomed or supported in this space. Instead, I felt like scum, like I was worthless. Bruises lingered all over my tan skin, angry black and blue spots forming on my legs and arms. My body was exhausted. Her words kept replaying over and over in my mind. Some of those words were the same ones I'd been hearing for ten years, while others were new and raw. I focused so much on these thoughts that I lost track of time. I put my remaining energy into figuring out why I was such a bad person, figuring out what I had done wrong.

All I could think was, "If I just hadn't done this, or this..." But those thoughts didn't last. I knew in my heart that what I did was exactly right. At age fourteen, I had a girlfriend of almost eight months. My aunt forbade me to see my girlfriend. I did what any other teenager on this earth would do. I continued to see her.

But now, I was lost. I doubted that I would be able to continue a relationship with my girlfriend. I doubted my relationship with my aunt was salvageable. That made me tear up. I had come to love my family in all its dysfunction. I curled up on the floor with my dog for a while, knowing she was one member of the family I could count on. As I stroked the little bichon-poodle mix, I talked out loud to her. "You still love me, right?" At the moment, it didn't feel like anyone in my family loved me. Why couldn't they support my decisions for once? They set me up to fail in anything I tried to accomplish. Though they may have loved me in their own strange way, I was getting tired of constantly being forced to be "popular" or to do things that "normal kids" do.

I stood and went to lay on the couch, a plan brewing in my mind. If this continued tomorrow, that would be it. I would run away to my father's house. My father and I didn't have a relationship, either. He saw me maybe once every week or so, but wouldn't call on birthdays and promised Christmas presents that never came. I also knew that he beat my brother. Through some miracle, when my mother died when I was four, my brother went with my father and I with my aunt.

I fought my drooping eyelids for hours on end, and I only realized that I had fallen asleep when my body hit the wooden frame of the couch. I felt a sharp pain on my side and through my legs. I yelped out some expletive and opened my eyes.

I jerked up to realize that she had pulled the couch cushion from underneath me, causing another sore spot to appear on my body. My eyes widened as she stomped her way into the kitchen and returned with a can of Lysol. I tilted my head like a curious animal, watching her movements closely. She stalked towards me like a predator, her knuckles ghostly white as she gripped the can.

"Get the hell up!" She barked, waving the Lysol can around wildly. Often a victim of inappropriate humor, I found this scene extremely amusing. Still, I obeyed.

She began furiously spraying the couch I had slept on with Lysol. I shifted my weight awkwardly from one foot to the other as she sprayed before finally deciding to settle down on an adjacent couch. I realized my mistake as she grabbed me forcefully by the arm, throwing me off the couch. I cringed as she came closer to me. I could feel my heart racing, feel the heat on my cheeks as she glowered down at me. I couldn't even bring myself to look her in the eyes. Instead I started a little mantra in my head, "Get your shoes and leave...get your shoes and leave..." The hard part of this would be finding my shoes. My aunt had hidden them the night before. She knew I was a flight risk.

"You don't get to sit there." She literally spat these words into my face, small specks of spittle falling across my cheeks.

After she had finished Lysol-ing everything I touched, she went into the kitchen for breakfast with my grandmother. It was strange to me how neither she nor my uncle spoke a word to me. I floated, invisible, in the background as they went about their day. I sat, confused, on the living room floor. I took the time to take in my childhood home. I can't say it was all filled with wonderful experiences, but it was all I had known. My aunt, whom I believe to be bipolar, would go on rages that involved screaming at me. I was never, ever good enough for her. Everything I did was wrong. All of this negativity from her just made me feel terrible about myself. In her own words, my body was too fat, and my behaviors weren't "normal."

It was simple enough. I carefully put on my favorite pair of sneakers while she wasn't looking. She purposefully hid them in the closet, thinking I wouldn't look for them. According to her, I was only allowed to wear sandals. She was worried about me running. Once my purple laces were tied, I headed for the door as calmly as I could.

I stood at the door, my trembling hands gripping the cold metal of the door handle. I kept giving glances back at my childhood home, already missing the sense of family that I once had.

In a flash, she came barreling at me from the kitchen, her face red and puffed up as she yelled. Her blond hair cascaded all around her face, her wrinkles accenting the ugly look in her eyes. I pushed the door open, let it slam against the railing and ran like hell. I ran for a long time, my thoughts racing. Every car that drove by looked like hers. My adrenaline was pumping, and fear was surrounding my every thought. I wish my father didn't live so far away. I felt my body dragging as I slowed to a jog, breathing heavily. I could see my father's house out in the distance, and I was so relieved when I approached the door. I gave a few soft knocks, then a series of louder ones.

My father answered the door in boxer shorts, his shirt off, looking as though he had the world's worst hang over. Some random brunette lay on his floor, the AC running full blast, and there I stood. It took me a minute to process everything, to go over what had happened in my head.

"What the hell are you doing here this early?" My father asked, rubbing his eyes. "What's with your clothes?" He motioned to the stains on my shirt and the strange boxer shorts I was wearing.

"I—I need to stay here for a little while." I watched as my father stood aside and let me in. The door slammed closed.

I can't say I never looked back.

When I was sitting, freezing on my father's bed, the heat off in the middle of the winter, I looked back. I stared out the broken window in the room, feeling another cold rush of air, my eyes falling on the stars. I had spent nights on the street, and this wasn't much better. I could hear my brother pounding angry fists on my door.

My father's drunken voice echoed up the stairs, his words indistinguishable. The light from the hallway seeped into my room much like the cold did, finding its way in through holes that my brother punched in my door. I could hear his angry voice, feel his anger as it too seeped into my room. I wondered what would happen when he finally broke the door down. I lived in constant fear of my father overdosing on whatever it is that he took, or my brother breaking down the door. As time went by, I felt more and more unsafe, like a scared little child hiding from the boogeyman. And that's exactly what I did. I turned off all the lights, curled up under my blanket and prayed that he would stop banging. But my brother never stopped.

He was about as violent as they got. My brother threatened to kill him or me with a butcher knife one night because I wouldn't give him the phone. Another time he made a hole so big in the door that he could fit his hand through it. He terrorized me everyday that I lived under that roof.

I looked back again when I forgot one night to lock my bedroom door. I looked back as an unfamiliar body pressed my bed down, cologne overwhelming my senses. I looked back, and I looked at the huge hole in the middle of the door, focusing all of my attention on that. For a while, that was all I remembered. I remember being so very afraid of him. I remember trying to push him off the bed. Most of all, I remember my father coming in, grabbing my brother by the hair and throwing him into their bedroom. The next morning, my father didn't look at me.

I wondered, once I finally realized the full extent of what happened to me, why I left. I had picked what I assumed to be the lesser of two evils, but instead I brought more pain and heartache on myself than I thought possible. I was solely responsible for the events that happened on all of those nights. I was responsible for the abuse, neglect and pain. As I told these thoughts to my therapist one brisk morning, my body folded up into my chair, and she reminded me of something.

"You had to." She explained calmly. "You had no other choice. You didn't choose to leave. You were forced."

Though her words were simple, they sunk into me. I had spent such a long time blaming myself for everything that happened to me that these words never crossed my mind. These refreshing words brought a sense of peace to me that I hadn't felt in years. I wish I had realized that sooner. But even with her comforting words, I still thought in the back of my head, "If only I had done something differently."

But, doing something differently would mean letting go of my sense of self. Letting go of my pride, my passions and who I was as a person. I was not ready to give any of these things up.

Every time I go to my mother's grave, I stand on the dirt and stare hard at her last name. I let my fingers trace patterns over the engraved stone, and I make sure to leave a rock on the top to let her know I was there. I never leave without talking to her. My mind always asks the same questions.

"Why?" I speak to her out loud for the first time. When I get no answer, when all I can hear is the whisper in the trees, I tear up.

I look back each time I walk down the street in the winter, snowflakes dancing around my head, my hands pressed into my pockets, and I see a family decorating a Christmas tree. It makes every inch of my body ache. Each time I see a mother hugging her child, I look back. When my fingers press to my mother's tombstone, when I feel a part of me is missing, I wonder if I ever should have left. Even now, five years later, I still try to think of ways to fix that lost, dark feeling that I get in my chest when I see a family together.

I don't know if I will ever change that.

Will Exchange Wisdom for Shelter, Food or Love*

Mx. Mirage

Editor's note: During the editing of Kicked Out, I lost contact with Mx. I believe Mx. is couch surfing, a common survival strategy for homeless youth.

On the Horizon

I am a mirage.

People call me Mirage, and I like it. I am a pre-op FTM tranny, and more often than not, I identify as pansexual. I write too often, dye my hair too much, say things I know will get me in trouble, and live life spontaneously. I take pictures of people inside malls and shopping centers. I sing and dance and perform in public places. I teach people who need to be taught about seeing queerly. I live in Maine 90% of the year. So, if you ever see some guy with hair that looks like Skittles just puked in it, running around the mall, having people pose with mannequins, say *hi*. I love making new friends.

Practical Knowledge

First of all, if you're a homeless queer youth, I hope you're somewhere safe. I know firsthand how cold it gets outside at night. Whether you've been kicked out or you just *had* to leave due to the situations going on at home, know that people understand. I understand. And no one should patronize you for the decision, if you chose to leave rather than being kicked out. Either way, I hope you are safe at a friend's house or a homeless youth shelter that is also considered a safe zone for LGBTQQI[1]. If you're out sleeping in public places, what's called being "without a bed," stay warm, stay hidden and eat lots of

---

1. Lesbian, Gay, Bisexual, Transgender, Queer, Questioning, Intersex

carbs. Dumpsters behind bakeries and places like Panera are great for bread. It's not gross; they just don't resell food a day old. Keep that in mind.

If you're someone who is still living at home but can't handle it, contact some friends and relatives of yours; see if it would be alright to stay there for a bit. Maybe you and your parents just need to take a break. If it ends up being a longer break than you had anticipated, try to help out the families you're with— if not by working and pitching in money-wise, then by doing dishes, trash, cleaning and things like that. They will appreciate your efforts a lot more than you think. More often than not, people are very willing to take in their friends/ family when in need, so find some good people, and don't be afraid to ask. This isn't the time to claim your independence; even if you think you're ready for it, you're probably not.

Don't ever forget that people love you. Never forget there are people who love you. Honestly, your parents are probably some of those people, even if they've been bad at showing you they love you.

You're not immoral, hedonistic, sick, bad, wrong or anything else for being queer. That's just the person you are, and you can't change that. Neither can people who say those things. Live your life the way you want to. Don't let others dictate your loves, wants, needs. And enjoy life! Don't use excuses. Work hard for what you believe in.

Learning to Raise Myself

The hardest thing for me was continuing to go to school while homeless. A lot of responsibility and attention shifts because you have to become your own parent in the eyes of the school. That's when it finally hit me that it was all real: I was homeless when the school declared me homeless. The nights I slept outside (or *didn't* sleep) weren't what convinced me. Maybe by that point, I was already insane. It had built up for a long time, though, this knowledge that I would one day huddle up in someone's pool shed to get away from the cold rain and to sleep an hour or two before school.

My mother and I never had a healthy relationship. She was very needy, sick both mentally and physically, and in most ways, I raised myself. All she did was feed my two older siblings and me, pay the rent, etcetera. She wasn't around a lot, and the older I got, the more we fought. I can't say it was completely her fault, but there were things she just wasn't willing to accept. She didn't understand why I dated a queer boy, who ended up breaking up with me because I was ill-equipped, but he knew going into the relationship that I was a queer tranny-boi. It was eighth grade—come on, I wasn't having T^2 that early.

She couldn't accept that I wanted to cut my hair or dye it blue, no green, no… pink! No maroon and violet. We fought about everything under the sun and moon, no matter how insignificant. Eventually, it got to the point where she was calling the cops on me and blaming things that she did on me (after all, I was the crazy, scissor-wielding fifteen–year–old out to get zir poor, defenseless mother!). Had they listened to me, they would have found a knife under *her* pillow and a taser on top of her dresser. Scissors don't beat tasers in this game, even if I had had them. She threatened to kill me, commit suicide, throw me out windows, etcetera. I've been stabbed, told to commit suicide (which I attempted but failed), choked, burned, tasered, abandoned and otherwise emotionally scarred because of her.

All in all, it was definitely better when I got kicked out. At first it was hard, I will admit. I didn't have any money and very little food. I hate to admit it, too, but I'm a really good thief. I stole from stores the first three weeks so I would have something to eat, even dry granola and tap water. It's not that bad, though. I slept in Wal-Mart a few times (they've got comfy pillows and heat), outside for about a week, and ended up sleeping in the costume loft at my school. It's somewhere no one goes, so I was safe amidst the old costumes and weird sounds.

Once the school was aware of my situation, thank goddess, I got some real help. They had a copy of my birth certificate, so I could get a job and health care. The school helped me with college applications and will help me get my driver's license. Even now that I'm eighteen, I get help from resources through the school, though I was never a ward of the state.

And Now

Currently, I live with my friend and their[3] mother. She accepts me, and I pay rent, although most of the time, she tries to give it back. As hellish and hectic as my life has been, I've survived. I don't know how, but I know why. I survived so I could tell others that there is an end to the tunnel.

It does stop raining, and cars do stop hitting you on the freeway.

---

2. Testosterone.

3. Their is used here to indicate a singular, gender–neutral pronoun.

My Days of Judgment*

Taylor L.

Editor's note: The program/shelter (Gay and Lesbian Adolescent Social Services in Los Angeles) that helped Taylor has since been closed. I have no contact with her, but I wonder about her all the time.

As a young child, I felt myself judging people as they walked by—especially girls. I never thought I'd like girls, but my feelings for them told otherwise.

My name is Taylor, and I'm a seventeen–year–old lesbian. I grew up in a Christian home. My mom wasn't religious, but my grandmother was. I went to church from the time I was a toddler until I was nine. Even though the church taught me that same-sex relationships were bad, starting out at nine I found myself looking at parts of girls and loving everything I saw. But I never considered myself "gay."

From then on, my life became hard. Me and my family started having problems. One day my sister threw away my mom's boyfriend's personal papers. He got mad and hit her in the face, and then he broke every light in the house. That's when we went away to foster care. My mom decided she didn't want to take care of twelve kids anymore. Her boyfriend convinced her that we were a distraction to their relationship.

I was in and out of foster homes all my life. There were always plenty of girls around. This furthered my suspicion about my sexuality.

Life moved on while I remained in foster care. In my fifth foster home, I found myself liking this girl named Marlene. It was just a sexual attraction. Between ages nine and thirteen, I had to learn to handle all of my lifestyle changes because of being in so many different houses. I could tell if a home was just in it for the money, or if they were in it to help the kids. A lot just want the money.

I've been through everything from verbal to physical abuse. In my third foster home, the foster mom used to get the other kids to jump on me—for no reason at all. I was mentally hurt because it never felt like "really being home."

Things got tougher and rougher. I got thrown into juvenile hall for making a "terrorist threat to a staff member." It's crazy because I was only a kid, and I was just yelling because I was frustrated and angry. Still, they put me away. One day my best friend got into a fight at school with all the other girls in the group home. She got sent home. When I finally got home, the cops were already there. I started to argue with the staff because they said I was in on the fight. The cops stopped the argument, and the staff member told the cops that I'd threatened her.

That was a turning point in my life.

Most people would think juvenile hall would be a scary place for a thirteen–year–old. But not for me. I loved it! I met a girl named Porsche who I was really attracted to—actually, I think I fell in love with her. Porsche left juvenile hall, and then times got difficult. I started to get into a lot of fights in the halls and to talk back to staff all the time. Porsche and me had fallen off track. I started cheating on her with a girl named Maliza.

Now, when I first met Porsche, I thought she was the most beautiful girl I'd ever met. Everybody fought over her. In the beginning, she was just a normal beautiful girl to me, but then, she drew me into her world with all her might, and I fell for it. I decided that I needed to have what everyone was wanting from her—which was just her. She was 5'7" and she always wore individuals in her hair. She had glasses and a lot of tattoos, which attracted me to her even more. She had this kind of "whip appeal," which you just can't resist. But, when she left and I met Maliza, it was different.

Maliza and me—we were into this same kid-shit-drama; we were on the same level. We were always breaking up and making up with each other. I didn't really like it because there was no true commitment. Our relationship didn't last long. After falling out of love with her, I started having only open relationships with all of my girlfriends.

When I became open about my sexuality I told my sister, Jasmine, first. She thought I was playing. But when she found out I wasn't, word got out to the rest of my family. They just all considered me a lesbian. They never once tried to disown me. However, the people who started to kick me out were the foster homes. No one wanted to accept gays or lesbians.

When I look back on these times, it makes me very upset. How can people judge others because of sexuality? That's discrimination. That's against my beliefs. Gay people are already judged by society. But for foster homes to discriminate against queer kids—that's just absurd! I don't think the foster homes were afraid of me. They were afraid of me possibly "persuading" some of their girls to "be gay," which was never my intention. I actually don't think you can persuade anyone to be gay or lesbian. It is just human nature.

In August 2006, I was placed in an LGBTQ group foster home. It is the best placement I've ever been in. It allowed me to be myself. It was my first placement out of juvenile hall. Being in a home surrounded by nothing but gay and lesbian youth made me feel comfortable.

On November 10, 2006, however, once again I was arrested for "making a terrorist threat against a staff." It was only based on accusations—false accusations. I was told to do standards, which is a kind of punishment where you write "I will not do this" over and over, so many times. I refused to do them. I started to draw things because I was upset and didn't want to be forced to write. Then, after ten minutes, I finally cooled off and started doing the assigned standards. I had already begun doing my punishment, but the cops had already been called. When they came to the home, they said I was accused of committing a crime—"making a terrorist threat." They said they had been told by staff that I'd told the staff I was "going to beat your ass." (I don't even remember saying that!) I had to do ten months in jail based on these false accusations. I was just a pissed-off kid, but I still had to do the time.

When I finally got out, they let me off probation, and I became a regular department of family and child services kid. I took advantage of the deal and started in the foster care system again. But, at every placement, I ended up running because of the fear that when they found out I was gay, they would reject me. I started kickin' it with friends, on the street, in the 'hood, around Hollywood. But it got old. One day I decided to turn myself into my social worker. Life felt totally meaningless. I was drinking and smoking every day and fucking everybody I walked past, but going nowhere. My own life didn't do me any justice.

On November 1, 2007, my social worker heard what I was saying and got me back to the LGBTQ group home. This time I am stable and doing well. I'm still trying to find myself, find out who I am in a lot of different ways. I know I'm a lesbian. I know that I love girls, but what I don't know is what my future holds. When it gets here, I will live it like I've always lived it, but smarter. One day at a time.

Sylvia's Place Resident

Samantha Box

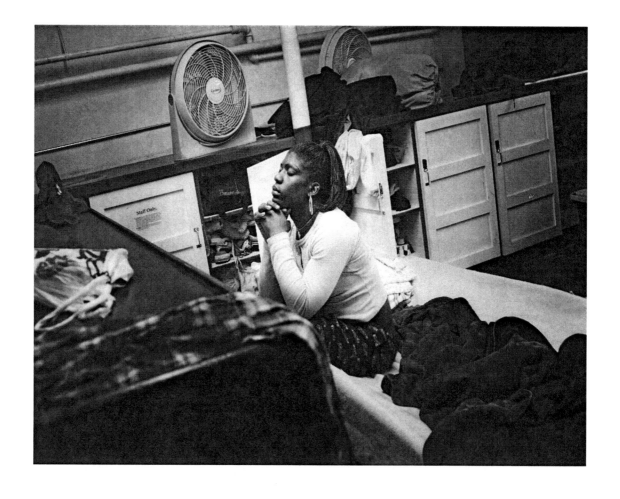

Tangled Hair

Booh Edouardo

The author wishes to thank Sassafras Lowrey; Dominika Bednarska; Sarita Cannon, Ph.D. and Catherine Ragazzi for reading and offering suggestions.

Curled up in the corner on a hard wooden pew in a church that reeks of incense and the sweat of grownups, I listen to the priest in the pulpit decrying the "hippies" at the Summer of Love and the "effeminates" who had rioted at Compton's Cafeteria the year before. While my parents had moved our family across the bay from San Francisco, we had not escaped from the immoral who had come into our neighborhoods. Looking up at the ceiling painted with clouds and angels, I listen to the priest who seems to have come down from heaven to remind people at church to "be vigilant of the menace" in our backyard. I wonder why he has chosen to yell at us in a dark, rumbling building when I can feel the power of the universe, the power of God, in the bright sunshine among giant redwoods and the cool, green grass.

As the priest speaks, I fiddle with the bottom of my pajamas that I have rolled up my thighs as high as I can in order to hide them under my dress. When I had gotten dressed in the morning, I decided to leave them on so that I could pretend that they are a pair of boy's pants. My parents don't allow me to wear male-like clothes. More than anything, I want to run and play outside just beyond the locked, stained-glass windows that, with the mid-morning sun, form shadows of odd creatures across the beige, spackled walls of the mission.

When church is over, my parents walk my older sister and me back to my father's blue Chevy Impala; we climb inside its wide backseat. After my father closes the door, I turn around and peer out the back window at the trees that line the parking lot while my parents get into the front seat. I want to get the smell of church off of me by running in the sunshine, climbing up the limbs of the big oak in the far corner of the lot and peering down at the world.

I slip off my toddler-sized, black patent leather shoes with matching bows on the top and stand on the soft vinyl seat, but even on my toes, I cannot reach the warmth and safety of the back dashboard. My hands reach for its top, a long, narrow cardboard-like surface that runs parallel to the large, slanted back window. I lean towards the dashboard as far as I can and jump with my arms outstretched, firmly grasping its center. Slowly, my hands pull me up, and I wedge myself so that my whole body is resting on its top.

I look out the back window and wish I could cast a spell to press through the glass and to transport myself outside. My eyes trace the twisted trees reminding me of the ones that I have seen in a picture book of Grimm Brothers' fairytales. The grass shoots out from the ground in browns and greens. Their individual stalks point towards the sky in anticipation of the summer's end. I want to sit, leaning against the big oak, to feel its roots, the grass and dirt under my short, skinny legs.

I imagine wearing a pair of jeans and a boys' t-shirt, which I can get as dirty as I like when I play instead of my perfectly pressed dress and perfectly groomed, bobbed hair. My mother tries to control my curls with hairspray and bobbi pins. But I wish my hair could grow however it wants in wavy curls like the twisted branches of the big oak.

I lie in the heat on the back dashboard, look through the window and listen to my parents whispering in the front. After awhile, I turn towards the noise. My mother adjusts the rearview mirror, shifting its slant from a horizontal to vertical position. From the mirror, my mother's eyes meet my gaze, and then she and my dad start whispering again.

After they finish, my father twists his body around towards my sister and me. His fingers press down on the button locking the back door. Then his hand reaches across the backseat, and he grabs my foot, dragging me down from the dashboard. At the last moment, I turn towards the big oak and the rest of the world and try to squirm away, but it doesn't work. He drags me down and slaps me with such force that the skin on my leg welts. His imperfect, red imprint serves as a tattooed claim, proving ownership over my body.

As he hits me again and again, he yells about how my wearing pajama bottoms to church has embarrassed our entire family. I explain as I cry that I didn't mean to embarrass anyone. I simply hadn't wanted to go out of the house feeling undressed. My mother and I look at one another again through the rearview mirror, and she smiles.

My father tells me that he, and the rest of my family, will beat my desire to act like a boy out of me if it is the last thing they do. He says that I am exactly the kind of person that the priest has warned the family about during his sermons. By the end of the beating, I feel ashamed of what I have done without knowing why. I promise never to wear pajama bottoms as pants or to mention wanting to wear boys' clothes again.

I sneak into one of the corners of the blue vinyl car seat. As my father drives, my sister, who is four years older and twice my size, scoots over, socks me hard in the ribs and then sticks her tongue out at me. I clutch my chest, slip onto the blue floor mat and huddle into the corner as far away from everyone as I can. My fingers lightly touch the welted, reddish-blue handprints on my bare legs.

I wonder, if the priest had sermonized about something else, would my father still have beaten me? Why am I like the hippies and the effeminates whom I had seen before we moved from San Francisco? Why is it a sin to want to wear boys' clothes, to run and play and to climb trees?

I never heard a biblical story that explained the sinfulness of wearing a pair of pajama bottoms to church. If I had worn boys' pajama bottoms, would that have made a difference? If the priest is supposed to help people, why did he give a sermon that encouraged my father to beat me? The answers to my questions don't seem like something I would find in the bible.

My parents decide that my desire to be male is about more than clothing. Although I try to keep my promise, they still beat me on a regular basis. At school if I choose to play with a toy fire truck or sports with the other boys, some of the teachers and children pick on me, and my parents hear about it.

My family tells me about other things that I do that are bad. They create new rules that keep changing that seem to be based on my instinctual choices. My parents become dedicated to beating all of the differences out of me. After they permanently injure me, I stop exercising my sense of choice.

The violence in my family grows as I do.

Often my parents bring me into their fights even when I am not in the room. Sometimes they fight over my father being "mulatto." My mother slaps or punches him and tells him to keep his voice down because someday I will write down their secret and tell everyone that they are an interracial couple, and they "pass" even though their marriage is not yet legal in many states. My father cries and says that my mother doesn't understand because she is white—that he, my sisters and I will always be different from her, different from the rest of the world, always misunderstood.

After their fights, my father paces up and down the long, narrow hallway. He talks to himself about how much he hates "niggers." I promise myself that I will never hate the color of my skin or anything else that is a fundamental part of me.

My father speaks to the many voices that only he hears. Sometimes he talks to the one that he thinks is God, the one that has told him to rape and kill me. Speaking in "tongues," he tries to carry out the Lord's will.

I spend time imagining how to escape my predicament. My family doesn't want me around, and I want to run away. Sometimes my mother and/or father kick me out of the house for a time.

When my parents lock me out overnight, I walk about two miles to the children's park and sleep on one of the benches painted brown to match the picnic tables attached to them. I lie on my back and watch the stars twinkling above me independent and free. During the day, families come to the park. They sit together at the picnic tables and benches laughing and eating their lunches. The children play in the park or visit the animals at the rescue zoo next door.

After my father has beaten me, I run away about two blocks from our house. The manicured lawns and pruned gardens end, and the wilderness takes over for a few hundred yards. Big oaks and firs grow along the embankment. I veer from the dirt path and slide down to a trickling creek under a bridge where I can hide.

My hair, which hangs past my thighs in a straightened ponytail, catches on a tree branch. As I pull my head away, pieces of the branch come off in my hair, and strands of it are left behind on the tree's limb. I slide down the embankment under the bridge that is falling apart from the hundreds of cars that drive over it everyday and wait in the dirt and mud. Vines of ivy and tall ferns grow out from each side of the creek.

After dusk, I clutch the plants and crawl up the embankment onto the other side of the stream. My back was re-injured when my father hit me, and I can't stand upright. It is now stiff from squatting for so long.

I hobble towards the paved road. In a few steps, I am back in suburbia. My shoeless feet shuffle pass the planned gardens with rows of flowers, patches of grass all cut the same length and into squares or rectangles. The bushes, trimmed into neat hedges, demarcate one property line from another.

My dress is too short and too small in the shoulders. Dirt and mud smudge my clothes, and I have bruises on my face and neck. My long ponytail has come undone part of the way, and twigs hang from its tangles just beginning to curl.

I remember seeing a police station near the library after we had come to this new town. Even though I'm in the fourth grade, we have moved so often that I have never gone to the same grade at the same school for more than a year at a time. Policemen help people in trouble, I think, people like me. Perhaps one of them can talk to me about what to do and protect me from further harm.

My hand reaches up onto the guardrail, and I walk down the six concrete steps. With both hands, I pull open the glass door framed in metal that serves as the after-hours entrance. The only policeman in the station glances away from his work and peers down at me from over the counter. Then he reshuffles his papers, picks up a pen and begins to write. Without looking, he asks what I want. He doesn't seem to notice my appearance or that I am out after dark.

My throat is dry, and I have trouble swallowing. I tell the policeman that my father has hurt me, and that I am afraid for my life. I push my tangled hair back from my face and look up at him, but he doesn't seem to notice me.

The policeman glances down and then continues to write. He says that I can file a police report if I want to, but that it won't do any good. Perhaps I have made up my story and need time to rethink it. He tells me that after I make the complaint he has to lock me up in juvenile hall where I will stay for an indefinite period. As I climb back up the stairs, I try to fill myself up by gulping in the warm evening air.

The Catholic Church that my parents belong to is nearby, I think. Perhaps the priests will help me since they know my parents, and my parents like them. As

I walk across the entryway, the lights over the front door of the rectory come on as if to welcome me. I ring the bell, and a man answers from a box that hums.

"Can I help you?" the voice crackles. I explain how I am a student at the school and a member of the church, and that my father has injured me. I ask for help and wait for the man's answer hoping that someone will open the front door. Finally, the box hums again and the man says, "Go away. No one here will help you."

I stand for a few seconds staring at the box wondering what to do. After awhile, it crackles again. The man tells me to get away from their private property, and then the humming stops.

As I hobble away from the rectory, I smell the spice of the big pepper tree. I have sat under the tree many weekday mornings waiting for the school bell to ring. I put my arms around its trunk and feel the rough edges of its bark press into my arms, chest and cheek, and I cry.

The wind tangles my ponytail that hangs in a curly mess down the middle of my back. It blows through the only clothes I own: a stained t-shirt, patched overalls and a fisherman's turtleneck sweater. My fingers lightly fiddle with the political button that I have pinned on my sweater, the one of Harvey Milk.

When I had turned eighteen, I was finally free from my parents' grasp. They could no longer kick me out. They could no longer order me back under threats of arrest. They could no longer try to have me committed to the state's mental institution at Napa. They could no longer force me to move with them from town to town and from state to state.

I watch the gay pride parade pass by, the first in San Francisco since Harvey Milk and George Moscone were shot, and the murderer was convicted. A man walks by in black leather: pants, boots, jacket and hat. He has pinned gay political buttons onto his jacket and red t-shirt. He holds up a bullhorn and says to the crowd, "Join in! Harvey is dead. This is no time to stand on the sidelines."

And so, I march. I march in a queer event for the first time. I march to remember Harvey Milk, whom I had never met. I march with the other people who weren't in contingents. I march even though my balance isn't good, and I'm not steady on my feet. I march past the police who stand on the sidelines with their batons ready in case I misstep.

A woman whom I have never seen before comes up from behind and touches my arm. We look at each other for a moment. Her straight gray hair frames her face with a square cut, and her blue eyes squint to avoid the pieces of trash and dust that blow around us. Her stomach rolls slightly over her belt and jeans and protrudes from under her white t-shirt. Between the edges of her green, puffy down jacket, the front of her shirt has a red fist inside a woman's sign. Without speaking, she puts her arm around my back, and I put mine around hers, as we walk towards Civic Center where the shootings took place. She disappears a few minutes later, and I never see her again.

I have come back to San Francisco for the first time since my family moved away from the area for good. I missed the shootings and consequential violence caused by the assassinations. I missed a local jury convicting the murderer of manslaughter. I missed the throngs of queer people blaming all local San Franciscans. I missed the riot caused by the police in the Castro.

It's as though I was absent from my own personal history, my own life. I have saved up some money to get something to eat after the parade is over. I decide to go to the Castro and look around.

I had left less than a year and a half earlier, but so much has happened: I assume that I will see visible signs, but it looks almost the same. A few storefronts painted their windows in memoriam to Harvey Milk and nothing more. I am disappointed that I cannot see the history I have missed.

I walk into Auntie Mmm's and stand near the door waiting to be seated. The diner is empty, and the only waiter stands at the cash register adding up the morning's receipts. After awhile I decide to seat myself and choose a booth near the window.

The waiter does not come over, so I say hello and give a shy wave. He does not notice. Eventually I get up, walk over and ask for a menu. He tells me that he will not give me a menu and to get out. I explain that I just want to get something to eat. He orders me out, points at the door and then walks away.

When the door closes, the bell on the doorframe tinkles. As I leave, I tell myself that the waiter is not important enough to cry about, but I cry anyway. I want to feel as if I belong somewhere, but I don't.

He is probably not from San Francisco or he wouldn't have acted the way he did, I think. Why does he hate me? Maybe I should hate him back. I want to run away, to climb a mountain, to walk among giant redwoods, to run through a meadow, to stomp through a creek in the rain. But I can't.

Instead, I wait for a trolley car without knowing where I'm going. My index finger traces the surface of the round two-inch button of Harvey Milk. It is his first campaign button for an election he lost. He wears a ponytail and smiles.

I am at a crossroads. I can fill myself with anger and hatred and become a bigot, or I can challenge myself to become someone better. Which will I choose? I wonder.

The trolley pulls up, but the driver keeps the doors closed. He stands and begins to clean up trash from the aisles. I think, the woman at the parade who put her arm around me never heard about the "out" queer youth movement since I am among its first generation, but she welcomed me anyway.

I realize that Harvey Milk and the woman symbolize the ability and effort of the queer community to embrace our differences. Perhaps I am unlike my father and the waiter, and that's why they hate me. Maybe their differences make them feel vulnerable, and when they see me, they see their weaknesses.

I think again about the woman who put her arm around me, and I smile. I went to my first gay day with a sense of aloneness, which I have carried with me all of my life. Yet, I will leave choosing to feel either rejected or accepted.

When the trolley door opens, I get on. I realize that the police have the power to imprison people like me. The priests have the power to spread hatred with sexual violence against children and their sermons about the effeminate "criminals" who threaten "family values." My parents and teachers have the power to listen to what they hear at church and on television, to close their eyes to reality and to pretend that it is truth.

My only power comes from deciding whom I look up to and how I live my life. I will never know why the waiter refused to let me eat at the diner or the real reasons why my family treated me the way they did. Yet, I don't want to walk around my whole life hating everyone just because some people have treated me badly.

Perhaps the little moments are the most important ones, like when the woman at the parade put her arm around me. The enemy isn't my father, the waiter or even the people who taught them to be hateful. My holding onto hate and a hateful attitude is the real enemy.

The trolley pulls away from the Castro. I think about how I have the power to belong somewhere. To make a place for myself in the world even if I can't always say where that place is, and even if I don't feel welcomed by everyone in my community. Then I realize that when I had marched in the parade, I had already chosen my path.

Many winters have passed since I marched in my first pride parade. Now, I am about the same age as the woman at the parade and Harvey Milk when he died. Like them, I try to reach out to queer youth, people I don't necessarily understand, people with differences from my own.

I don't have position or power or money, and I don't represent anyone's point of view but my own. Nonetheless I wish to pass on the common legacy that Harvey Milk and the woman at the parade passed onto me. All of us, including queer youth, have the right to exist, to be ourselves even if other people in our community work against us. We should have the right to live, to love and to die without fearing the callous hatred and violence that continues to emanate in the United States and in the world beyond.

I still feel the coolness of the grass under my legs. My body still warms under the sun when I lean against the big oak. My calloused hands still grasp tree branches and tree trunks. But I no longer climb trees in dresses—unless I'm also wearing a tiara.

And, most of the time, my hair hangs in long, curly tangles.

I Used to be Daddy's Girl

Nat Roslin

1)

I spent two and a half happy years confident that I had made the right decision in coming out as bisexual, but then the doubts started to creep in. I realized that the more I looked at men, the less I found myself attracted to them. I knew within me that I was using the label of bisexuality as a safety net. If I still liked men, then my friends and family would still accept me; there would be no judgments, and I would be given the benefit of the doubt.

At the age of twenty-two, I had again reached the crossroads in regards to my sexuality. I doubted my identity and myself, and I hated not knowing who I was anymore. After a night out, I had a long chat with my surrogate sister, a woman I have known since birth and who has been like an older sister to me throughout my life. Then I phoned one of my drag queen friends and asked if I could meet up with him and talk. It was thanks to his advice, and the advice of one of the other drag queens at the local drag cabaret club, that made me realize that the only one who was holding me back was me.

One of them stood me in front of a mirror and asked me what I saw. Every time I came back with an answer that was how I thought other people saw me, he told me to look again. Several hours of frustrated crying later, I looked into the mirror and finally answered with, "I see Nat." It was that simple answer that made me realize my sexuality is a part of me but not the only part of me. I had hung everything, every ounce of who I was, on appearing to be acceptable.

It was through my surrogate sister introducing me to the club a little over a year before that I was able to meet a lot of wonderful queer people whom I began to see as my extended family.

2)

Coming out to my father, however, had begun to cause me a feeling of dread. Every time I thought about it, my stomach would clench; my nerves would shatter, and my head would spin. The idea of telling him that I wasn't the girl he thought I was left me nauseous.

3)

I had come home after a Sunday evening at the club, happy and tipsy. I went up to my room, turned on the light and started to look for clean pajamas. My father came charging into my room and demanded to know where I had been. I told him, and he flipped out. He started yelling the same things he'd yelled a thousand times before—telling me that my friends would give me "the gay disease"; that I'd end up hurt, dead or both.

The ticking time bomb inside me exploded. I had had enough of the abuse, enough of the judgments. My fists clenched at my sides, my body drawn up to its full height, I looked at my father and yelled back, "I will never fall in love with any of them!"

4)

The atmosphere in the house was unbearable. I stayed out as late as possible, came in after he had gone to bed and left before he even got up. It was easier than dealing with the looks and the snide comments he'd whisper under his breath that he thought I couldn't hear. On the third day, he started talking to me again, but it was stilted and as if he didn't recognize me. He no longer saw the little girl he'd raised, and my fears had been proven. I no longer recognized the man whose roof I lived under as my dad. My dad had been the one to pull me into his arms if I'd had a stressful day, the man who had convinced me that it was okay to still be afraid of the dark long after most kids outgrew it. He had understood when I wouldn't let anyone sit in my mother's chair or drink out of her mug after she'd died.

One fight had changed all that. The atmosphere continued for another two days, and then on the sixth day after our fight, he told me to get out. I wasn't his daughter any more. In that moment, it felt like a knife had been stabbed into my heart. I packed what I could carry and headed out the front door, tears in my eyes, feeling as if I had become an orphan overnight, my little brother telling me he would always love me.

5)

I won't be asking him to walk me down the aisle at my civil partnership ceremony. I may invite him, although that's looking more and more doubtful. If I do, he won't be sitting with us at the reception—that's for sure. It hurts to know that he will never accept me for who I am, and the metaphorical knife he stabbed me with when he kicked me out digs in a little deeper when I think about the way I used to imagine getting married, my proud dad giving me away.

But I know that in order for my civil union to be a happy day, I can't have him there as the person to give me away. He lost my respect and trust the day I was left to fend for myself.

My relationship with my dad died the day he kicked me out. To have him at my civil union would mean a miraculous recovery of our lost relationship. As much as I long for that to happen, I am beginning to face the fact that it won't. Memories of the past and the actuality of the present clash in my heart and mind. Reconciling the two is a painful process that may never have an ending. Thoughts of inviting my father to the happiest day of my life are just that—thoughts.

Every time I think about the possibility, I end up remembering why I can't. He *wouldn't* come. I have recently discovered through my brother and family friends that he is getting remarried and isn't inviting me because he doesn't want my stepmother to know his eldest child is a lesbian. His shame is why I cannot have him at my ceremony.

My dad, the man I love, the man I remember, is the person I want at my civil union. But I know he is just a memory. While in name my father still exists, my dad is gone.

Sylvia's Place

Lucky S. Michaels

Director of Metropolitan Community Church of New York Homeless Youth Services

In the autumn air of 1985, I was walking home from school in Detroit City, thinking about Mrs. Black's class and how cool it was finally to be old enough to go to school, unlike my two younger brothers who were then four years old and three months old. We lived on Elm Street at the time. I remember running up the dirt driveway, past the rusty car that sat next to our house, and then up the wooden steps of the porch when I collided with the step–parent who was controlling my mom and us boys as he rushed out of the house. That was when I experienced my first flight out of the nest: I found myself being tossed into the yard, a sudden sharp pain and blood gushing down my face. A lot of yelling, dirt, door slamming, the leaves all around me suddenly felt like spring for some reason, despite the orange and blood red of the fall season. I don't know how or when I picked myself up, but I did. I started thinking about doing my homework and couldn't wait for the next school day to come.

What seemed like a lifetime later in the mind of a five–year–old may have just been a few months of yelling and hitting and crying and pain, and then it happened: he left the house and wouldn't be back until late. Like clockwork, my momma, wounded and shaking, packed up enough for the baby, and we packed our bags too, going on what we believed to be a trip. It turned out to be a trip that saved our lives as she checked into a women's domestic violence shelter, not knowing we would need to be saved again and again. The people in the shelter were the most interesting people I had ever met, including one whom I believed to be an older guy with long hair and makeup; he claimed to be an artist. That was when I began to believe that I would be an artist when I grew up.

We escaped from my stepfather for the time being and found ourselves on Three Mile Road when we were first introduced to the person who would become the only dad we would ever know. He brought us "Dog Nuts," and let me tell you, doughnuts were thrilling after living off what we had been eating. Of course, he was not really in the picture yet, and it would take many years of trials with the stepfather bearing witness to broken windows, ribs and dishes. More and more I discovered that my extracurricular life was more satisfying than my life at home.

I got my first job when I was eleven to buy my first car which, little did I know, would serve as a roof over my head during the adolescent years I spent coming into my own, or more accurately put, coming out. Deciding to finish school and to become successful was my goal as I worked all night long at a twenty–four–hour diner and attended school during the days. Good thing I finished school in spite of the aching in my gut caused by trying to swallow my emotional scars and pain, which led to unsuccessful suicide attempts. The day I received my diploma, I was crying so violently on the inside. I could only really cry when I broke away from the crowd, not out of joy but out of the great sorrow in my life.

In 2001, my life brought me to New York City, where I struggled fiercely to be an independent adult. I studied at Parsons School of Design, where I had to find my own way through an educational system that depends so much more on familial and monetary support than it should. This journey brought me to the steps of the Metropolitan Community Church of New York at a pivotal point in its history and mine at the end of 2002 and into the start of 2003. It was a place that I could call home. At that time, the Church had just embarked on the enormous task of founding Sylvia's Place, a shelter for homeless LGBTQ youth that was open three–hundred–sixty–five days a year since it opened full time.

"This," I thought on my first day as an Overnight Counselor at the shelter, "this is my dream job." The perfect marriage of my artistic nature and passion for LGBTQ youth resulted in my first world–wide distribution of a published photo essay titled, "Shelter," which launched in December 2007. It has brought me overseas to London and Germany on exhibition, and there was a full–length article in the *New York Times* on April 17, 2008. If I can do that, then other queer youth certainly can put their passion and talent together and live the dream that is aching to get out.

Only one man in our household ever earned the title of "Dad," and it was not my biological parent, nor my abusive stepfather, but rather the one man who managed to stick with us through the years and to take care of my mom and us four boys in spite of none of us being his biological children. That title was given to the man who brought "Dog Nuts" into our life.

Somehow the few years of abuse as a child always seemed to dwarf the ten years that followed with this man. Perhaps this is due to my perception as a child at five years of age compared to my adulthood, which seemed to start shortly thereafter: I was driving cars by the age of eleven because it always seemed somebody was too drunk to drive to the store for another "40."

Dad passed away a couple years ago, sitting on the couch. Glad to hear he was there instead of falling asleep on the washing machine as he had done on many occasions during my youth. I was lucky to have reconnected with him and the rest of the family when I started school at Parsons School of Design. I spent my summers photographing my family in an attempt to understand them better and to make peace with where I came from. The resulting photo essay, titled "Child Support," has taken considerably longer to produce given my dad's death as I have yet to get through transcribing his interviews. My biggest realization through doing this work was that they too were exactly who they were supposed to be and were happy living their lives; it was just different than the life I found within myself. I had to come to terms with them, just as they had to come to terms with me and my boyfriends. After all, I must admit that I was a little bit of a mama's boy.

I wasn't kicked out, but coming out often feels that way to those of us who struggled to find someone to whom we could relate. Many of us left home as a protection mechanism—regardless of whether home was the safest or most dangerous place at that time in our lives. One in fifty American children becomes homeless, according to the news that just rolled out from CNN and the Associated Press on March 10, 2009. Think about your classes in school, and start to calculate the number of kids who will become homeless or are already homeless and couch–surfing, living out of their cars, in a shelter, or even on the streets—yet they are sitting there in class. A graduating class in the thousands, like mine, could have had forty or more such kids, without even counting the sophomores and juniors, yet I did not know at the time that there were definitely many others just like me.

Reconnected: An Interview with Anthony and Sassafras

Anthony

Anthony and I met on a sagging, soiled couch at our local queer youth recreation center. As always, there were heated games of pool happening in the middle of the room, communal food simmering in the kitchen and a dance party starting near the stereo. Anthony and I found ourselves in a short conversation before he had to leave. Though our connection was brief, it stuck with me, and our friendship continued to grow over the next few years. I was living in a rented room a few blocks from the community center and visited there every night. Anthony was able to attend rarely because of his living situation.

Anthony and I lost touch for about a year, only to reappear in the same community of Portland punk houses. It was during those years when Anthony and I became closer: we shared stories of family rejection, substance abuse, the creation of chosen family and our dreams for the future.

When I began *Kicked Out*, I knew that I needed to find Anthony. Several years had passed since we had been close: I had finished college, and my partner and I had relocated to New York City. I knew that Anthony was in school and was working with at–risk youth. Getting back in touch with Anthony was important to me not only because I wanted to include his experiences in the foster care industry, but also because there are too many kids with whom I have lost contact. As I have grown older, maintaining these contacts has become even more important to me because these are the people with whom I shared some of the most difficult and formative years of my life.

Much to my delight, Anthony was thrilled about the idea of being interviewed for the anthology, but completing the interview proved complicated. With a three–hour time difference and completely different sleep cycles, we had to get creative. Early one morning while Anthony was nearing the end of his graveyard shift and I had just woken up, we connected for the interview below.

Sassafras: Do you want to start with giving background about your childhood?

Anthony: I was adopted when I was almost four years old. I had been in the foster care system from about seven months old to the time I was adopted by a middle–class family who already had three boys. The parents really wanted a girl, so they adopted me.

Sassafras: Wow, you weren't quite what they were expecting, to say the least.

Anthony: Yeah! I guess that's what they get for trying to handpick a kid of a certain gender!

Sassafras: Yes! I assume that your not being a girl must have come as quite the shock to your adoptive parents?

Anthony: I feel like in a lot of ways I was a "typical" case. I think their denial was very deep–rooted though. But I can remember as early as preschool battling over the dress for picture day. Finally my mother agreed to make me wear the dress only for pictures. Then I was allowed to change.

Sassafras: Wow, so was gender always an issue in their home?

Anthony: Always. In grade school when I got in trouble, my mother would make me wear dresses for punishment. Needless to say, I was always in a damn dress!

Sassafras: That's intense.

Anthony: Yes.

Sassafras: How old were you when you had to leave their home? What did that experience look like?

Anthony: I left home at the age of fourteen. I went into a residential treatment program that dealt with drug, alcohol, behavioral and emotional issues in teenagers. By the time I left my parents' house, I was using drugs heavily, always getting into trouble, running away, getting into fights. My parents and I couldn't even be in the same room. It wasn't my choice. However, it was the best thing they ever did for me. My home was really abusive, and it got me out from underneath their reign. It let me deal with my earlier childhood trauma, the ongoing abuse I faced in their home, and figure out who I was and what I wanted in my life because I was miserable, acting out all the time and using drugs. It wasn't fun for me.

Sassafras: How did things change for you after leaving their home?

Anthony: I was able to look at my earlier childhood, start to take responsibility for my actions and myself. It also gave me the room to explore gender and sexuality. However, I didn't have the language for that until I moved into the group home, but I was in charge of how I dressed.

Sassafras: When did you move into the group home?

Anthony: I was fifteen, almost sixteen. I was supposed to go back to my family's house after treatment, but things had only gotten worse since I had left their house. A lot of that was due to the fact that I was figuring out who I was, and I realized how abusive and volatile my relationship with them was.

Sassafras: Was the group home a good place for you? I know that you had some really intense experiences with CPS [Child Protective Services] and other state agencies. Can you talk about what that was like in your case?

Anthony: Oh my! That is quite the question. It was a mixed bag. At the group home, I met some staff who were really supportive and actually flat–out asked me if I considered myself trans and/or queer. However, the program director was a totally different story!

Sassafras: Wow.

Anthony: He told me that staff could respect my preferred name and pronouns if I came out to my parents. Mind you, I had been out for less than two weeks and was not ready for that, but I felt like I had spent soooo much time hashing out my gender stuff that I really needed people to respect my gender identity. I came out—against my better judgment (also, keep in mind the program director was gay himself).

Sassafras: How did your parents react when you came out to them?

Anthony: The program director sat in on a meeting with my parents and me. When I came out, he basically talked them into believing that "it was just a phase"—"you know how those teenagers are," etcetera, and said that my chosen name was a "nickname." However, I made it really clear in that meeting that it was not a nickname, nor a phase, and that if they wanted to believe that, they would be in for a big surprise when I turned eighteen. My parents believed the program director and said they would support me when I turned eighteen, but not any sooner, and that I was not allowed to talk about it, especially in our family therapy sessions because "it was not a family issue." And my DHS [Department of Human Services] worker did not help the situation!

Sassafras: How so?

Anthony: It was very clear to me that he was homophobic and transphobic, and he didn't understand why I would "hurt my parents like this." He thought that I was "doing it for attention."

Sassafras: Wow, talk about a lack of sensitivity! What was life like in the group home while all of this was going on?

Anthony: It was really difficult. The program director gave staff a choice as to whether or not they wanted to respect my name and pronoun, so there was tension between the staff who respected me and those who didn't. The girls were great though [it was a girls' group home], and the program director told me I was not allowed to access any LGBTQ services. I wasn't even allowed to go to my GSA [Gay–Straight Alliance] or to continue to see the counselor through the LGBTQ youth center.

Sassafras: But the program director was gay?

Anthony: Yes! That's what was so fucked up about the situation. For a whole year, I was really isolated. I didn't meet any other trans people until I started sneaking around and lying about where I was.

Sassafras: Was there ever discussion of moving you out of a girls' home?

Anthony: Nope, never. When new girls would come, they always thought I was a biological boy, so there was always "that" conversation.

Sassafras: Wow. You talk about sneaking around to meet other trans folks. Where did you go, and what became the role of the larger LGBTQ community in your life?

Anthony: I had been involved in twelve–step programs, so I would leave really early to go to my weekly meeting, but would stop at the trans youth group on my way...and the twelve–step group I had found was an LGBTQ young people's meeting. I believe this is where I got to know you more maybe...

Sassafras: Yeah, I think we met the first time at the trans youth meeting.

Anthony: Basically, the LGBTQ youth center saved my life at that time. I really don't know what I would have done without that connection while in the group home. Staff tried to be supportive, but they also weren't my peers, though a lot of them were young queers! I also cut off communication with my family at seventeen, so I started to form my own family.

Sassafras: Wasn't the LGBTQ center part of that chosen family for you? Can you talk about the process of creation of family?

Anthony: At that time, yes! I would go whenever I could (once the program director pulled his head out of his ass). I met so many amazing young queers there. I knew that I always had someone to talk to.

Sassafras: So he eventually started to let you go to the center?

Anthony: Yes, after a year of complete isolation. It was once I wrote the Executive Director and also informed him of what the program director was doing, which was completely illegal in Portland where trans folks have a lot of protections. Not to mention, the behind–the–scenes stuff that the line staff were doing...

Sassafras: That's incredible that in the middle of that, you thought of writing to the Executive Director! What sorts of behind–the–scenes stuff was going on?

Anthony: Yes, I was desperate. Staff would do things like print articles and photocopy sections of books about best practices for working with trans clients—they would highlight important paragraphs and leave it all on his desk on a weekly basis. They would continually bring stuff up in the staff meetings mostly, just reporting how depressed I was, my suicidality, the fact I was completely shutting down.

Sassafras: It sounds like they were some major allies for you amongst the staff. Did the youth center staff know what was going on? Were they in communication with the group home?

Anthony: Oh yes, they knew what was going on well; the LGBTQ youth center counselor (who later became the program director) was communicating with a couple of the line staff. He was attempting to be in touch with the program director, but it was like talking to a brick wall.

Sassafras: Wow, that's really great that you had that sort of support from the staff of the youth center. When were you finally able to leave the group home?

Anthony: When I was seventeen, we had a big family meeting because it was pretty clear that my parents and I weren't going to work things out enough for me to go back to their house, so I advocated for myself to be able to move into a transitional housing program. Originally, they were just going to keep me at the group home until I turned eighteen!

Sassafras: Wow!

Anthony: Also, my LGBTQ youth center counselor was there, line staff, the program director, the milieu director, my DHS worker, my parents, and the house treatment coordinator.

Sassafras: How did the meeting go?

Anthony: Hahaha. I wish you could have been a fly on the wall. Well, aside from half of the people in the room referring to me by my preferred name and pronouns and the other half of the room not, it went well...sort of; there was a lot of tension. I think the best part about the meeting for me was when my DHS worker was surrounded by three gay men.

Sassafras: That is so fantastic!

Anthony: And when the treatment coordinator informed my parents that I probably would not want to talk to them for a while, and they should just accept that. I can't remember what exactly my parents said, but it was really offensive in regards to my ability to function and to be a productive member of society—to be successful. They were still treating me like a fourteen–year–old, and I had grown so much! I was working full–time and completing my high school diploma a year early.

Sassafras: I remember that. You were doing a million things at that point and were so together. It's really intense that they were not able to see that. So they let you go to the transitional living program?

Anthony: Yes! I got on the wait list. I actually was the catalyst for a cool change in the transitional housing program. They were run by the same agency. And they had heard about all I had been through in the group home, and they wanted to make it a more trans–friendly place. They asked me how I thought they could do that, so they got rid of the gendered waiting list and had the girls live upstairs and boys downstairs.

Sassafras: That's incredible, especially when I think about the size of the young trans community in Portland. I'm sure that you made it much safer for so many other youth. How old were you when you entered into the transitional housing program?

Anthony: I was still seventeen, and I only lived there for five months, actually, before moving in with a friend.

Sassafras: How did that move change your life?

Anthony: It was amazing! It allowed me to really be in charge of my own life—and all the decisions being made about my life, where it was my decision, not the state's or my parents'. It also allowed me to get more involved in the community, and I met some of my friends whom I still consider to be family regardless of how much we get to talk or see each other. In a sense, it was a big "fuck you" to my parents. They told me I would never be successful, never be able to live independently, never graduate high school, never have relationships, etcetera.

Sassafras: Being able to prove people wrong and have the successful life you have always dreamed of is such a personally transformative experience. Did your relationship with your parents ever improve?

Anthony: No! I actually cut off contact while I still lived at the group home. Over that next year, we wrote a couple of letters. They were never productive, so I waited until after I was eighteen to let them know I was alive, well and starting my physical and legal transition. Then I didn't contact them again until about a year ago. I got in touch with one of my brothers, and he guilt–tripped me into writing my mom. He said she had been addressing her mental health, and it had really improved their relationship; I wrote her. As usual, I took ownership for my faults and bad decisions and was pretty offended by her response. I didn't write back, and my brother stopped talking with me.

Sassafras: How do you think your life is different or has been altered because of the experiences you had as a youth?

Anthony: I wouldn't be who I am today! I know that seems like a really standard response. Let me explain more. I wouldn't have learned how to advocate for myself or others. I wouldn't have had such a drive to work in the social work field. I wouldn't have learned how to be truly independent. Everything I have in my life—whether it be relationships, materials, education, my job—I've had to work my ass off for. I also wouldn't have learned how to let people into my life and to accept support.

Sassafras: Absolutely. What sort of advice do you have for kids who might be facing similar situations, or who are being forced to leave home?

Anthony: That is a tough one! I would first let them know there are people out there who understand what they are going through. Learning how to advocate for themselves will be an invaluable tool, and networking may save their ass. Also they are beautiful people, and no matter how much people have told them they are worthless, won't make anything of themselves, etcetera, that they can make something of themselves. They can tell the unhealthy people in their lives to fuck off. They don't have to keep family in their life who will be abusive—they can create a community of supportive people. I don't feel like I'm articulating myself very well at the moment, but I hope the sentiment is there.

Sassafras: No, I think what you are saying is really great stuff and makes perfect sense, especially to folks who have experienced that or who are currently in a similar situation. What are your thoughts about the epidemic of queer youth homelessness? How do you think this population could be better served?

Anthony: I work with the homeless youth population. I think it is tragic that these youth are being forced to leave their homes based on their sexuality and gender identity. I think that there is always a need for more resources. One of the hot topics in my agency right now is, do we need to push for LGBTQ–specific housing or just LGBTQ–friendly housing. We have LGBTQ–friendly housing currently—and I think some of the youth *could* benefit from more culturally specific services...but I go back and forth on the issue. We could acknowledge that there are differences in culture for some of these youth. I think we tend to take the stance (we being providers in general) that everyone is treated equally, and we treat and approach every youth in the same way. And I think that is problematic. We need to be seeing our youth on more of an individual basis and really acknowledge the cultural differences, which seem to be having such a clear effect on the youth—especially if their culture is the reason they are on the streets in the first place.

Sassafras: Yes, absolutely! I think that's it for my questions. Is there anything else you want to add?

Anthony: I talked about the gender identity stuff a lot—because that was a huge struggle during my teenager years. But I wanted to point out that I'm now in a place in my life that I live mostly stealth. In fact, one of my housemates doesn't even know my trans history, so doing this interview should be interesting.

Sassafras: Wow, it definitely will be interesting when the book comes out! That's something I realized I forgot to ask you in the beginning: how do you identify?

Anthony: Haha!

Sassafras: Name, pronoun, all that jazz…talk about memories.

Anthony: Oh wow. Well, I go by Anthony, male pronouns, and really my gender actually isn't a part of my identity but is a part of my history. I identify as queer with gay tendencies [laugh]...or as a fag. What I mean by "queer with gay tendencies" is that I am very queer politically, but when it comes to attraction, I don't find myself attracted to a whole spectrum of genders. I would love for that to be the case, but you can't help whom you are attracted to.

Sassafras: Very cool—thanks for clarifying that one. I think it will help people to better understand where you are coming from.

Eighteen, Down and Out (and Back)

E.F. Schraeder

My fingers, caught in the white screen door, squirm for a moment, then relax once the burning sensation of metal on skin turns to numbness. I stand at the door, confused tears welling in my eyes because of the combined stinging of physical and psychological pain. My mother's eyes peer through me from the other side, her hand on the inside, firmly rejecting my access by pressing the door shut even tighter while my hand reddens.

Our hands could be touching. The glass could be a fun–house mirror, with the eighteen year difference between us noticeable only up close. With unflinching malice, her green eyes watch my wriggling fingers between the frame and door.

I clutch my aching hand as I walk away in a stupor. Unable to speak, unable to pause, I collapse dejectedly into my rusty blue, compact car after gathering the few books she hurled at me along with some insults not worth paraphrasing. I leave without realizing I have seen the inside of her house for the last time. I start the car, and frustrated tears cloud my eyes. As I drive away, bags filled with random clothes and a teddy bear rustle against the window in the backseat. Detached, I suddenly recognize the pain in my swelling hand, which overtakes me as I veer into a parking lot. I stumble through the doors of a bright, sterile bank, my hand bleeding, and I faint.

Since I have no health insurance, I do not go to the hospital as the clean–cut ambulance drivers suggest. I wait until I feel less pressure in my hand and return to my car. Then I drive to where a friend and her mother live to stay for the night, creaking up the steps of their duplex with my bags clumsily jostling against the wall. In the course of one hour, my life and choices shake under the new weight of isolation. Vacant numbness settles me to sleep that night on what proves to be my initiation into "family–free" life.

My frame of reference for the world suddenly shifts into two categories: things I can and cannot afford. The part–time minimum wage job that provided "book money" for college abruptly becomes my top priority. The hope to transfer into a private school for my second semester escapes my grasp in seconds. Goals evaporate into curiosities to store someplace undisturbed; my ambitions and confidence ephemerally float out of reach quickly. As if the world lost gravity, grounded things twist into chimeras that haunt my perceived options for more than a decade, only noticeable now in hindsight.

When filling out the so–called "financial aid forms," my age renders me ineligible to qualify as a financial independent even with proof, and each year the joke of "expected family contribution" on the government's calculation of familial support reminds me of my alienation, looming financial instability and the idiosyncrasies of being socially invisible. As months pass, wedges of frustration, confusion and anger plant themselves permanently between "self" and (what I thought of as) "family." More months render rent and bills as disappointing replacements for aspirations, and ideas about the future drift away like little clouds of smoke on the horizon.

I never once wondered about the origin of my mom's hostility, forcing the ridiculous drama on the front porch. Technically, I knew it was not something I had *done*, and despite my confusion, I felt no guilt. I knew instead that something I *wanted* broke the unsteady conviction of her commitment to parent me, revealing the fast lie called "maternal love." I liked a girl at college more than the guy I was dating. A lot more. When I saw her, I felt my body flush and face blush in a wave of exuberance; my heart fluttered, my words stammered, and I shifted on my feet like a nervous schoolgirl. When I saw him, I said a sensible hello. No physiological signs of excitement: it was hardly like I had a body at all. Is that what love is supposed to feel like? I hoped not.

I never went out with her. In fact, I waited a full year before dating any girl at all. More than I wanted that flush to overtake me, I wanted to be sure of myself. I wanted to find a place within myself with slightly less anxiety, enthusiasm and perspiration on my palms. Besides, I like to read about things before doing them. I spent nearly twelve months curiously meeting women–loving–women and nurturing friendships in this new world. I scouted women–owned bookstores, cafes and theaters. My nerves jolted each time I stepped into spaces defined and maintained by sheer grrrl power. Picking up the queer quarterly newspaper felt, each time, like picking up a ticket to transform my universe. I excitedly sought "a women's community," maybe something like the one I read about in Women's Studies classes, circa the early 90s. I entered on cue: the quiet, long–haired, guitar–strumming, granola type looking for lesbian feminists. Maybe I was looking for a stereotype; maybe I was a stereotype, but the Indigo Girls and Salt–n–Pepa were on the charts, Ani DiFranco was playing at the bookstore and Sweet Honey in the Rock had feminist anthems worthy of paragraph–length tattoos. I found friends who led women–centered lives. I spent that year reading, drinking coffee, camping, telling stories and flirting. It felt something like home, and resilience began to fill the spaces between fear and growth.

Although upheaval sped my full immersion into this new culture, I learned quickly the value of being present. Alternative potluck events with friends inspired new recipes and friendships, and private anti–holiday plans reminded me of options, like taking walks with my dogs on days when banks and post offices were closed instead of spilling out an awkward afternoon at a picnic table with distant cousins, or feeding seagulls at the lake while most families were carving into birds. I began to distinguish the difference between family of origin and family of choice. Admittedly, there were times I wished that my chosen family were my "real" family, but these folks (dogs and cats included) have continued to fill the spaces in my life for unconditional love now fifteen years later.

I spent my twenties exploring my sexuality with playful caution, and my girlhood shifted slowly between forms of femininity and androgyny, varying teasingly among shades of girlhood, boyhood and womanhood. I took care to become the woman I wanted to date, with the steady support of friendships sustaining me through the predictable break–ups. Packaging and repackaging myself into versions of this new self became as familiar as packing and unpacking my life along the timeline of twelve–month leases on rentals. Mobility became second nature, though there was nothing upward about it. I relocated across the city with regularity, passing through my sophomore, junior and senior years at college.

In retrospect, the eerie clarity of the connection between my sexuality and my economic class looks obvious. Yet, caught in the framework of actions and reactions at the time, each choice seemed a matter of necessity. I thought little about the meanings of the mental transition from "student" to "wage worker," or about the (perceived) difference between a degree from a public college and a private one, since some "opportunities" closely wed themselves to affiliation and pedigree. Although I enjoyed and rejected the idea of educational elitism, the ride sure wasn't pretty: instead of lavish old brick and ivy buildings beset by rolling hills, I took a bumpy bus ride downtown to a concrete architectural nightmare. Caught in the snafu of life traps and pressed regularly to the verge of the cliff called "going under," I clutched onto the one thing that made sense: I clung to school, continuing to register for classes each semester that I could afford, until I finally had enough credits stacked up to have a little piece of paper sent in the mail. When the diploma arrived, I wished it had arrived in an envelope emblazoned, "You go, girl!" since I skipped commencement and the regalia.

The consequences of life (tritely) without a net took a toll. I worked multiple jobs to get by like so many folks and still struggled. Health insurance looked as unattainable then as it does now. The privileged securities and comforts of being "a middle–class white kid from the suburbs" vanished with the onset of a sudden adulthood. The sense of promise was replaced by an awareness of the need for endurance. Hetero friends began to marry into the safety of retirement plans, social security benefits and tax breaks, clarifying the link between "success" and sexuality. I noticed that seventy–two cents on the dollar goes much further as a second income. Yet I also noticed how easy it was for me to establish a "good" credit rating in spite of my just–above–poverty income. Sure I always paid my bills on time, but no doubt perceived social expectations and the biases of whiteness impacted this arena. Even if my "wealth" didn't grow (or show any life signs of the sort), bankers and their institutions seemed oddly prepared to assume it would.

Ironically, beset by the demands of my independence, life on my own allowed little time to cultivate or to nurture intimate relationships. I came down with a bad case of autonomy, unwilling to rely on anyone again and hopping from place to place as needed. I consistently avoided commitments through various combinations of un/conscious methods. I "unwittingly" dated "players" and ended up dumped after several months of exclusivity and mindless fun. I spent wholly innocent weekends with groups of well–matched couples, guarding against any potential threats to my un/intended seclusion. I developed a mild penchant for the unavailable girlfriend (preferring thinking to doing) and truly fell for a confused (and married) gal I later met in grad school. The predictably disappointing desire for the unattainable finally ceased when I realized it was a tedious knot yoking me to unfaltering dissatisfaction with relationships, mirroring what I felt about my so–called "real family." Eventually, I resigned myself to focus on activism, politics and other sorts of community engagement that consumed my "free time" in gobbling chunks. Besides, based on what I was paid at most of my jobs, all my time felt like free time, anyway.

In reality, I was afraid of closeness. Everything a child "ought" to learn about love, I learned in reverse. Being loved meant being threatened; trust led to disappointment. Being alone mitigated my fears. None of that early learning made for easy intimacy without a whole lot of help from late night talks with those folks who became my precious chosen sisters. My priority at the time was finishing school while staying housed; finding a lover was superfluous.

Eventually, I stirred to move further away from the place I once called home. Finishing my undergraduate degree led to an occasion to pack myself into boxes yet again: the promise of Grad School (ta da). My desire to "go all the way," at least in school, sprang from my ability to excel with far greater ease than I had with women; I never outgrew my shyness anymore than my tomboy preferences. So, no more than two months after finishing my undergraduate degree, my dog and I headed West.

After the drive across what felt like the world, I set up life all those happy miles away from my family of origin. I felt lucky everyday for the freedom that distance brought with it. I unpacked my things into the spare room of a recently divorced and newly "out" woman and her girlfriend who needed light "handygirl" work done. In lieu of rent, I painted the reclaimed rooms of the recently husband–vacated house: neutral creams fading beneath bold queer hues of lavender and lilac. I admit I enjoyed the softly butch arrangement of setting up ladders, removing hardware from windows, patching holes and applying smooth primer in sheets of glossy white. I found a new women's community through coffee shops, cafe concerts, activist organizations and poetry readings, and I maintained old–fashioned written relationships through the handy U.S. Postal Service.

With the life of school, family conflict (and exes) secured thousands of miles away, the distance boosted my optimism. With a combination of luck, supportive friends and persistence, my options eventually changed for the better, and my confidence grew in the unfamiliar terrain as I recognized the unexplored (internally and externally) as a trajectory of possibilities.

Now with lessons learned, I find myself with a Ph.D. and a "real job." Two decades later, my chosen family blossoms in all directions: two queer sisters, a partner and her siblings, inherited nieces and nephews from the daughters and sons of long–time friends who have become parents, a furry flurry of cats and dogs (worthy of their own stories entirely), and a handful of people whose regular presence adds guidance, perspective, support and humor—everything needed from "family." I know that many LGBTQ folks find acceptance within their families of origin, but my experience shows that acceptance is not always "out there" for all of us to reach. The sweet truth exists in that acknowledgment: I am uninterested in them and happy with what is. The door to my biological family has been closed and locked, this time from my end.

In Their Own Voices: The Youth who Call Sylvia's Place Home*

Kenyatta, Bella, Etern!ty, Anonymous

Editor's note: The following pieces were written by youth living at the Sylvia's Place shelter in New York City and submitted to shelter director Lucky Michaels for publication in Kicked Out. In order to preserve the authors' voices, these pieces are unedited.

Untitled by Kenyatta

Through the ups and downs of my life, there has always been a constant: my survival. I've always been able to survive. When my mother's abusive husband forced me to eat, then beat me for regurgitating the food, I survived. When the kids at school would pick on me for being feminine, I survived. When my grandmother died of lung cancer, I survived. When I was informed of her cancer. When she died. When my mother found out I was gay and met my significantly older boyfriend. When my boyfriend and I broke up. When a piece of me died. When I was a heavy participant in drug use. When I became homeless and lost all my inheritance. When I was raped. When men would hit me and use me.

It's okay though because through all of this, I have survived and will carry on being who it made me be through all the lies and deceit and stares from people who don't even know me but thought they did. It doesn't matter that I have no money or a steady home to lay my head because I know that I can survive and conquer these challenges.

I'm a transsexual woman who has done that and been through a lot in the small amount of years that she's been here. I am who I am, and that's all I can be. By working hard and staying focused, I know that I will achieve what I deserve.

◊ ◊ ◊ ◊ ◊

Close Your Eyes by Bella

Listen to the rain, imagine NYC loud hustle and bustle.

Picture a young preteen, struggling to keep on

her wet torn clothing.

She gets into an empty doorway.

Dialing, raining harder, thunder, loud hustle and bustle.

Crying, sobbing.

Daddy please.

I don't want to talk.

Come get me.

Daddy, I need you.

Her phone dies.

Alone, afraid, thunder, sobbing, running.

A pay phone.

Daddy!

Screaming, sobbing.

Please, he hurt me. I need you.

I feel weak. I need you.

Falling, falling darkness, crying, sobbing,

screaming, sobbing, shaking.

Daddy…it's raining.

◊ ◊ ◊ ◊ ◊

Editor's note: The following piece was written in the form of thirty–five text messages to Lucky Michaels, the Director of Sylvia's Place. Because the author wanted her story to be told, she wrote her experience using the only medium available to her: text messages. The original text is important, as her language, spelling and convention all are part of her unique story and thus remain intact. In order to make the piece more accessible, her story is translated below each paragraph.

Untitled by etern!ty

well my nayme iz etern!ty i guess my l!l st0ree startz wen i wuz a b!t yunger. letz rewynd 2 wen i wuz 13. i fell hard k0re in l0ve w!th a 7th grayder, letz kall her k. 0k well u all kn0w ub0wt the r00lez in sk00l. un kn0w u kant dayte a 7th grayder if ur a 6th grayder ryte, well anyway i fell hard k0re in l0ve with her & az 4 me, well i wuz!nt ev!n a bl!p in her raydar any way. letz fast f0ward 2 wen i wuz 16. i had just kayme 0wt 2 my sister C. she t00k it pr!tee well. aksh00lee she wuz the 1 that t0ld me that i sh00d talk 2 her & i d!d. we h!t th!ngz 0ff & we g0t 2gether relee fast. 7 th!ngz wur g0!ng g00d unt!l the wuman that rayzed me m. f0wnd 0wt. she axed me if it wur tru that i wuz dayt!ng a gurl & i sed yes. i sed it pr0wd 2 :-) after that she left it ul0ne s0 i thawt she wuz try!ng 2 aksept it. but dayz turned in2 weekz & she wuzn!nt talk!ng 2 me. then 1 day she went 2 wurk & left me & J. in the kare uv her new f0wnd hubby naymed h. well that m0rn!ng my gurlfrend kalled me 2 ax wut wuz the plan 4 the day s0 we sp0ke & we wur meet!ng up at 4. well that d!dnt happ!n bkuz H drunk az he alwayz wuz t00k it up0n h!mself 2 smash the f0ne 0ver my hed it wuz 1 uv th0ze b!g ugly pay f0nez that sum st0rez had. well any way he kraked my hed 0p!n lyke a p!nyata & i wuz bleed!ng ul0tt s0 i went madd kuz uv all the bludd s0 i ran upstarez 2 my s!s unt!l M. kayme bak frum wurk & wen she d!d we had wurdz. yea me & her had ul0tt uv wordz.

Well, my name is Eternity. I guess my little story starts when I was a bit younger. Let's rewind to when I was thirteen. I fell hard-core in love with a seventh grader—let's call her "K." Okay well, you all know about the rules in school. You know you can't date a seventh grader if you are a sixth grader, right? Well, anyway, I fell hard-core in love with her, and as for me, well, I wasn't even a blip on her radar anyway.

Let's fast-forward to when I was sixteen. I had just come out to my sister, "C." She took it pretty well. Actually she was the one who told me that I should talk to her, and I did. We hit things off, and we got together really fast. Things were going good until the woman who raised me, "M.," found out. She asked me if it was true that I was dating a girl, and I said yes. I said it proud too. =) After that, she left it alone, so I thought she was trying to accept it. But days turned into weeks, and she wasn't talking to me.

Then one day, she went to work and left me and "J." in the care of her new-found hubby, "H." Well, that morning my girlfriend called me to ask what was the plan for the day, so we spoke, and we were meeting up at four. Well, that didn't happen. Because H.—drunk as he always was—he took it upon himself to smash the phone over my head. It was one of those big, ugly pay phones that some stores had. Well, anyway, he cracked my head open like a pinata, and I was bleeding a lot. I was mad because of all of the blood, so I ran upstairs to my sister until M. came back from work, and when she did, we had words. Yeah, me and her had a lot of words.

i t0ld her that k kalled me & h. thawt the kall wuz 4 h!m & wen i tryd 2 xplayn 2 h!m the kall wuz 4 me but he went in2 a rayge & well the fakt that he wuz drunk all the tyme d!dnt help anyth!ng any way wen m. st0pped us frum rgu!ng she t0ld me i had 2 ch00z btween l!v!ng there & bee!ng w!th k. & well i ch0ze her. 4 a wyle i d!dnt kare kuz my s!s w00d tayke kare uv us. f00d sh0wur & kl0thez wyze. well 4 me at leest kuz k wuz m0re uv the dress b0y type. any way it wuz the summer s0 i d!dnt kare that we wur 0wt all the tyme & az tyme went by we g0t 2 each uther kuz we spent all 0wur tyme 2gether but then 1 day we walked passed th!s kreepee aband0ned h0wse s0 we mayde it 0wurz & s00n after she g0t a j0b. then i bkayme the h0wse wyfe & th!ngz wur g00d unt!l we had 2 leeve kuz the p0l!ce f0wnd us. i t00k the blaym & g0t k 2 leeve b4 the k0ps g0t her 2. appar!ntlee u kan g0 2 jayle even if the playse iz aband0ned any way i wuz in jayle & me & k had spl!t up. wen i g0t 0wt i d!dnt kn0w ware i wuz gunna g0 0r sleep. my s!s had m00ved uway & i wuz ul0ne. s0 i mayd my way 2 k'z awntz h0wse & she let me l!ve there 4 a wyle but then i had 2 g0 kuz there wur 2 many peepul l!v!ng there s0 here i wuz aga!n h0mel!ss. s0 i mayd my way 2 th!s laydee that new my awntz in fl0r!da. she t00k me in & start!d wurk!ng at her bar w!th her. it wuz grayt but just lyke b4 i had 2 leev kuz well 1 uv her s0nz wuz a m0nster.

I told her that K. called me, and H. thought the call was for him, and when I tried to explain to him the call was for me, he went into a rage, and well the fact is that he was drunk all the time, [and that] didn't help anything. Anyway, when M. stopped us from arguing, she told me I had to choose between living there and being with K. Well, I chose [K.]. For a while, I didn't care because my sister would take care of us food, shower, and clothes-wise. Well, for me at least, because K. was more of the dress boy type. Anyway it was the summer, so I didn't care that we were out all the time, and as time went by, we got to each other because we spent all our time together.

Then one day we walked past this creepy, abandoned house, so we made it ours, and soon after, she got a job. Then I became the housewife, and things were good until we had to leave because the police found us. I took the blame and got K. to leave before the cops got her too. Apparently you can go to jail even if the place is abandoned. Anyway I was in jail, and me and K. had split up.

When I got out, I didn't know where I was going to go or sleep. My sis had moved away, and I was alone. So I made my way to K.'s aunt's house, and she let me live there for a while, but then I had to go because there were too many people living there, so I was again homeless. So I made my way to this lady that knew my aunts in Florida. She took me in, and I started working at her bar with her. It was great, but just like before, I had to leave because, well, one of her sons was a monster.

0ver the next few munthz i wuz jump!ng frum k0wch 2 k0wch frum 0ld frendz 2 frendz uv frendz gett!ng s!k fr0m n0t eat!ng 0r sleep!ng. but i wuz sm0k!ng a h0le hell uv al0t uv s!gerettz. kutt!ng m0re than uzuall... it wuz h0rr!bull. sh!t i wuz h0rr!bull.. then sum guy hand!d me a k0ndum but i wuz lyke what d0 i want wyth that but !t had !nf0 0n !t & an 0ld x uv myne j. dr0pped me 0ff at th!s playse kalled s!lv!uz. he t0ld me that he w!ll alwayz l0ve me & that he wantz the best 4 me. s0 he gayve me a k!ss. hugged me tyte & sed i h0pe that wut ever ur l00k!ng 4 u fynd it here & l0ng & bh0ld i d!d :–) i f0wnd a m0m naymed T. that kared enuff 2 l!s!n 2 me & a dad naymed lucky that wureed ub0wt my ware ub0wtz wen i wuz layte. my m0m l!s!nz 2 everyth!ng i had 2 say 2 h!m, my dad pr0tekz me just lyke a dad iz supp0ze 2. ne!ther uv them judged me n0 matter wut it wuz. th!s wuz all then bak frum 2003 t!ll n0w 2009. i talk 2 them 2 let them kn0w im 0k, ware im l!v!ng & w!th wh0. az uv june 1 2008 i've b!n l!v!ng w!th 1 uv my best frendz letz kall h!m K.L.A. k!ng laff ulott :–) but kall h!m dadee kuz he tayx kare uv me. i've kn0wn h!m 4 7 yeerz & he'z grayte. sumtymez wen we rgue lyke bestfrendz 0ft!n d0 i go 2 my awntz h0wse her nayme iz p. ev!n th0 she'z n0t my reel awnt she playz the r0le & i lyke it & t!ll th!s day i st!ll g0 see my m0m & dad 0ver at s!lv!uz. xsept n0w my dad iz the dereckter w!ch iz s0 k00l & my m0m iz the k0wnsuler w!ch iz s0 grayt. i d0nt kn0w ub0wt my burth muther 0r much uv my burth father but 2 me my m0m & dad are my reel par!ntz :–) i l0ve them 4 everyth!ng that they've tawt me 4 everyth!ng that they've helped 0verkum. itz kuz uv the!r guyd!nse that helped me h0w 2 lurn 2 sleep itz kuz uv the!r guyd!nse that i lurned h0w 2 st0p kutt!ng s0 much. & it wuz kuz uv the!r guyd!nse that helped me h0w 2 deel w!th the l0ss uv my s!ster & the d!ssapear!nse uv my nephew d0nav!n. h!z m0nster uv par!ntz m00ved uway & n0w i d0nt get 2 see h!m anym0re. but sh00d he ever kum akr0ss th!s b00k i want h!m 2 kn0w, d0nav!n ur t!t! l0vez & m!ss!z u veree much... & 2 u m0m & dad thank u guyz 4 everyth!ng i l0ve u guyz :–) i h0pe u g0t them all dad:–) & i h0pe i d!d a g00d j0b

Over the next few months, I was jumping from couch to couch, from old friends to friends of friends, getting sick from not eating or sleeping. But I was smoking a whole hell of a lot of cigarettes. Cutting more than usual...It was horrible. Shit, I was horrible...Then some guy handed me a condom, but I was like, "What do I want with that?" but it had info on it, and an old ex of mine, J., dropped me off at this place called Sylvia's. He told me that he will always love me, and that he wants the best for me. So he gave me a kiss, hugged me tight and said, "I hope that whatever you are looking for, you [will] find it here," and lo-and-behold, I did! =)

I found a mom named "T." who cared enough to listen to me and a dad named Lucky that worried about my whereabouts when I was late. My mom listens to everything I have to say to him; my dad protects me just like a dad is supposed to. Neither of them judged me no matter what it was. This was all then back from 2003 until now 2009. I talk to them to let them know I'm okay, where I'm living, and with whom. As of June 1, 2008, I've been living with one of my best friends; let's call him K.L.A.—King Laff Alott =), but [I] call him Daddee because he takes care of me. I've known him for seven years, and he's great. Sometimes when we argue, like best friends often do, I go to my aunt's house; her name is P. Even though she's not my real aunt, she plays the role, and I like it, and till this day, I still go see my mom and dad over at Sylvia's. Except now my dad is the Director, which is so cool, and my mom is the counselor, which is so great.

I don't know about my birth mother, or much of my birth father, but to me my mom and dad are my real parents. =) I love them for everything that they've taught me, for everything that they've helped me overcome. It's because of their guidance that helped me how to learn to sleep. It's because of their guidance that I learned how to stop cutting so much, and it was because of their guidance that helped me how to deal with the loss of my sister and the disappearance of my nephew, Donavin. His monster[s] of parents moved away, and now I don't get to see him anymore. But should he ever come across this book, I want him to know, Donavin, your "Titi" loves and misses you very much. And to you, mom and dad, thank you guys for everything. I love you guys. =) I hope you got them all, dad =) and I hope I did a good job.

Love by Anonymous

Beat down life all fucked up.

Being gay is the hard thing

To ever believe for my father.

He really does not like me.

He always says

I did not make you like this.

I made a girl who likes boys.

Tell him I like girls.

Make me feel like I am the Bad Person.

Dark night. I start to go to sleep.

Rapes me and tells me this is how

It feels to be with a man.

Didn't I tell u—u are not gay.

Makes me swallow his shit.

Think in my head I can't do this any more.

Try to live.

It keeps on happening.

13—get on my feet and go to the shelter.

Think in my head

If he can't love me, somebody else will

And won't do shit to me.

Meet this girl and give her five

Years of my life.

Think it going good.

Four years passed and my life was back

Where it started.

Beats me like he used to do.

Half–way dead.

Say I can't take this anymore.

I remember that girl told me

If I was to ever leave

She was going to kill me.

Come home from work

And it just got worse for me.

Gunpoint. *Where the fuck have you been?*

I can't do this anymore.

Dishonoring the Family

Tommi Avicolli Mecca

On two separate occasions, Papa forced me out of my house. The first time I left to get as far away from him as I could. The second time, he actually kicked me out.

I grew up in working–class Little Italy in South Philadelphia in the 50s and 60s. We were poor. Papa and his oldest brother operated a small gas station two blocks from our house. They made a decent living, but not enough for Papa to support four kids. Lots of sacrifices had to be made. I wore hand–me–downs for my entire school life. Mama pinched pennies to keep us fed.

I spent summers trying to earn extra money either by collecting newspapers and bottles to bring to the local junk yard (we didn't call them "recycling places" in those days) or washing cars and doing other odd chores around the gas station.

Being at the gas station was tough. The retired, macho, Italian guys who hung out there sometimes hassled me about being effeminate.

My Uncle Charlie was the worst. He was a Philly cop. He ridiculed me every chance he got. "When're you gonna start acting like a man?" he asked. I usually ignored him. So did Papa.

I knew I was different. I liked to play fashion models with my sister. I jumped rope with the girls. I didn't know exactly how odd I was until one night when a neighborhood kid talked me into helping him steal a copy of *Playboy* from a drugstore. I was scared, but I didn't want him to think I wasn't cool. After all, most of the other boys ignored me or called me names. I didn't know why he wanted to hang out with me.

We paged through the magazine in a dark alley. He was really turned on by the naked, pink–skinned women with big boobs. I wasn't. I knew that I had to pretend that I was. I was a teenager. I was supposed to like to look at pictures of naked girls. It scared me that I didn't. I tried not to think about the fact that it probably made me some kind of freak of nature.

Then he put my hand on his crotch and told me to unzip his pants.

That first brush with gay sex left me looking over my shoulder all the time. I kept expecting that god was going to strike me down for being a sinner. I couldn't confess it and gain absolution. It was unspeakable.

Relief came after my brother introduced me to the writings of French existentialist Jean–Paul Sartre, who believed that there were no absolutes, no good or evil, no wrong or right. I was "condemned to freedom." I decided I didn't have to be ashamed anymore of who I was.

I met someone at a bowling alley one night and developed a strong friendship with him. I was happy. Happier than I had ever been. That boy and I were inseparable. We even kissed. We vowed to go off to college and live together after we graduated high school. I thought I had found the love of my love. Unexpectedly one night he told me he couldn't see me anymore. I was devastated. When the depression and suicidal impulses went away, I vowed I would find others like myself.

I knew they existed. I heard them mentioned when my parents spoke Italian with their friends and family. They were called *fanuk* (short for *finocchio*, Italian for fennel). They were guys who liked other guys.

I found them at a Gay Liberation Front coffee hour at Temple University, where I went to college to avoid the draft. When I walked into that room, I felt a weight lift off my shoulders. Within weeks, I was secretary of the group. In no time at all, I was chairperson. As chair, I helped to organize a gay liberation forum that drew hundreds, among them a man named Bill. I went home with him that night, and the next morning we declared ourselves boyfriends.

It couldn't have been more than a couple weeks later that Bill asked me to move in with him. To understand why I did it without hesitation, you would have to know Papa, the original raging bull. Anything could, and did, set him off. There was no predicting what that would be.

Papa was also star of his own sitcom: *Everybody Loves Papa*. The original Mr. Nice Guy. He would literally give someone the shirt off his back if the person needed it. He was the neighborhood Republican committeeman. He helped guys get their tickets "fixed" and their problems with the cops "resolved."

At home, he ruled his castle with anything but benevolence. There was no room for dissent. I was the enemy: a hippie. I was growing my hair, which sent him into regular tirades. I listened to rock music. I worked at a record store. I expressed radical ideas at the dinner table, such as opposition to the Vietnam War and support for the Black Panthers.

Papa adored Frank Rizzo, Frank Sinatra and Richard Nixon. I idolized Karl Marx, John Lennon and Angela Davis.

It wasn't a good position to be in. I knew that if Papa discovered I was queer, my life was all over. As a preemptive measure, I moved in with Bill. I couldn't just take up and leave. Southern Italian families used to have this rule: you didn't leave home until you were married, or you died.

I told Papa that Bill was an editor at a South Jersey weekly (he was actually an ad rep), and that I was going to be his apprentice for the summer. I was majoring in journalism at the time. After grilling Bill for almost two hours, Papa reluctantly gave the nod for me to leave home.

About two months into living together, everything came crashing down around me. I was in the living room watching TV one night, when Bill and a friend came home from a night at the bars. They obviously had too much to drink. I decided to go to bed. Bill insisted I stay with them. He also told me that he wanted me to have sex with him and his friend. I refused and headed for the bedroom. Bill and his friend followed.

There's only one word for what happened after that: rape. I didn't want his dick in me; he rammed it in anyway. I was in excruciating pain from the lack of lubricant and the size of his member. He didn't care. Neither did his friend, who continued pawing me as Bill fucked me until he came.

In the morning, there was blood on the bed underneath me, and my ass throbbed. I was in a panic, convinced I was going to die. I asked Bill to take me to the hospital. He refused, saying that it was just a little cut. I called a friend who drove me back to Philly to see my neighborhood doctor.

I spent the next week or so in bed recovering. Bill didn't offer much sympathy. He insisted it wasn't his fault. When I felt strong enough to pack, I called my friend again, and he took me back to my parents' house while Bill was at work.

I told my family that I didn't like working at the paper and had decided to change my major to creative writing. Life went back to the way it was before I met Bill. No one at home was the wiser. I came out to my siblings one at a time. They were cool about it. I knew I could never come out to my parents.

Fate had other plans. We received a call at the Gay Liberation Front office that a local TV talk show wanted to host a debate between gay liberationists and a doctor doing aversion therapy on gay men at a psychiatric institution funded by Temple University. The Gay Liberation Front had been fighting the cruel practice for years. Aversion therapy involved attaching electrodes to the dicks of gay men and zapping them with electricity when they were shown pictures of naked men.

As chair of the group, I was the logical choice to represent us on the show. With great hesitancy, I agreed.

I knew I had to tell Mama. I found her ironing in the basement and dropped the news on her. She was horrified, not because I was gay, but at the thought that Papa would find out. Mama would become my greatest ally in the family, but that afternoon she could only think of the mistake I had made in taping the program.

The night it aired, I stayed with friends. I was too scared to go home. I prayed Papa wouldn't see the show, which aired at one in the morning. I was right. Papa didn't see it. But he heard about it from Uncle Charlie.

When I got home the next morning, Mama told me that Papa was gunning for me. He caught up with me a while later in my room. He read me the riot act. I had disrespected him. I had shamed my mother and sister. I had destroyed the family's honor.

I was no longer his son. I was banished from *la mia famiglia*.

The real meaning of that exile didn't hit me until I was gone from the room in which I had spent my childhood. Until I had to face holidays without going home. I was devastated, but relieved that I didn't have to face Papa everyday.

I stayed in contact with Mama and my siblings. When I saw Papa at one of my brother's houses, he didn't talk to me. If I called and he answered, I hung up. I learned to phone at times when he was likely to be at work. For years, I suppressed the feelings I had about the situation. I tried to pretend that it didn't affect me. I was a rock; I was an island. The anger and the hurt were too overwhelming to face.

I had regrets, too. Every once in a while, they surfaced in my thoughts. If only I hadn't done that TV show. If only I had been more discreet. If only I had tried harder to get through to Papa afterward.

To compensate for the loss of *la mia famiglia*, I created my own. I gathered around me a wonderful and eclectic bunch of folks who became surrogate brothers and sisters. We had dinners at my place, especially on holidays. Lovers came and went, but my chosen family didn't. My oldest brother visited me often. He even lived nearby for a time after he left his wife and took up with a girlfriend (now his second wife).

I kept thinking Papa would relent and invite me back home. He never did.

One Christmas in the late 80s, my oldest brother talked Mama and Papa into letting me come home for the holiday. I arrived with my brother and his girlfriend. The three outcasts. Papa wasn't thrilled that my brother was "living in sin."

The house seemed strange. Frozen in time. Little had changed since I left. My old bed and bureau were still in my room as was the desk where I wrote my first poems and short stories.

Papa sat at the kitchen table and said little at first. The tension was unnerving. My brother kept saying silly things to get us to laugh. I just wanted Papa to say something to me. Even if it was, "Look, you little shit, you made my life a living hell all these years, but I love you anyway, and I know you're a good kid."

He finally asked me if I was working. I assured him I was. He wondered if I had enough money. Papa was the money man when I was small. Usually it was quarters. He gave those out as a token of his affection. I told him I didn't need any money. It wasn't much of a conversation, but it helped make me feel more at ease.

As we started to go, Papa went to the dining room closet. "It's cold out there. That coat you're wearing is not warm enough." He pulled out an old jacket.

"Take this one," he said.

I fought back tears as we headed down the steps, Papa watching from the doorway. I was clutching the jacket as if it were made of gold.

It was the last time I would see Papa alive.

A few weeks later, he was lying in the emergency room bloated from an aneurysm. Mama gave the order a few days later to have him removed from life support. He died within twenty–four hours.

It was over. "Ding dong, the witch is dead," my friend, Philip, sang when I told him. Philip had a lunatic of a Papa who once pulled a gun on me when I arrived at his house in drag.

"You don't understand," I said. He didn't. No one could. The emotions were so complex. They still are. Love and hate are two sides of the same coin. They're inseparable.

It has taken years to realize how much I loved the part of that man who took my sister and me to Steel Pier in Atlantic City to ride the ferris wheel. Who won me a pink elephant at one of the game booths. Who gave me a quarter to buy comic books at the local newsstand. Who fed the homeless guy who slept in the alley behind his gas station. Who went to neighbors' houses to make sure they had enough to eat. Who took care of us, even though he made little working so hard at that gas station.

I didn't know what to say to him when he lay dying. I wanted to assure him it was okay between us. I just stood there speechless, unable to articulate what was going on in my head. At the funeral, I was numb. There were no tears.

There still aren't.

Letting Go of the Pain

Angie Guerra

My story is one we hear much too often. We know the character and identify with the "victim" on so many levels.

Unfortunately, at the age of seventeen, a young, naive version of myself awoke to the screams of my parents fighting again. This time, however, was different: the anger was clearly directed towards me. The anger was so fierce and so violent! I wondered to myself, *what could be causing all of this commotion at 7 am on a Saturday morning?*

On this particular Saturday morning, my parents were getting ready for a yard sale. They started their morning like any other. Mom was making dad his coffee and breakfast, and they were readying themselves for a busy weekend ahead. However, on this Saturday morning in late May 1991, things were surely about to change for all of us…forever.

In preparation for the yard sale, accommodations needed to be made; tables needed to be set up; lawn furniture had to moved out of the way; the cars rearranged.

Soon, I would know what all of the ruckus was all about.

I heard the footsteps on the stairs. "Angie get up!" The sound of my father's voice again: "Angie, I said get up!" I responded, "I'm coming—give me a minute." I didn't recall this tone of voice coming from my dad before, and I had heard him angry many, many times. I thought, *I didn't come home drunk last night.* I had hidden my pack of cigarettes. What could I have done that was so bad?

He was now standing at the bottom of the stairs, asking, "Is it true? Is it true what your mother told me?" I stood there with a stunned look on my face, not entirely sure what was going on. I ventured down the steps, very, very slowly. I looked at my mother's crying face, and I saw a note in front of her swollen eyes.

Oh my God! Where did they find that?

With all of the yard sale preparations, my mom moved my car. She inadvertently stumbled upon a note from my girlfriend! There it sat, staring at me. At that moment, everything was a blur. I didn't know what to say. At this point, it was too late not to say anything; I was backed into a corner. I looked at both my parents and said, "Yes, it's true."

What happened next was something I will spend the rest of my adult life trying to forget. The cruelest words I ever heard came from the mouths of the people who were supposed to love their children unconditionally: "You are not my daughter! Get the fuck out of my house!" There were certainly other precious things said, but that is the phrase that has stuck with me. I looked to my mom for support, and there was nothing. She sat there crying and looked so far out of reach, like she was a million miles away.

I felt lost. I pretended not to hear. I got myself ready for work that morning, trying to pretend that everything was normal, but when I returned "home" after the work day, it was true: I really was being kicked out. I couldn't believe this was happening to me! I really thought my mom knew that I was gay. My mom and I had more of a friendship in addition to being mother and daughter. She always had my back, even when my dad and I didn't see eye to eye on things. I could always depend on my mom to be there for me. Not this time. She wouldn't even look at me. I felt so hurt, so angry, so betrayed and so alone.

Where was I supposed to go? I was seventeen years old, still in high school. I wasn't ready to support myself. I was more concerned with SATs, ACTs, applying to colleges and going out on the weekend.

I went to my room. It all felt like a horrible nightmare. I wished that I could lie in bed, fall asleep, wake up and the nightmare would be over. I could start the day fresh without facing what was now my reality. It was in that room that I had learned so many of my coping mechanisms. I learned to run away from my dad's anger. I learned to step away when my mom was drinking. I learned that when I was dreaming of a brighter future, I could stare out the window and wish I were anywhere but standing in my own skin. Unlike many of my friends at the time who were contemplating suicide or ending up in drug and alcohol rehab, I always had my wits about me. I was always the responsible one.

It seemed as if I always knew when to say "when." And now, even when my world was being turned upside down, I learned a new coping mechanism: how to swallow my emotions, how to hold everything in, so that no one else could see my pain.

But there I was, seventeen and just kicked out of the house. I felt so alone and more scared than I'd ever felt in my life. Things at home were never perfect, but it was still home. I still had two parents who were married. I had a stay–at–home mom who cooked dinner for the family everyday and did my laundry. I had parents who bought me my first car. I didn't need for anything, and now I was being told to leave, with nothing, all for being gay. It hardly seemed real.

I started to pack a bag. I kept hearing my father's words in my head, repeating themselves over and over, "Get the fuck out of my house–get the fuck out of my house–get the fuck out of my house!" I was numb. I didn't want to feel all of this unbelievable anguish. *Where am I going to turn for help? Who can I call? What am I going to take? Am I ever coming back? Will I ever see my brother and sister again? Are they really kicking me out? What does this all mean? How did they not know? Where am I going to go?* I sat on the floor in my closet, not knowing what to do.

My bag was half–packed; my mind was a jumbling mess. I didn't cry yet. I was still in shock and trying to figure out what was next until my two–year–old baby sister came into my room and asked, "Can I come?" She always wanted to go wherever I was going. She was more like a daughter than a sister with our fifteen year age difference. It was then that I lost control. I started sobbing uncontrollably, and I don't think the pain from that moment has ever gone away. My mother had to pull her from my arms and tell me to leave. She said, "Enough already! It's time for you to leave!"

I called a friend whose mom tended to take in "strays." I asked if I could come over for a few days. I didn't have a plan; I just knew I needed somewhere to go in that moment. That moment turned into a trip to the liquor store. I thought maybe alcohol would drown my sorrows away. Later that evening, my friends found me walking around the neighborhood incoherent and crying. I was so much of an emotionally empty being that for the next several days, even the school counselor wouldn't let me attend classes. I'm sure the school counselor thought it might be easier on me not to attend classes than have to explain to my classmates what was going on, and thus having to "come out" to everyone. However, I was lucky: most of my high school friends already knew of my sexuality, and for the early 1990s, I suppose I was lucky. I was the only out gay person in school and very well accepted.

I leaned on the school counselor, friends and their families for support. Their guidance and encouragement are where I found strength. The high school counselors continued with their message that I could attend college and find scholarships, even without the support of my parents. I think they were trying to keep my focus on something other than on this enormous tragedy, and it was actually helping me keep grounded. Graduation was so close: it helped to keep me in school, and I never thought about dropping out. *How am I going to make it to college now, given my circumstances?*

I was nearing high school graduation, and I was bouncing from one friend's house to another. I had no contact with my parents, but my parents were making threats to anyone who attempted to help me. They tracked down my girlfriend and threatened statutory rape charges. In the midst of getting kicked out, I found myself getting dumped because my girlfriend was scared of my parents' threats.

I noticed that everyone around me was feeling so much happiness. We were in the midst of graduating from high school. This was what we had all worked so hard for. Many of us were getting or had already received our college acceptance letters. This was the group of friends I had. We lived in the suburbs; we all admittedly partied a little too hard, but we were all smart kids. We had goals and aspirations. Sure, some of us had problems because we were teenagers and were consumed by the usual angst. But what I was dealing with seemed to be too overwhelming, even for my friends. I felt like I was a downer to be around because I needed too much support. Additionally, we were all going in different directions. It was not just another summer break: this was when we were all supposed to find our own way. It was a very transitional time, and I felt like I was lost.

I ventured off to a new group of friends who were a bit older and were mostly gay and lesbian. I was looking for support wherever I could find it. I was trying to find anyone who could understand what I was feeling and for someone to be a sounding board for me. This person came to me by way of an older woman who stepped in the picture and offered her condolences.

She offered a then eighteen–year–old but still lost and lonely young person a listening ear, a helping hand, a place to live. She offered to share her bed. The offer seemed too good to be true to someone who had suffered so much. It seemed like just what I need at the time—finally someone who could help me through this difficult time.

But at eighteen, the naiveté of life was still there. Less than a month into the relationship, I started seeing signs that things might not be all that I thought they were. The relationship quickly turned verbally and physically abusive. Now, I had gotten myself into a situation, but I had no one to turn to. I remember wanting to blame my parents—*see what you made happen!* I thought that if they hadn't kicked me out, I wouldn't have been in that situation; it's all their fault. Of course, that wasn't true, but after all the hurt they caused, it was easy to stay in a situation that was unhealthy. I felt unworthy of anything else. At times, my partner was taking care of me, which was what I needed from her. But I also felt trapped because I didn't feel confident enough to leave her. I had no support system.

After spending six years in a severely unhealthy relationship, I later discovered that I was living with a woman who struggled with bipolar disease. She struggled with anger issues and possessiveness, and I was the target. Of course, I realized all this in retrospect. At eighteen, I didn't recognize these signs. I didn't know what was going on. I just knew that things were not good, so much so that she had threatened to kill me.

That was a wake–up call!

At twenty five years old, I was determined to make things right in every way. I needed to forgive my parents, and I needed to forgive myself. I needed to move forward and to let the past go. Over the past several years, I once again established a minimal relationship with my parents. It wasn't easy, and it was still strained. At least we were trying.

I decided to move back "home" at twenty–five—literally into my parents' house. I thought this was going to be the only way to make amends with each other and to know each other again. We each had the choice to accept each other or not. Really it seemed that simple. I missed them, and I believe they missed me. It worked! We had found a way to mend our broken relationship. Today, my parents are very accepting of my lifestyle. They have accepted people I have brought into my life.

While mending the relationship with my parents, I also took time to better myself and finished my bachelor's degree. I earned a degree from the University of Wisconsin–Milwaukee in Journalism and Mass Communication. I started an internship program at a local company and started volunteering. Through my volunteer efforts, I became connected with the Milwaukee LGBT Community Center, where I served as Director of Development and Marketing for four years.

Through my journey, the Milwaukee LGBT Community Center has played an integral role in my life, although not in the typical way that a community center can provide a safe space. When I reached the point in my professional career when I could give something back, I realized that I wanted to do more. I have now decided to pursue an advanced degree and to earn a Master's Degree in Social Work in hopes of counseling LGBT youth, young adults and their families.

The world has changed so much over the past ten years. The Milwaukee LGBT Community Center, among many other LGBT community centers nationwide, now offer programs serving youth who share my story—those who get kicked out and who are homeless. The numbers are astonishing. I resonate with their tragedy, and I can't help but want to do more!

My struggles have impacted who I am and what I do today. I feel fortunate that I have been able to reconcile with my family and that I found the courage to go back to college and to find a career that suits me.

As far as surprises go, my mom even volunteers at the LGBT Center's events every year!

P(ie)C(e)S

Kestryl Cael

2000: Does it still count as being "kicked out" if you tried to leave first?

I am a teenage escape artist. Not even the overpriced security system that my parents just installed can fulfill its sole purpose of keeping me in. I cheat the sensors with tape and guile, slide open the window and vault onto the second–story deck. Wary of tripping the motion–sensor floodlights, I creep down the stairs through mottled moonlight and edge towards the gate. Footsteps soft on bark dust and pine needles, I slip out of the yard. I hope they haven't noticed. I hope I'm safe. I stride to the end of the block in silence, ears alert for footfalls on the pavement behind me.

At the bus stop, I feel secure. I stare down the empty street, searching for evidence of the last #52 bus of the night. I don't have much of a plan, but it's more than last time. Last time, I left without thinking and found myself shivering in an abandoned train station at 2:00 am, hoping the sirens outside weren't looking for me. At least I have somewhere to run tonight.

On the bus, a man sits down across from me and tries to make small talk. He's at least twice my age. I pretend to be older and wiser, and he gives me a hand–rolled cigarette and his phone number, tells me to give him a call "if things don't work out." The bus reaches the end of the route, and I'm not nervous. Really. Walking to Corey's house, I imagine myself as independent, debonair, rakish. I steal up to the window, knock twice on the glass and creep into the darkened room.

We talk nervously in the basement until caresses lead to something more, and then we fall asleep. In the morning, we approach Corey's father. Over coffee and oatmeal, he addresses me: they want to take me in, want to look into fostering me. The catch? I have to call my parents, tell them where I am and receive their blessing, or, at minimum, their consent.

I am back in the maximum security, suburban prison by noon.

2006: How were you "kicked out" if they say it was for your own good?

I have no proof it was because I was queer. They've denied it every time I asked, every conversation *cum* familial breakdown that I've initiated since my discharge.

I suppose it's just a coincidence that three of the four people I've found who were locked up with me there now identify as queer. I suppose it's just a coincidence that one of them is trans.

I suppose it's just a coincidence that I was required to grow my hair long there. I suppose it's just a coincidence that we were required to wear pink as a punishment.

I suppose it's just a coincidence that my counselor, Dana, focused more of our weekly sessions on the page in my journal that described my girlfriend than she ever did on my cutting and scars. I suppose it's just a coincidence that so much as a hug between two girls on the unit was punishable with weeks on Investment. We were encouraged to spend time with the boys.

Enough of the coincidences.

I was sent to Peak's Crest School, a lockdown institution disguised as a residential academy, one month into my sophomore year of high school. The brick walls of that building in the desert defined my universe until the end of April. For seven months, I hardly saw the sky.

We were there for a motley host of reasons: drugs, sex, violence, disrespecting our elders, being too much, too fast, too young. Or so we were told. I can't attest to the veracity for the others. We weren't allowed to discuss our "issues" with fellow inmates, lest it lead to one–up–man–ship and war stories, but I can testify now that the common excuses of drugs and violence had little to do with my confinement.

As I've been told, my original diagnoses related to depression and being "out of control." The fact that I had left home multiple times didn't help. The fact that I held a 4.0 GPA, played first clarinet in the marching band and starred in school plays didn't matter.

The fact that I was about to start one of my school district's first Gay-Straight Alliances may have been the last straw.

2000: Can you call it "kicked out" if they're steadily draining their bank accounts to keep you locked up?

I didn't know what was happening until after the plane landed. I'm still not sure I understand. I had been told we just had a layover here, and then we were catching a flight home. I see the two men in uniforms approaching as we deboard the plane, greeting my parents. Their hands grip my shoulders as my parents tell me, "You need more help than we can give you. You're going to go live at Peak's Crest for a while." The guards lead me forcefully through the airport, half–dragging me as I scream curses and epithets at the passersby. My parents trail behind as the guards shove me into an unmarked van. I won't see my family again for several months.

We drive in silence for over an hour. My seatbelt feels like it's choking me. Eventually, we pull into a parking lot, down a long drive and far from the main road. I get my first view of Peak's Crest School. The building seems unassuming and bland, a brown brick bunker with growths like octopus arms stretching out over yellowed grass. The guards' hands become vises on my shoulders, yanking me out of the van, across the parking lot, through the portentous glass door and into the lobby. The room is modest and pink, hospital furniture and disinfectant masquerading as a grandmother's best parlor.

We pass through vacuum–sealed doors—I don't know how many—locks sliding seamlessly back in place behind us. The hallway seems much longer than the building's profile suggested. I descend into a blur of terror. After several flights of stairs and more doors, we arrive in a partially darkened room. There are more people here, wearing badges. Someone orders me to remove my clothes.

I want to maintain my dignity. Somehow, I force myself to stop crying. Arms crossed, I hold my ground, my jeans feeling like my last shred of autonomy.

I refuse to strip, so they do it for me. With surgical scissors, they cut off my sweater, my shirt, my pants, my bra, my underwear, the cord of a necklace that I wear with loving devotion underneath my clothes. At some point, I start screaming. The room goes black.

I awake sprawled on the floor of a small room, my cheek pressed against cold, gray concrete. My arms and legs look like someone else's, clad in hot pink sweats that are ragged and frayed at the cuffs. A heavy metal door with a small square window dominates one wall. The rest of the room is empty.

I wait, sore and confused. I don't know for how long; it can't be more than a few hours, but time has little meaning. At some point, someone comes to give me a tray of room–temperature iceberg lettuce and orange juice, but she won't talk to me. Later, she gives me the rules.

She tells me that all of my problems stem from a lack of structure. Society is based on rigid structures, the rules assert, and if I refuse to comply with social structures, I will never be a productive citizen. Peak's Crest will cure me by training me in the structure I lack. She gives me a manual describing the structures: a specific way to stand in line, a protocol for addressing staff, a method for folding my underwear and arranging my laundry in my drawers. Any misstep—walking too quickly or improperly making my bed—will be punished by time on Investment.

The Investment Unit makes the rest of Peak's Crest look like summer camp. Girls on Investment spent their time seated, back straight, hands in their laps, feet flat on the floor, eyes staring straight ahead. They do not move unless someone tells them to. Girls who were there long enough seemed afraid to think without being granted permission. Some girls were on Investment for months. Some girls were on Investment for years.

When they release me from the small gray room, they place me on Investment because I am "high risk." I don't get any privacy. I don't get to go to the bathroom alone. It doesn't take me long to learn that playing by their rules means I can earn the privilege of unchaperoned showers. It doesn't take me long to learn that the girls who play by the rules get out the fastest, as long as they convince the staff their performance is sincere.

I become a model patient. Total surrender is the only path to discharge; there are girls who rebelled and have been here for years. One girl, sixteen years old, has been here since she was twelve. She tells me she'll be here until she turns eighteen and can sign her own discharge papers. She claims her integrity is more important than escape.

They assign each of us to specific therapy groups based on our treatment plan and our "issues." In Self–Esteem Group, we learn how to apply "natural" makeup and compliment each other's appearance. Every so often, they bring over some well–behaved boys from the young men's campus and tell us to socialize, to make friends and to send letters after the event ends. They are helping us to feel normal, the staff tells us, because when we feel normal, we won't have low self–esteem.

After seven months, I am told to prepare to be discharged. I'm unsure why: either they think I'm performing "normal" well enough, or the money has run out. I can't be sure which, though I suspect that the two factors are acting in tandem. Other patients tell me that Peak's Crest costs between five– and seven–thousand dollars a month, and I doubt that my parent's insurance has been contributing. Years later, my father answers my questions: "At some point, we had to decide how much our daughter's life was worth."

They never specifically said that it was a bad thing to be queer. They never *officially* said anything about being queer at all, as if it weren't even real. My counselor had momentary obsessions with the part of my journal where I had rhapsodized about my girlfriend, but she never explicitly told me I should be straight. She didn't need to; the structure did it for her. Queer life was messy. It didn't fit into Peak's Crest's boxes.

2001: *How were you "kicked out" if you couldn't wait to break free?*

I'm terrified of ever going back. I've had a taste of the repressive power of the normative world, and I, isolated and fifteen, am in no position to take it down alone. I'll toe the line. I'll keep my hair long, even curl it occasionally. I'll wear skirts. I'll be inconsolable when the boy I claim to have a crush on doesn't invite me to Homecoming.

All of my energy focuses on counting. I have twenty–six months left, twenty–six months until I will be eighteen, and free. At twenty months to go, my parents decide I have "stabilized" enough not to need constant, direct supervision. They let me get a part–time job. I save every penny I earn, planning a permanent and legal escape.

Twelve months left on the countdown, and I start making purchases for my own home: towels, sheets, dishes. I make no secret of my preparations; my parents know I can't wait to leave.

Two months left, and I start to get cocky. I take a girl, Michelle, to prom. She's a good friend, I assure my mother, a disappointed junior who can't buy a ticket for herself until next year. We both know I'm lying, but as long as I play it straight, it's fine. I know the rules, and I've learned to follow them.

I celebrate my eighteenth birthday with a trip to a drag show, and stay the night at my gay boyfriend's apartment. My mother expresses concern at my choice to spend the night with a man, and I relish in the phone call: "He's queer, Mom." It will still be months before I manage to tell her that I am.

2008: Can you ever stop feeling like you've been "kicked out"?

I want to believe that my parents didn't lock me up because I was queer. I really do. I don't want to blame them. But the evidence seems murky—the most I've gotten from them, when I've asked why they sent me there, was that they were trying to save me. Save me from what? I've yet to hear a satisfactory answer.

Even their own protestations—that I was depressed, suicidal, a danger to myself—mask the full story. I could cite the numerous statistics of youth who suffer depression because they are queer in a homophobic environment. I won't. I'll refrain from assigning retrospective motivations to my teen angst, as obvious as the correlation now appears.

I wish I could distill a lesson, some moral of the story to pass onto others who find themselves in parallel situations. It would be easier if my life read like a fable. I have trouble assigning blame; as bitter and pained as I still am about my parents' decision to banish their child from their home and into an institution that desired nothing more than to break hir, I cannot render them as simple villains.

My parents genuinely thought they were helping me, the only way they thought they could. Peak's Crest seduced them with glossy brochures of smiling teens and parent testimonials, promising healing and comfort. I do not (cannot) believe they would have sent me there if they knew what I would experience. Perhaps that's naïveté on my part, but I have trouble faulting their choice. As far as they were concerned, they were trying to save the only daughter they had. I'm not sure that even I was aware, at that point, that perhaps being their *daughter* was part of the problem.

I don't know that I can claim I was *kicked out* because the phrase implies being forced to leave somewhere that you wanted to stay. Their house had stopped being a home before they sent me to Peak's Crest. Once, when I asked why they sent me away, my father replied, "You said we needed some time apart." It's true: we did…but I needed to leave on my terms.

Coming Out and Coming Home, or: You CAN Choose Your Family

Anne Giedinghagen

"Home is where, when you have to go there, they have to take you in." —Robert Frost

"But what if they don't?" —Anne Giedinghagen

When you're young, your family makes you. I mean this in the most literal sense—the mixing and melding of your parents' genes and whatever happens afterward creating your body—but also figuratively. They mold your personality, affect your self–esteem and impart their values. For some people, that process never stops; in some cases, it's great, while in others, it's not so wonderful.

Some eventually move from being made to making themselves. I am one of those.

I am one of those because I finally realized that the mold my parents kept trying to force me into was too constricting and painful; and that fitting into it would require carving off and discarding significant portions of myself. When I knew that the life, the love, the family I wanted to make was beyond their understanding, I began making my own family. In some ways, it was easier than bringing together a "normal" family. There were no weddings to plan, no antagonistic in–laws to appease, no fights over curfews and dating. Yet in other ways, it was profoundly more difficult: it meant starting from square one, a place few people ever really find themselves. It meant stepping out into the unknown with few plans and even fewer guarantees.

In hindsight, I began assembling my chosen family even before my parents ejected me from theirs. I had to—not just for comfort, but for survival. Otherwise I could never have endured the violence, the disdain, the chaos that marked life at "home." By the beginning of high school, before I even came out, I had managed to collect an assortment of mothers and almost–aunts. These wonderful women offered the kind of acceptance and compassion I hungered for. Even the word *hunger* seems like an understatement; it was a profound starvation, yet I'd become so accustomed to it over the years that I no longer really noticed the pangs. They noticed, though, and I suspect the need that was so hidden from me was as raw and apparent to them as the sound of my voice or the color of my eyes. Foundling that I was, they took me in.

Colleen ushered me through middle school, cheering me on at track meets and listening to my outpourings of teenage bitchiness. I felt guilty for burdening her sometimes, but when guilt wrestles with the primal, desperate need to be loved and understood, need wins every time. Johnna made me blueberry muffins to keep in my locker during that period when (obviously) I wasn't eating breakfast at home. Sharon read my hackneyed seventh–grade poems. Once, when talking about my family reduced me to tears, she got a compact out of her purse and handed it to me saying, "Look at those wet eyelashes. Look at how beautiful you are. There are women who would pay a lot of money for a mascara that did that." Finding humor in the pathos is essential to survival; in absurd and surreal circumstances, sometimes the healthiest response is to be a little absurd yourself.

Yohanna watched from a distance since she lived an hour away. Still, she wrote me often and consoled me by phone when dealing with my first family got to be too much. Yohanna was also there for, and a catalyst for, a lot of my firsts. She was the first person to tell me that being gay was okay (when I brought it up in that evasive way unique to thirteen–year–olds—I was ashamed of it at the time, of course; I had been brought up to be ashamed of any kind of desire, much less one labeled "deviant").

She was the first to suggest the vision of God my parents and church had presented—the distant judgmental father who punished me "for my own good"—wasn't the whole story. Her voice replaced the constant refrain of my dad's criticisms in my head: "You worthless whore. You stupid bitch. Lazy, selfish, ungrateful, disgusting…" Often his words were punctuated with slaps or shoves, something no one in our house ever discussed. I learned to numb myself to his impact, but with the process of coming out came a sudden thaw and an accompanying rush (as long–frozen emotions grew mobile again) of dread, anger and elation.

I had always fended for myself, but suddenly I needed comforting. I needed consoling and support. In short, I needed a mother, and the universe brought me just that: a bisexual Pagan, simultaneously nurturing and strong, to tell me that I wasn't crazy; someone to declare that my thoughts and desires were not only acceptable but worthy of celebration. I couldn't have imagined a woman better able to address my peculiar mix of adolescent independence and injured neediness. Yohanna was the first person ever to be firmly, militantly on my side. Her outrage on my behalf—"Your father said what? How dare he! He hit you? He can't get away with that!"—was something I had never seen from the mother I was born to. It was another first: when I first stood up for myself, if only in my own head, following Yohanna's lead.

I didn't meet Lisa until later in high school, when I was teetering on the cusp of coming out. We strategized, considered the possible consequences of freedom versus the painful (but safer) strictures of the closet. Was it worth a broken heart, a broken home, possibly a broken jaw? Was it worth forfeiting a group of friends or the esteem of my more conservative teachers? If those welcoming arms withdrew just because I came out as gay, how welcoming had they been to begin with?

Lisa also introduced me to the basics of queer culture, such as it was in Missouri at the time: *Hothead Paisan* and *Dykes to Watch Out For*, the hairy body–painted wonder of the Michigan Womyn's Music Festival and Pride in June.

"You really need to go to New York or San Francisco for a Pride march, though," she said. "Kansas City doesn't even have Dykes On Bikes, and that's something you've gotta see." She also passed along some of her favorite "dykey" CDs: Catie Curtis and Melissa Ferrick. For the first time in years, I felt excited about something—maybe there was a life out there for me. More than a mode of wary survival, a life in black (and blue) and white: now, there could be a life in Technicolor. Meanwhile my own mother, not quite hip to my increasingly close friendship with a senior girl, was still harassing me to wear a bra and to shave my legs.

"And would it kill you to get a purse so you aren't always hauling that backpack around?" she demanded. Dad would probably kill me if a copy of *Rubyfruit Jungle* fell out of a zipperless purse versus the more secure backpack with dozens of zippers where I'd been stashing such "perverted filth." Maybe he wouldn't have killed me; he would just have screamed for a while, socked me a few, maybe raged around the house a bit. Still, I wanted to avoid his wrath if I could.

I'd spent years tiptoeing around my father's rages, trying to avoid flying words and fists; why tempt fate? Eventually, of course, he did find out. Luckily I had already laid the groundwork, and I had several pairs of arms flung open to receive me. This isn't to say it was easy to face the rejection—it wasn't. Parents are supposed to offer unconditional love, right? I stayed up nights doing mental acrobatics, trying to understand or justify what my parents had done. If my own parents—the people practically required by law to love me—couldn't stand me, how could I expect anyone else to? Fortunately for my emotional (and physical) survival, my other mothers poured the love on thick.

Again, I know: I was extravagantly lucky. Years of feeling unlovable coupled with this final, utter rejection took their toll. I still went to school, still played my flute and oboe, still went to debate tournaments. What very few people knew was that I was living like an emotional burn victim—raw nerve endings exposed to the world. Several times during high school, I seriously considered taking a swan–dive off the Broadway Bridge. My mothers held me in; they held me up. They literally saved my life.

"Everything happens for a reason," my mother used to say. Though I agree with her—I know that a lot of my maturity, grit and strength has come from dealing with my identity and with other people's reactions—it doesn't excuse the way my parents treated me. Nor does it let society off the hook for nurturing an environment where parents feel justified in abandoning and abusing their own simply because they're different. I was forced to grow up faster than I should have, without the support a "family" is supposed to provide, and I won't lie. It sucked royally, completely, totally. At the time, I assumed it would hurt forever, that the pain would always be there, red–raw and insistent. Fortunately, nothing is forever.

In some ways, it was like being blinded in an accident. At first, I groped in the dark and stumbled into things. I accumulated quite a collection of bruises and scars. Among those injuries was the feeling that because my first family didn't accept or nurture me, I was unworthy and unlovable. If love was conditional, being cared for meant carefully monitoring my every action to make sure I never caused offense; I never let people see the real me for fear that they'd kick me out of their lives or run screaming from the room. That, I think, is every person's secret fear: the question that lurks in the inner recesses of the brain, the monster in the shadows. *Will I be loved, and am I worth loving?* What's the point of getting close to someone only to be tossed away like a used Kleenex?

For the average person, these questions get hammered out naturally; family provides at least a basic template of love and acceptance, and society affirms their (heterosexual) relationships. They never hear from the pulpit or Senate floor that their desires are depraved. They have a fighting chance, at least. I had a fighting chance too, I guess, but only because I've been a fighter from the beginning and because I never stepped into the ring alone. My mothers were always behind me. Kathleen and Annette, with a hug or dinner: for my high school graduation, they took me to a restaurant where, despite trying my damnedest to be thrifty, I couldn't finesse a meal for under twenty dollars. I hoped the low light concealed my blushing as I finally understood the phrase "embarrassment of riches." Annette in particular seemed to recognize my hunger, though she took it as literal and responded with that Midwestern emotive substitute, food. To be fair, she fed everyone, not just me. Kathleen was like a rock, and her inexhaustible patience and staid enthusiasm always comforted. Suzanne, with words of encouragement, a reserved strength and a warm bed to fall into. Janet, whose couch was a place to settle when nowhere else felt safe.

Slowly, abilities I never knew I had came to the surface. Like a person whose other senses become exquisitely acute to make up for lost vision, I developed surprising resourcefulness and determination—even, eventually, a sense of pride. Did it make me a better person to have my parents turn their backs on me? I'd like to think it's made me more independent, and I know it's made me more compassionate. Were the gifts worth the heartache? I don't know, but my new family is one of those gifts. It has become as dear to me as the family I was born into: my parents' genes may have constructed my body, but my chosen family makes up my heart and soul.

I still wish my lot in life had been different, but that longing is less frequent and less painful than it once was. Of course, I still have twinges of self–doubt and wild insecurity, still feel that insatiable love–hunger. How much is simply the reality of being human, I'm not sure, but each day it recedes a little more. I am becoming the woman I've wanted to be, and I can make anywhere feel like home.

The Psychic Cheesegrater: What I Learned on the Streets

Tenzin

Homelessness during youth can dramatically alter our sense of identity and can have lasting effects throughout our lives. Even formerly psychologically healthy people can develop mental illness in response to the stress of homelessness. The impact of these experiences is compounded for already marginalized queer youth. We can never entirely replace what we lose on the streets—namely, a sense of innocence, safety and security. Our faith in people and the world can become irrevocably damaged. Yet the aftermath of adversity is not exclusively negative, since we have the potential to derive strength and wisdom from suffering and to witness and embody humanity's more exalted qualities in a world characterized by narcissism, cruelty and exploitation.

I offer these words for those still living in toxic environments (whether literally or psychically). As a fellow queer survivor, I would encourage you not to devalue the unique skills and meaning you may derive from an experience that is rare in the Western world.

Positive Side Effects of Adolescent Homelessness

Despite the physical and mental damage I incurred during adolescence, my exposure to deprivation and violence imbued me with a sense of gratitude and equipped me with qualities and abilities that I would otherwise lack; I am better able to benefit others, my child and myself as a direct result of living on the streets.

In a culture consumed by rampant materialism, I am easily contented by a simple life. I have a deep appreciation for things that most people in the Western world take for granted, such as food, shelter and warmth. Being homeless during my formative years allowed me the opportunity to provide resources and protection to those more vulnerable than myself. I was among the fortunate minority who managed to hold jobs for periods and fed younger people to prevent them from having to generate income through dangerous alternative venues.

A premature exposure to violence and abuse equipped me with a high threshold for pain and a fighting ability that enabled me to protect others in dangerous situations. This exposure also simultaneously (and paradoxically) desensitized me, yet it instilled an empathy for survivors that enabled me to work on behalf of abused children, torture victims/political prisoners and people oppressed due to their sexual and/or gender identity.

Confrontations with mortality, coupled with stigmatization as a freak and second–class citizen during my adventures in foster care and on the street, were integral to my spiritual development and the direction my life took. I empathized with people with AIDS who were hated, feared and abandoned to die without love. I began volunteering in AIDS organizations when I was sixteen and cared for numerous friends with the disease when I was no longer homeless. Multiple exposures to threats of imminent bodily injury and death not only gave me the psychological fortitude to be present for the terminally ill, but helped me to recapture the numinous sense of the sacred I experienced spontaneously as a young child; I felt a profound sense of expansiveness, safety and love not connected with any external person or thing when climbing trees in my backyard. Although I felt temporarily disconnected from spirituality during the turbulence of adolescence, the connection was abruptly regained when someone threatened to kill me. I felt flooded with the same love and tranquility as I contemplated my imminent death (although the endogenic opioid response triggered by a body preparing itself for injury may better explain this phenomena) and prayed aloud for the would–be murderer in a way that shocked him so much that he stopped. Having friends die and experiencing repeated murder threats imparted an understanding of the precariousness of human existence that renewed my interest in life's spiritual dimension. Eventually this interest culminated in my decision to ordain as celibate Buddhist monastic clergy in the Tibetan Drikung Kagyu tradition in 2000.

The Buddha's first noble truth regarding the ubiquity of suffering resonates deeply with those who have experienced hardship and loss. Although Buddhism is often criticized as a pessimistic, depressing religion for its focus on suffering, the Buddha was merely pointing out something that is obvious to anyone paying attention to the horror and misery experienced by all sentient beings during some point in their lives. One could argue that Buddhism is inherently optimistic since it not only describes the problem of suffering, but offers a systematic method to transform our subjective experience of suffering through mind training and meditation. Buddhism posits that mental afflictions are not intrinsic to the nature of our mind, but are merely temporary illusory states that seem to obscure our true nature.

Although I lack profound spiritual realizations and am not an exemplary Buddhist practitioner, I have derived immense benefit from spiritual practice. I am intimately acquainted with the factors that drive people to seek spiritual nourishment, after having discovered at a young age that everything that one is taught to rely on for personal happiness, safety and security is entirely unreliable. Parents, possessions and friends provide no ultimate refuge due to their transitory, mercurial and often volatile nature. Buddhist teachings on impermanence and suffering meshed well with the disenchantment with temporal existence I derived from watching people get beaten and shot, and losing friends to AIDS, murder, overdose, prison and suicide. Exposure to neglect, cruelty, homelessness and violence during my formative years and beyond were instrumental in shaping my identity and fueled my spiritual predilections.

Buddhist practice has transformed my life. My practice is a form of spiritual excavation; I examine and strip away the illusory afflictive emotional states and habitual propensities derived from traumatic experiences that obscure my intrinsic spiritual nature to reveal something primordially clean, compassionate, resilient and indestructible. Although a cursory examination of human behavior does not easily lend itself to the belief that people will exercise their ability to treat each other civilly (or even avoid bringing the human race to extinction through nuclear catastrophe or environmental destruction), I have faith that all human beings are capable of amazing transformations, provided they are willing to do the work. The power of wisdom and compassion exceeds that of greed, hatred and ignorance.

Living With and Overcoming the Past

Although I am still haunted by the physical and psychic effects of my time on the streets and am not successful by the economic standards of Western American culture, I am far happier and healthier than I would ever have anticipated. After actively contemplating suicide between the ages of nine and twenty–eight, my present contentment and happiness are likely the result of extensive therapy and spiritual practice. Despite prolonged struggles with physical illness and debilitating post–traumatic stress disorder, I recently graduated *summa cum laude* from the University of Oregon. I have worked to benefit others whose suffering surpassed my own in the fields of human rights, hospice, AIDS activism and spiritual practice. Although my intellectual development was adequate (despite numerous interruptions in my education), I still exhibit deficits in social functioning related to inadequate/unorthodox socialization, innate or inculcated reclusive tendencies, post–traumatic stress disorder and issues related to my transgendered status (such as difficulties accessing surgical and hormonal interventions that allow greater physical gender congruence).

Despite having life experiences so far out of the range that most people consider normal and lacking appropriate parental role models, I have been a nurturing, effective parent to my child with Asperger's syndrome. Although my negative experiences during my early life made me concerned about bringing a child into the world, I was determined to raise my child lovingly and consciously, free from the contamination of my own legacy of betrayal and abuse.

My history profoundly affected my parenting in positive ways. Not being adequately loved and valued by my parents during my formative years makes me cherish my child all the more. I have the luxury of direct knowledge of the consequences of being mistreated and discarded. Lacking salvageable parental templates required me to exercise creativity when learning parental skills. I read books, utilized community resources such as Healthy Start and emulated altruistic people in the AIDS caregiving circuit, mentors, friends and characters in novels to acquire the skills to raise my child. I love him and try to provide a good example as an activist, a Buddhist clergyman and an unrepentant transgendered person. I want to instill the strength, compassion and social conscience in him that I acquired in my life; to encourage him to stand up against intolerance; to be true to himself; and to care for others and the planet. Most importantly, I want him to feel safe, accepted and loved in a world that can seem ominous and confusing.

The Kindness of Strangers, Vampires and Angelic Crack Whores

I saw an unexpected side of human nature on the streets. The compassion and charity I encountered while homeless were all the more striking due to their rarity. The people who attempted to ease rather than to augment my suffering stand out in my mind as an inspiration even today.

I remember a benevolent elderly man covering me up with a blanket when I was sleeping on the porch of the Basque Hotel in San Francisco, rather than telling me to get the fuck off his porch as I was expecting. Hunger and malnutrition were salient since I had been a vegetarian since age nine and stubbornly remained so during my protracted homeless sojourns. Sometimes the only vegetarian options at food kitchens were nutritionally sparse selections like bread, iceberg lettuce and cake. I ate bread off the ground or discarded veggie pizza since I was too embarrassed to panhandle. Sometimes I gathered pennies off the ground until I had enough to buy steamed rice at the Chinese restaurant; a man who watched me went into the restaurant and bought me food.

Another time a man brought $20 to give to a homeless person in Golden Gate Park. As hippies, punks and growly bums surrounded him like ravenous geese and began begging and whining for the money, I thought that his generosity was commendable even if it only resulted in someone getting drunk or stoned. At that moment, he walked over and gave me the money that enabled me to purchase food for myself and my friends. One of my fondest Christmas memories is sitting around a barrel fire in Golden Gate Park and being blessed with gifts of oranges and thick socks by some amazing people. These simple acts profoundly affected me; I was touched that strangers showed more concern for me than my biological parents, foster parents or the child welfare system had.

Severe illness during homelessness made me feel extremely vulnerable, and many unlikely people provided assistance and intervention that allowed me to remain on the planet. I remember lying on Market Street, delirious with a high fever resulting from a prolonged, untreated kidney infection. Passersby ignored me, probably assuming that I was merely inebriated or on heroin, rather than suffering from renal failure. It was strange to feel so isolated in such a public setting, and I thought it was ironic that I would die alone even though I was surrounded by people. I was haunted by the account of a friend with AIDS who was unconscious in a gutter on Market Street for eight hours before anyone stopped. I felt disposable. I ruminated dismally on human nature. The only person who stopped was a disheveled crack whore who knelt down and lovingly offered me a hit off her crack pipe. When I explained that I didn't partake and needed medical attention, she called an ambulance for me.

I think of her often since she not only probably saved my life, but did much to restore my precarious faith in humanity. I believe crack is evil, but the love and generosity the woman exhibited by offering to share it was not lost on me. Her compassion and basic decency shone through the fog of addiction when she offered to share a substance that normally makes people so desperate that they will sell their bodies, steal from loved ones or kill.

My gratitude goes out to these helpers in unexpected places, particularly the deceased whose kindness still resonates in my psyche: Jason Blore, who was one of the sweetest people I knew underneath his superficial veneer of vampiric malevolence, and Turk le Clair, who fed us and provided shelter without expecting anything disgusting in return. Their scattered acts of compassion were often enough to maintain my faith in people.

Advice for Those Still Living on the Streets

For those of you still living on the streets, find places that help queer youth where you will be understood and cared for rather than exploited. There are queer youth centers and youth shelters in many cities. Stick together with other people in your predicament, and try to avoid becoming addicted to toxic substances that ultimately exacerbate the difficulties they once seemed to alleviate. Remember that you have value, and that anyone who judges you for being queer and homeless wouldn't last a day in your situation; nurture a sense of superiority towards those who would judge and blame you for your predicament in an attempt to insulate themselves from guilt and to excuse their lack of compassion. Try to remember that the whole world is not as pestilential and cruel as it can seem on the streets. One would hope that your parents would have behaved differently if they knew what would happen to you on the streets; my hope in writing this is that other parents will choose to accept their children for who they are rather than subjecting them to homelessness.

Advice for Parents Struggling with Their Child's Sexual and/or Gender Identity on Religious or "Moral" Grounds

Life is difficult for all queer people, even the fortunate queer children blessed with supportive PFLAG parents. For those without the safety net of a supportive family, the effects can be catastrophic (as evidenced by the elevated rates of suicide and homicide among queer people). Conversely, the harm inflicted upon queer children and adolescents by an intolerant society can be mediated by a parent's unconditional love, acceptance and understanding. Although some parents find it difficult to reconcile the tenets of their religious traditions with their child's queer identity, particularly if the religious tradition expresses ambivalence or hostility towards lesbian, gay, bisexual and transgender people, Christians can look to Christ's example in the New Testament for guidance (rather than the Old Testament where those who eat shrimp platters at Sizzler's are similarly condemned to Divine punishment): Jesus enjoins his followers to show mercy, charity and love toward all people fearlessly, even when they do things we don't understand or agree with. If one is supposed to love even one's enemy, how much more so should parents love their own queer children.

Ousting queer children from the family and onto the streets may expose them to deprivation, assault and possibly murder; subjecting one's offspring to such suffering based on religious grounds is antithetical to the fundamentals of Christ's teachings of compassion and social responsibility. Religion is ideally a source of strength and comfort for both adherents and those with whom they come into contact. Conversely, if adherence to a religious faith makes followers more judgmental and fearful and less compassionate and accepting, perhaps we can conclude that they are not practicing it properly.

Transmutation and Transcendence

Periods of adversity and deprivation have the capacity to transform the human psyche in profound and unexpected ways. Many of the world's mystical traditions advocate the deliberate adoption of poverty and asceticism. Even our involuntary time on the streets can be re–contextualized as a spiritual education from an alternative perspective. The Buddha, Jesus, Gandhi, St. Francis and numerous adepts from many disparate sacred traditions throughout the world were homeless wanderers during portions of their spiritual quests. Even atheistic secular humanists derived meaning from times of hardship and suffering as evidenced by Victor Frankl's accounts of his incarceration in Nazi concentration camps in *Man's Search for Meaning*. The value of such experiences is still salient today: a Vietnam veteran who later became a Buddhist monk spent time homeless as a component of his spiritual practice, and a revered Buddhist lama spent seven years meditating in a cave in Tibet with little food and developed spiritually as a result of this experience.

My intention is not to minimize or to romanticize our experience of adolescent homelessness and its resultant exposure to deprivation and cruelty, but only to illustrate that many of the most revered people in human history spent time either voluntarily or involuntarily homeless. Although homelessness was not volitional for most of us (but rather the result of a lack of familial and societal love and responsibility), we can still derive meaning from our experience. The psychic scarring and developmental disruption are profound for young people when the illusion of safety and refuge ideally provided by parents is abruptly shattered (whether through being kicked out for being queer or due to abuse and/or neglect). In addition to the horrors we encounter when we are thrust onto the streets, those who survive can gain an indomitable strength, rare insights into the human condition and compassion.

Remember that you are not alone. Many queer youth have walked this dangerous, tedious and often lonely path before you and not only survived to tell the tale, but thrived.

Shifting My Pack

Sassafras Lowrey

If I were to tell my story to you simply, it would go like this: when I was seventeen, I left my mother's house. She drank too much. My stepfather raped me. My mother beat me up. The police weren't much help. I moved in with friends. They kicked me out because I was gay. I lost everything important.

I don't think about it much now.

For a long time, I let that be the story I told to friends who asked if I was going "home" for Christmas. I told this story to anyone who asked careless questions that assumed I had a biological family expecting me on Thanksgiving like they did. It's a simple story. It's a quick story that I can tell without thought or feeling.

That is not the whole truth of what happened to me. My life has never been simple. My family has always been incomprehensible. My experience defies the narratives both of how children are supposed to grow up and who homeless youth are believed to be. Like the story of my childhood, my memory is complicated. It doesn't come easily or chronologically.

Sometimes it is in the complexity that the truth is most evident.

My parents have never been prosecuted for the war crimes they committed. They strode free as I hunted for the scattered puzzle pieces of the war–torn land that is my mind. The aftermath of greedy hands are forever etched onto my topography. Boundaries redrawn, borders erected, but the old maps remain, buried in my cerebellum. Yet still, hands grope wildly in the night. Bombs drop within my temporal lobe, their screeching plummet also a piercing screaming. Hands reach for me through tangible darkness, pulling me backwards to that house with the arborvitae and the brown paint that hid all their secrets. I wake fearing that the last seven years are only a dream, and that I'm back, my body a general's pawn.

◊◊◊◊◊◊

But there was a life outside of the war too. The apparent life of a kid.

I was a dog kid, a show kid. I could name any breed of dog accepted by the American Kennel Club (AKC) and identify it on sight. I was agilitygirl200@ hotmail.com, an elite level competitor. I was an Honors English A student. I was a Future Farmer of America—a red, white and blue country, beef–eating hick. I could spit and cuss and flip a lamb.

My mother's home was never stable. My bedroom closet held evidence: it looked like a recycling center stacked high with her attempt at hiding the green, glassy aftermath of two bottles of cheap grocery–store wine a day.

Fermented grapes are the smell I associate most with death.

My mother has been committing suicide since before I was born. Every day a slow–motion fall towards drowning. Her body submerged, pickled, trapped below the surface. On benevolent days, I think of her as a helpless lab experiment, body locked in a mason jar of ethanol, the prop of a professor's lecture or the victim of a mad scientist. But there is no denying she slid into the sparkling liquid, no pretense of a held breath. She has never gestured for the surface.

Living with my mother was never easy, but within the confines of her home, came my first shaky attempt at created queer family. Ultimately I wanted no part of the humans who had borne me. I was never one of them. We all knew this. They tried to deny it, then bound me to them with claims of blood right and honor. I knew family could mean so much more.

I left the first time at four, finding kinship in the drooling grin of every dog on the playground of my preschool. I'd press face to withers and inhale. In my heart, I left forever at six. I built my own family, my own pack. It didn't matter that I was still forced to live within her home. My dog, Peepers, became the only family that mattered. For years, I refused to speak to people. Sitting silently in the back of every classroom, I longed for the chance to run away from the crowds on the playground and back to my house, back to my room where we could play catch and hide under the covers.

My mother knew what was most important to me. From second grade on, she made sure I remembered that foster care wouldn't heed how much I loved him. My created family kept us trapped. Late at night, I whispered into Peeper's drooping ears that we would leave as soon as I could figure a safe way out. When I walked down the brick stairs for the last time Sunday, September 9, 2002, at age seventeen, I carried his ashes with me.

Sunday, September 9, 2002: I destroyed my first family. The truth bursts vessels, soaking my mother, grandmother, grandfather, stepfather, aunts, uncles, cousins and brothers in my blood. By the time the clots were washed away, I was gone. People always say the truth will set you free, but it is also a prison. The truth–teller becomes the criminal.

I was the only kid I knew who had someone arrested, let alone a parent. Polaroids whizzed in oversaturated interrogation rooms, bruises fresh on my face and arms. I was seventeen and terrified as officers recounted stories of how her acrylic nails clung in desperation to the chipped white molding of the doorjamb before her body was dragged down the red brick stairs. Her knuckles, still white with strain, groped for the black wrought iron banisters. Her eyes were gray, glazed, unable to focus on the flashing lights or the golden badges glimmering under the porch lamp. I'd betrayed her, and now she sat sobering in the county jail. She'd made me promise no matter what, I would never tell all the secrets that lived within the walls of our pretty, little house at the edge of suburbia. There was no going back.

My mother pleaded guilty to felony assault. I was her victim, but then I signed the paperwork, crisp, white and in triplicate to set her free. I refused to testify. The district attorney told me if we went to trial, she would go to jail for a long time, and that her teaching license would be revoked. She had worked hard for that license. When I was four, my mother went back to school and became a teacher. Education was everything to her. It was supposed to save her from a crumbling marriage, from the physical violence she suffered at the hands of my stepfather, from her own working–class roots of which she was so deeply ashamed.

The district attorney told me if I we went to court, she would be convicted for first degree assault and endure those consequences. Instead, I gave her a plea bargain: she spent the next six months in outpatient recovery where she pretended to get sober. She kept her teaching license and still drinks herself to sleep. I say I couldn't bring myself to destroy my mother's dreams, but really I stayed silent to save myself. Leaving with my freedom was revenge enough.

◊◊◊◊◊◊

Cindy knew things at home weren't good.

She was the first adult I'd ever told about the years of constant abuse I'd witnessed. For the first couple of years of our relationship, I only told her about my stepfather, how I'd watch my mother's body crumple at the bottom of the hall stairs. It was Cindy's voice I repeated like a prayer when, at fifteen, I looked him in the eyes and told him to leave for good. My mother lay cowering at his feet. He'd never expected me to stand up to him. My mother's jewelry box splintered against the sheetrock, and then he stormed past me, out of the house and out of my life.

A year later, I started to tell Cindy about my mother. My mom hated the dog shows, so she let me travel all over the region with Cindy, who loved them. On late night drives, we'd confess pieces of our pasts. She started to fear for my safety.

The summer before my senior year of high school, the last summer I lived with my mother, things got worse. Her behavior became more erratic, and I became more isolated. I made the mistake of first outing my gay male best friends to her, and then in August, myself. Things were bad before she knew I was gay, but once she did, everything got worse. The only time I left her sight was at dog shows.

For the first time, Cindy and others began noticing the bruises. I halfheartedly tried to save my mother, made excuses. I said I had run into things. No one believed me; I didn't want them to. I started to fear if I didn't find a way out soon, my mother would devour me.

Sunday, September 9, 2002: we left a dog show event at the Vancouver fairgrounds, and Cindy drove me straight to my county sheriff's office. She sat with me as I filed charges, my arm swollen and discolored from being flung into the entertainment cabinet the night before. My eye black and puffy from where her fist had landed when I tried to go to bed.

◊◊◊◊◊◊

Where I come from, kids don't get kicked out. There aren't programs, systems or shelters.

Where I come from, we're suppose to keep our family secrets. No one saw the signs because they didn't want to. We were the perfect family. Dogs were the most important thing to me and were the only reason I told.

When I left my mother's house, I took my pack: Snickers, a miniature schnauzer and Flash, a shetland sheepdog. I moved in with my coach, Cindy, who was more than a coach to me. She was my best friend and the first butch I ever loved. I never told Cindy I loved her. She never loved me the way I wanted her to, but that didn't matter.

The foster care system never got a chance to own me. I disappeared deeper into Oregon wilderness with Cindy, and they looked the other way. Even the court hadn't known what to do with me. My school said they'd never had to "deal with a kid like [me] before." Since I would turn eighteen in nine months, the court told me it would be too much work to have me emancipated, and it wasn't worth the trouble to put me in the foster system. I was lucky to have an adult friend who wanted me and my dogs. "Stay out of trouble" was the best advice the victim's advocate could provide.

Cindy and I left the sheriff's station together, drove past the dump and turned left at the Oregon Trail memorial, past where the streetlights ended. To the left was a llama ranch, and to the right, the shell of a flooded–out trailer. We made a left on the first road past the fork, wound our way down the hill and turned on the gravel drive behind the horse arena. Home.

From my bed, I could see the creek that ran vein–like through the property. On a hill overlooking the rainbow of dog agility equipment, I found paradise.

◊◊◊◊◊◊

That first night, her husband cooked us steak, the bloody meat sizzling on the grill as I sat in borrowed sweats. When we were alone, she asked if I was "over that gay thing." Her eyes pleaded. I knew the survival of my pack depended on my lies. I gave her everything she wanted, but lying always catches up in the end.

I fantasized that Cindy was my lover.

I was the vice–president of my high school's first Gay–Straight Alliance. I'd just dyed my waist–length hair fuchsia. Classmates threatened to show me what it was like to be with a real man. I read everything gay I could find under "homosexuality" in the library. I was rainbowgirl2002 on AOL instant messenger. I changed the "he's" to "she's" in every country love song I fell asleep to.

On Friday, February 8, 2002, I came home from school to find my room ransacked: drawers upturned, with library books that were always neatly piled between dresser and window, now splayed open and vulnerable across the floor. My journal lay open upon the bed, turned to a page about desire—a story I'd written about being cradled in the arms of a masculine woman on a snowy sleigh ride like the one we'd taken with friends the week after Christmas.

I put my room back together before we sat down to dinner with her husband. Cindy never spoke of what she saw—lesbian love stories stacked carefully between faded math and science books, snuck out of the Oregon City Library, shoved deep in my backpack after check out.

My world was rewinding; I kept my heart leashed in a controlled formal heel. I wanted to tell her it wasn't true, that it was all a joke. She knew better.

Cindy and I left the next morning for a dog show. Entrance fees were prepaid, and neither of us could comprehend not going. Five dogs crated in the back of the van, the silence was punctuated only by her occasional humming to the radio, her scarred forearms tense and those strong hands white–knuckling the steering wheel. When she thought I was sleeping, I stole glances in her direction.

We spent a mostly silent weekend together in Everett, Washington. The frigid fairgrounds provided little relief from the storm brewing within her travel trailer. We fought once—an altercation that landed me locked out of the trailer with my dogs in the middle of the night. I spent two hours walking around the fairgrounds to keep them warm before she let us back inside. I thought I could make it okay, that I could convince her to love me like the child she'd never had or desired. She could never forget what she'd seen.

Monday, February 11, 2002: I sat on the cracked linoleum. The grimy beige phone cord slinked around the corner from the student center of my sprawling semi–rural/semi–suburban high school. Classmates rushed past me, late to their third period classes. I pressed the receiver to my ear; I could hear Cindy's labored breathing. She told me never to come back. I picked Everett fairground dirt from my gray sneakers as she spoke. We'd fought that morning before she dropped me off at school, but I never saw this coming. She told me my dogs were gone to me. I thought we had created family. I thought I had a home and land, but she took that too. I had no family left to me.

Dogs had been my life. Going to live with Cindy was an assurance that I wouldn't lose my boys; that Snickers and Flash would be with me; that we would keep competing; and that most of all, we would never be separated. Living with my mother, I'd always been careful to make sure AKC registration was in my name. As a child, I'd always insisted on making the vet appointments to insure a paper trail of ownership. I couldn't lose my family.

When Cindy told me never to come home, she took my pack. I had no home, no job, no choice but to abandon them. Their small bodies strained at the leather leashes in her husband's hand. His knuckles grew white as he worked to keep them from following me down the long gravel drive the night she let me come to retrieve my belongings that she'd haphazardly packed for me.

Did you know that a pack will fight to the death to protect one of its own? They will forgo escape routes to stay behind. They do not leave, no matter the pain. The ultimate trust. They will never give up until their bodies fail.

Perhaps I was human after all. I'd saved myself, but failed my pack.

◊◊◊◊◊◊

March 2002: I spent the month couch–surfing with the family of my best gay boyfriend, Josh. His older sister was at college, so there was an empty bedroom in the bottom of the dairy barn turned house. Sympathetic ex–hippies, they had raised two queer kids. They weren't keen on me going to the group home that the county found in desperation when I was again homeless; besides, I did the dishes.

I called my court–appointed victim's advocate to tell her where I was. She said I should forget "the gay thing" and go home. She said I had a mother who loved me, that I should be "normal." She didn't understand leaving had been my one chance at survival. I stayed with them for four weeks, until I couldn't handle that county anymore. In every field was planted a memory of the life that was taken from me.

When I left Josh's house, the court officials told me just not to get in trouble in the remaining months before I turned eighteen. I was a minor living on my own. I became illegal. Survival became dependent upon being invisible. It required slipping into shadows when walking home later than city–imposed curfews. It meant being grateful for the ability to rent a room without windows. The house's owners were willing to turn the other way and to ignore the three months until my eighteenth birthday—so long as I stayed in the basement and didn't make much noise.

I stopped being friends with the kids at school. SAT scores couldn't have been more disconnected from the reality I was seeing in the city. I was paying rent, buying groceries and commuting two hours by bus each way to finish high school. My friends were sleeping under bridges and in abandoned buildings while everyone at my school was picking prom dresses. I found packs of kids like me. Together we walked down Burnside in big boots, studs, work pants, rainbow hair spiked high, our faces filled with metal. We called ourselves freaks.

For the first time, I didn't feel alone. I'd always chosen to hide the truths of my original home from childhood friends, but here, on late night walks past Paranoia Park, I wasn't afraid to tell about bodies ripped open and wine bottles hidden in closets. For the first time, similar histories were reflected back to me. Under the streetlights, we compared scars. In the darkness, we traced their borders running fingers and tongues over their edges. Human packs began forming. Our lives' discarded jigsaw pieces snapped together into a mismatched mosaic.

I survived because I created family.

◇◇◇◇◇◇

Family found me and grabbed me with thick hands, pulling me away from destruction, statistics and death wishes.

By the summer of 2002, I graduated from high school and made family of a butch couple who had built a life in the county that I'd had to flee. My moms fought to swagger. They made an old house a home, constructed 1,500 feet of decking with their callused hands. They built a pond for visiting ducks and kept careful records of every bird species that visited their property. They survived heart disease, cancer, seemingly uncontrollable diabetes and multiple knee surgeries.

My butch moms scooped me up and held me tightly, adopting me in our own queer way. Our family never wanted the validation of the courts. They risked everything to take me in. They chose me as their kid. I was a rescue just like their pack of beagles, taken from backyard chains and given a first chance at family, at home.

That first summer, I'd visit their house and fall asleep instantly on their couch, my new puppy nestled in my arms, their dogs at my feet. They had me over at least once a week, and it was the only time I slept. In my apartment, my dreams were punctuated by the sounds of screaming.

I lived in their house for a few weeks when I came back from a failed Southern romance that left my heart raw and my senses charred. I rarely slept in my little attic room. I much preferred to spend my nights on their couch — it was the only place I knew where I was safe, watched and protected.

From 2002 through 2004, I had an address, but I was still homeless. I moved fourteen times during those years. My friends stopped bothering to write down my address. The post office forwards took weeks to wind their way to my mailbox. I used wooden crates as furniture because they doubled as boxes when every few months, I would pile them high with books and clothes in the backseat of someone's borrowed car.

◇◇◇◇◇◇

In every apartment, every shack turned house, I was searching for an end to the fear. I have a friend who describes her panic attacks as the aftermath of a decomposing star. In some ways, that's the closest I'll ever get to describing the way it feels to unravel in the IKEA showroom because picking a living room set is an emotional experience bringing forth years of instability, of moving every few months to escape homophobic, transphobic neighbors who chased me out of neighborhood after neighborhood.

Around me, I see the bodies of fallen selves, all the lives I lived, or could have lived, and the life I have now. Suddenly New York City, seven years and three–thousand miles don't seem so far from Oregon farms and abandoned logging roads. Memories are the weapons I fear most. They sneak upon me as skillfully as any sniper, my limbic system seared by their gunpowder. Shrapnel comes to rest deep within.

This will be the third year my partner and I have lived in this apartment. We pay way too much rent; the security door is rarely locked; our walls shake with the neighbor's bass. But it's home.

It's the longest I've lived anywhere since I left my birth mother's house. This is my home. We chose the color that coats the walls. We own the furniture that fills each small room. In my living room sits an altar to the dogs lost, on my right arm a memorial to their presence in my life. I share my life with a dog who means everything to me. This is my family.

My biggest fear is that I will lose everything I have built.

Once you've lost home, you're never the same. You will spend the rest of your life questioning whether you had it to begin with, and if it's ever possible to find it again. I survived because I created family, because I found a pack that would fight for me.

This the closest to home I think I will ever get.

Lesbian, Gay, Bisexual and Transgender Youth: An Epidemic of Homelessness[1]

Nick Ray

Former Senior Policy Analyst, National Gay and Lesbian Task Force's Policy Institute

The stories in this remarkable anthology demonstrate all too clearly the terrible impact of homelessness on America's lesbian, gay, bisexual and transgender (LGBT) young people. Many of the stories recount episodes of abuse, neglect and withholding of love and affection. However, these stories also show us that young LGBT people affected by homelessness can be tremendously resilient, determined and focused individuals—determined to climb out of the dire circumstances in which they find themselves, and committed to building good, productive, healthy lives as contributing adult members of society. Some have found this challenge harder than others, while some have exceeded perhaps their own dreams for themselves.[1]

What remains true, regardless of the specific challenges they have faced or the outcomes they achieved, is that each story is part of the fabric of the collective LGBT homeless youth experience, which is not a problem that will disappear anytime soon. Indeed, the crisis of homelessness among LGBT youth has reached epidemic proportions.

LGBT Youth: An Epidemic

The U.S. Department of Health and Human Services estimates that the number of homeless and runaway youth ranges from 575,000 to 1.6 million per

---

1. Excerpted and edited with permission from the National Gay and Lesbian Task Force Policy Institute and the National Coalition for the Homeless. Ray, N. (2007). *Lesbian, gay, bisexual and transgender youth: An epidemic of homelessness*. New York: National Gay and Lesbian Task Force Policy Institute and the National Coalition for the Homeless. The report from which this essay is excerpted was published by the National Gay and Lesbian Task Force ("The Task Force") in conjunction with the National Coalition for the Homeless (NCH). It includes contributions from senior staff at five homeless youth service providers who perform amazing work with homeless LGBT youth. Each agency contributed material to the report based on a detailed discussion of the model programs they have developed to improve service delivery to this population.

year.[2] When it comes to counting or estimating the number of LGBT youth experiencing homelessness, the existing literature provides a wide range of figures. Despite this variance, there is a consensus that LGBT youth represent a significant proportion of the homeless youth population.

These numbers convinced The Task Force to investigate in collaboration with the National Coalition for the Homeless (NCH). Our analysis of the available research suggests that between 20 percent and 40 percent of all homeless youth identify as LGBT;[3] of these many studies, some studies have suggested that racial and ethnic minorities may be overrepresented in the homeless youth population.[4] LGBT youth experience homelessness at a remarkably disproportionate rate, one that might well be considered to have reached epidemic proportions.

Few cities have conducted a large–scale count of homeless youth. As of the late 1990s, advocates could only estimate that upwards of 20,000 homeless youth were living on the streets of New York,[5] while a 2002 report suggested the number stood somewhere between 15,000 and 20,000.[6] In 2007, the city council provided funding to underwrite some of the costs associated with a count of homeless youth living on the streets of the city. This most recent count shows

2. Robertson, M. J. & Toro, P. A. (1998). *Homeless youth: Research, intervention, and policy.* United States Department of Health and Human Services. Retrieved June 3, 2005, from http://aspe.hhs.gov/progsys/homeless/symposium/3–Youth.htm.

3. See pages 11–14 of the full report and the addendum beginning on p. 162 for a more detailed summary of the available research on the proportion of homeless youth who identify as LGBT. Regarding the proportion of the U.S. population that identifies as LGB, the 1992 National Health and Social Life Survey found that 4.9 percent of men and 4.1 percent of women ages 18–44 report ever having a same–sex partner. The 2002 National Survey of Family Growth found that 4.1 percent of 18–44 year–olds identify as LGB. Analysis of 2006 National Exit Poll (NEP) data found that 3 percent of voters identify as lesbian or gay (the NEP did not allow respondents to identify as bisexual or transgender). NEP and Voter News Service (VNS) polls since 1996 have found the number of lesbian and gay respondents to range from 3 percent to 5 percent. The available research on the proportion of the U.S. population that identifies as transgender is too limited to permit an accurate estimation.

4. McCaskill, P. A., Toro, P. A. & Wolfe, S. M. (1998). Homeless and matched housed adolescents: A comparative study of psychopathology. *Journal of Clinical Child Psychology, 27*(3). Cited in Robertson, M. J. & Toro, P. A. (1998).

5. Holloway, L. (1998, July 18). Young, restless and homeless on the piers; Greenwich Village reaches out to youths with plan for shelter and services. *New York Times.* Retrieved September 20, 2005, from http://query.nytimes.com/gst/health/article–printpage.html?res=9C05E5DE1330F93BA257.

6. Nolan, T. (2004). Couch–Surfers: Invisible Homeless Youth. *In the Family.* p. 21–22.

a total of approximately 3,800 youth living on the streets of the city—still a frighteningly huge number. In 2004, the U.S. Conference of Mayors suggested that unaccompanied youth make up 5 percent of the total urban homeless population, up from 3 percent in 1998.[7]

In 1985, the National Network of Runaway and Youth Services (now the National Network for Youth) estimated that only 6 percent of homeless adolescents identified as gay or lesbian.[8] They have subsequently revised this estimate upwards to a range of 20 percent to 40 percent.[9] Other studies from the early to mid–1990s reported that 3 percent to 10 percent of homeless youth were gay or lesbian. However, more recent studies and ample anecdotal evidence from social service professionals suggest that the proportion of LGBT youth in the overall homeless youth population is significantly higher than their proportion in the U.S. population as a whole.

In one study, Clatts et al. estimate that among combined homeless and street–involved populations,[10] 35 percent are LGBT, while among street youth only, the figure might climb as high as 50 percent.[11] A study of unaccompanied homeless youth in Illinois reported a statewide figure of 14.8 percent who identified as LGB, "questioning" or "something else." According to a report published in 2005, in the city of Chicago and immediately surrounding Cook County, the rate for these groups was 23.1 percent and 22.4 percent respectively.[12]

In Decatur, Illinois, a youth group surveyed homeless youth and found that 42 percent identified as LGB, while service providers in Los Angeles estimated

7. U.S. Conference on Mayors (2004). *A status report on hunger and homelessness in America's cities: 2004.* U.S. Conference of Mayors. Retrieved September 22, 2006, from www.sodexhousa.com/HungerAndHomelessnessReport2004.pdf.

8. National Network of Runaway and Youth Services [now the National Network for Youth]. *To whom do they belong? A profile of America's runaway and homeless youth and the programs that help them.* Washington, DC: National Network of Runaway and Youth Services.

9. Dylan, N. (2004). City enters partnership to assist lesbian and gay homeless youth. *Nation's Cities Weekly, 27*(10).

10. Street–involved youth are those who have a home to which they can and often do return at night. However, for a multitude of reasons, they choose to involve themselves with youth living on the streets, often becoming accepted members of the community of youth. In New York City, for example, there are youth who skip school and/or stay out late at night to hang out with homeless youth on the Hudson River piers.

11. Clatts, M. J. et. al. (1998). Cited in Dame, L. (2004).

12. Johnson, T. P. & Graf, I. (2005, December). *Unaccompanied homeless youth in Illinois: 2005.* Chicago, IL: Survey Research Laboratory–University of Illinois Chicago. p. 46.

that between 25 and 35 percent of homeless youth there are lesbian or gay.[13] In Portland, Oregon, one homeless youth service provider estimated that its LGB clientele climbed from 20 percent[14] to approximately 30 percent of youth between 1993 and 1994.[15] The City of Seattle's Commission on Children and Youth found that approximately 40 percent of homeless youth identified as lesbian, gay or bisexual.[16] The recent count in New York City did provide a concrete number: one–third of all respondents self–identified as LGBT.[17]

Unfortunately, because of the fear many young people have about acknowledging to themselves or others during a survey that they are lesbian, gay, bisexual and/or transgender, these figures are potentially an *undercount* of the true proportion of LGBT homeless youth. What is absolutely clear is that regardless of the actual number of LGBT people in the overall population, a disproportionate share of the nation's homeless youth identify as LGBT.

The Causes of Homelessness

Family conflict is the primary cause of homelessness for all youth, LGBT or straight. Specifically, familial conflict over a youth's sexual orientation or gender identity is a significant factor that leads to homelessness or the need for out–of–home care.[18] According to one study, 50 percent of gay teens experienced a negative reaction from their parents when they came out, and 26 percent were kicked out of their homes.[19] Another study found that more than one–third of runaway and throwaway youth who are homeless experienced a physical assault

13. Cited in Truong, J. (2004). *Homeless LGBT youth and LGBT youth in foster care: Overview.* The Safe Schools Coalition. Retrieved June 3, 2005, from http://www.safeschoolscoalition.org/RG–homeless.html.

14. Ibid.

15. Krisberg, K. (2002). Oregon clinic increases health care access for homeless youth. *Nation's Health, 32*(7).

16. Dylan, N. (2004). City enters partnership to assist lesbian and gay homeless youth. *Nation's Cities Weekly, 27*(10).

17. Freeman, L. & Hamilton, D. (March 26, 2008): *A Count of Homeless Youth in New York City.* Empire State Coalition of Youth and Family Services. Retrieved June 19, 2009 from, http://www.citylimits.org/images_pdfs/pdfs/HomelessYouth.pdfTbl.1.

18. Clatts, M. J., Davis, W. J., Sotheran, J. L. & Atillasoy, A. (1998). Correlates and distribution of HIV risk behaviors among homeless youth in New York City. *Child Welfare, 77*(2). See also Hyde, J. (2005). From home to street: Understanding young people's transitions into homelessness. *Journal of Adolescence, 28.* p. 175.

19. Remafedi, G. (1987). Male homosexuality: The adolescent perspective. *Pediatrics,* (79).

when they came out:[20] Hagan and McCarthy created a measure of "coercive parental control" (i.e., physical abuse) and found that a one–point increase on this scale correlated with doubled odds of a young person ending up homeless on the street.[21] In addition, parental or sibling drug use at home sets a dangerous precedent and creates a dangerous environment for young people.

Yet escaping abusive familial behavior necessarily leads to new forms of instability for youth.[22] In a study of homeless youth in Minnesota, 24 percent cited substance abuse at home as a reason for not being at home,[23] as did 30 percent in a study of homeless youth in Los Angeles.[24]

This kind of instability and lack of permanence in a young person's life can go back many years.[25] In and out of different care settings for all manner of reasons, including violence, criminality and drug or alcohol abuse in the home, many homeless youth do not feel a sense of belonging to the place arbitrarily labeled "home."[26] Indeed, all of these challenges combined can come to constitute an experience that leads to youth leaving a shelter or foster home because they actually feel safer on the streets.

Impact on LGBT Youth

A review of the research reveals that young people experiencing homelessness face a multitude of ongoing crises that threaten their chances of becoming healthy, independent adults, whether LGBT youth are homeless on the streets or in temporary shelter.

Mental Health

While all homeless youth are disproportionately prone to psychological issues compared with the general population, LGBT homeless youth are especially

20. Wilder Research. (2005). *Homeless youth in Minnesota: 2003 statewide survey of people without permanent shelter.* Author. Retrieved June 26, 2006, from http://wilder.org/download.0.html?report=410.

21. Hagan, J. & McCarthy, B. (1992). p. 547.

22. Sanchez, R. (2004, December 20); Thompson, S. J. et. al. (2001).

23. Wilder Research. (2005). p. 7.

24. Hyde, J. (2005). p. 175.

25. Kipke, M. D., Palmer, R. F., LaFrance, S. & O'Connor, S. (1997). Homeless youths' descriptions of their parents' child–rearing practices. *Youth and Society, 28*(4).

26. Miller, P. et. al. (2004). p. 741; Wilder Research. (2005).

vulnerable to depression, loneliness, psychosomatic illness,[27] withdrawn behavior, social problems and delinquency.[28] These findings are not merely the result of sympathetic researchers' efforts to highlight a problem. The U.S. Department of Health and Human Services acknowledges that LGBT youth live in "a society that discriminates against and stigmatizes homosexuals," making them more vulnerable to mental health issues than heterosexual youth.[29] This vulnerability is magnified for LGBT youth who are homeless.

Research has documented high rates of depression and substance abuse among sexual minorities as well as alarmingly high rates of suicide and suicidal thoughts.[30] One study in 2004 found that significantly more LGB youth had thoughts of suicide than did their heterosexual peers (73 percent compared to 53 percent), and one–half of LGB youth had attempted suicide at least once, compared to one–third of heterosexual youth.[31]

The results of other studies are equally disturbing. For example, in a study of youth in Massachusetts, half of the LGB–identifying youth had contemplated suicide.[32] In 2005, the National Runaway Switchboard estimated that a lesbian, gay, bisexual, transgender and/or questioning youth commits suicide every five hours and forty–eight minutes, and that 30 percent of gay and bisexual males attempt suicide at least once.[33]

27. McWhirter, B. T. (1990). Loneliness: A review of current literature with implications for counseling and research. *Journal of Counselling and Development*, 68.

28. Cochran, B. N., Stewart, A. J., Ginzler, J. A. & Cauce, A. M. (2002). Challenges faced by homeless sexual minorities: Comparison of gay, lesbian, bisexual, and transgender homeless adolescents with their heterosexual counterparts. *American Journal of Public Health, 92*(5). pp. 774–775.

29. Gibson, P. (1989). Gay male and lesbian youth suicide, vol. 3: Preventions and interventions in youth suicide. In *Report of the secretary's task force on youth suicide*. Rockville, MD: U.S. Department of Health and Human Services.

30. Safren, S. A. & Heimberg, R. G. (1999). Depression, hopelessness, suicidality, and related factors in sexual minority and heterosexual adolescents. *Journal of Consulting and Clinical Psychology, 67*(6).

31. Whitbeck, L. B., Chen, X., Hoyt, D. R., Tyler, K. A. & Johnson, K. D. (2004). Mental disorder, subsistence strategies, and victimization among gay, lesbian, and bisexual homeless and runaway adolescents. *The Journal of Sex Research, 41*(4). p. 334.

32. Wen, P. (2002, October 22).

33. National Runaway Switchboard. (2005).

Substance Abuse

The combination of stressors inherent to the daily life of homeless youth leads many to abuse drugs and alcohol. For example, in Minnesota, five separate statewide studies found that between 10 and 20 percent of homeless youth self–identify as chemically dependent.[34] These risks are exacerbated for homeless youth identifying as lesbian, gay or bisexual (LGB).[35]

In recent years, increased attention has been paid to how LGBT youth might be at particular risk for substance abuse and associated health risks. Social stigma is a potent force behind the substance abuse problems of LGBT homeless youth. In an initial study, Rosario et al. hypothesized that LGB youth might be more inclined to turn to drugs and/or alcohol to cope with emotional distress that results from the social stigma of homosexuality.[36] Of the 154 LGB young people in the study, 93 percent of the females and 89 percent of the males reported lifetime use of any legal or illicit substance. In their six–state, eight–city study of public health issues, Van Leeuwen et al. confirmed that alcohol abuse was more common among LGB respondents (42 percent of sample) than non–LGB youth (27 percent of sample).[37]

Risky Sexual Behavior

All homeless youth are especially vulnerable to engaging in risky sexual behaviors because their basic needs for food and shelter are not being met.[38] Defined as "exchanging sex for anything needed, including money, food, clothes, a place to stay or drugs,"[39] survival sex is the last resort for many LGBT homeless youth. A study of homeless youth in Canada found that those who identify as LGBT were three times more likely to participate in survival sex than

---

34. Wilder Research. (2005). p. 27.

35. Van Leeuwen, J. M., Boyle, S., Salmonsen–Sautel, S., Baker, D. N., Garcia, J., Hoffman, A., & Hopfer, C. J. (2006). *Lesbian, gay and bisexual homeless youth: An eight city public health perspective.* Unpublished work.

36. Rosario, M. et. al. (1997). p. 455.

37. Ibid.

38. Rosenthal, D. & Moore, S. (1994). Homeless youths: Sexual and drug–related behavior, sexual beliefs and HIV/AIDS risk. *AIDS Care,* 6(1).

39. Cited in Anderson, J. E., Freese, T. E. & Pennbridge, J. N. (1994). Sexual risk and condom use among street youth in Hollywood. *Family Planning Perspectives,* 26(1). p. 23.

their heterosexual peers,[40] and 50 percent of homeless youth in another study considered it likely or very likely that they will someday test positive for HIV as a result of their sexual activity.[41]

In San Francisco, researchers studied ninety–three youth ages thirteen to twenty–five involved in homeless youth behaviors. Sixty–seven percent of the participants were living on the streets or in a shelter or transitional living program, and 31 percent admitted they had worked as prostitutes to survive.[42] In a separate study of youth working the piers in New York City, stories confirmed that "they began hustling as a way to earn easy money, and many reported that they were curious about the sexual experiences." However, as one youth commented, "After [the curiosity] goes away, it's just about money."[43]

In a study by Gaetz, transgender homeless youth were about three times more likely to engage in survival sex than the rest of the sample.[44] One study of transgender youth in New York who used the Safe Space program in the 1990s estimated that half of the transgender runaways worked as prostitutes, and 20 percent had tested positive for HIV.[45]

Survival sex is a desperate, risky behavior borne out of isolation and the lack of any tangible resources. It causes negative health outcomes for any homeless youth, but especially for highly vulnerable LGBT homeless young people. Those who have been abused while younger, especially sexually abused males, are particularly prone to taking sexual risks.[46]

Victimization of Homeless LGBT Youth

LGBT youth face the threat of victimization everywhere: at home, at school, at their jobs, and, for those who are out of their homes, at shelters and on the streets. According to the National Runaway Switchboard, LGBT homeless youth are seven times more likely than their heterosexual peers to be victims

40. Gaetz, S. (2004). Safe streets for whom? Homeless youth, social exclusion, and criminal victimization. *Canadian Journal of Criminology and Criminal Justice, 46*(6).

41. Kihara, D. (1999). Giuliani's Suppressed Report on Homeless Youth. *The Village Voice, 44*(33).

42. Fagan, K. (2006, January 9).

43. Maitra, R. (2002). p. 11.

44. Gaetz, S. (2004).

45. Pratt, C. (1995, June 18). The perilous times of transgender youth. *The New York Times.* p. CY7.

46. Taylor–Seehafer, M. & Rew, L. (2005).

of a crime.[47] While some public safety agencies try to help this vulnerable population,[48] others adopt a "blame the victim" approach, further decreasing the odds of victimized youth feeling safe reporting their experiences.[49] In Des Moines, Iowa, a particular part of town popular with homeless and LGBT youth is a haven for violence, but youth still choose to congregate there. The city police officers believe that the kids who are harmed are "volunteer victims" because they know it is a tough, potentially dangerous area, but they still choose to hang out there. The fact that alternatives might be severely limited or themselves unsafe for many of the youth is not considered.[50]

The Juvenile and Criminal Justice Systems

While there is a paucity of academic research about the experiences of LGBT youth who end up in the juvenile and criminal justice systems, preliminary evidence suggests that they are disproportionately the victims of harassment and violence, including rape. For example, respondents in one small study reported that lesbians and bisexual girls are overrepresented in the juvenile justice system, and that they are forced to live among a population of inmates who are violently homophobic.[51] Gay male youth in the system are also emotionally, physically and sexually assaulted by staff and inmates. One respondent in a study of the legal rights of young people in state custody reported that staff members think that "[if] a youth is gay, they want to have sex with all the other boys, so they did not protect me from unwanted sexual advances."[52]

47. National Runaway Switchboard. (2005).

48. Dylan, N. (2004). City enters partnership to assist lesbian and gay homeless youth. *Nation's Cities Weekly, 27*(10).

49. Bounds, A. (2002, September 24). Intolerance discussed at BHS school offers week–long focus on tolerance. *Boulder Daily Camera*. p. C3. See also: D'Augelli, A. R. & Hershberger, S. L. (1993). Lesbian, gay, and bisexual youth in community settings: Personal challenges and mental health problems. *American Journal of Community Psychology, 21*(4). See also: Arnott, J. (1994). Gays and lesbians in the criminal justice system. In *Multicultural Perspectives in Criminal Justice and Criminology*. Springfield, OH: C. Thomas Charles.

50. Anonymous. (2002, August 14). Out of control: At downtown's biggest street party. *Cityview*, Des Moines, Iowa. p. 9.

51. Curtin, M. (2002a). Lesbian and bisexual girls in the juvenile justice system. *Child and Adolescent Social Work Journal, 19*(4).

52. Estrada, R. & Marksamer, J. (2006). The legal rights of young people in state custody: What child welfare and juvenile justice professionals need to know when working with LGBT youth. *Child Welfare, 85*(2).

Transgender Homeless Youth

Transgender youth are disproportionately represented in the homeless population. More generally, some reports indicate that one in five transgender individuals need or are at risk of needing homeless shelter assistance.[53] However, most shelters are segregated by biological sex, regardless of the individual's gender identity,[54] and homeless transgender youth are even ostracized by some agencies that serve their LGB peers.[55]

Homeless transgender youth face similar safety and privacy concerns on the street, where discrimination against LGBT youth is rampant. Shelters often create unsafe, hostile environments by imposing gender–enforcing behavioral rules and dress codes, causing many transgender youth to wind up on the street, engaging in risky survival and coping behaviors.[56] Like homeless youth in general, trans–identified homeless youth are often reprimanded for their survival crimes by the criminal justice system, which exposes them to further violence and abuse.

The Federal Response

Since 1974, when the federal government first enacted the original Runaway Youth Act, there have been numerous pieces of legislation addressing youth homelessness. Most recently, the Runaway, Homeless and Missing Children Protection Act (RHMCPA) was signed into law by President George W. Bush in 2003 and was recently reauthorized in 2008.[57]

Among the most important provisions of this complex piece of legislation are programs that allocate funding for core homeless youth services, including basic drop–in centers, street outreach efforts, transitional living programs (TLP) and the National Runaway Switchboard. While the law does not allocate funding for LGBT–specific services, some funds have been awarded to agencies who work exclusively with LGBT youth, as well as those who seek to serve LGBT homeless youth as part of a broader mission.

---

53. Cited in Mottet, L. & Ohle, J. M. (2003). Transitioning our shelters: A guide to making homeless shelters safe for transgender people. http://www.thetaskforce.org/downloads/TransHomeless.pdf. Retrieved June 12, 2006, from http://www.thetaskforce.org/downloads/TransHomeless.pdf.

54. Ibid.

55. HCH Clinicians' Network. (2002, June).

56. Mottet, L. & Ohle, J. M. (2003).

57. Public Law 108–96 for fiscal years 2004 through 2008.

Unfortunately, homeless youth programs have been grossly under–funded, contributing to a shortfall of available spaces for youth who need support. In 2005 alone, due to this lack of funding, more than two–thousand–five–hundred youth were denied access to a TLP program for which they were otherwise qualified.[58] Additionally, over two–thousand youth were turned away from Basic Center Programs, which provide family reunification services and emergency shelter.[59] Working with a number of coalition partners the Task Force helped to secure an additional $10.5 million of federal funding in 2008, though this is still woefully short of the true level of investment that the government needs to make if it seriously wants to tackle this epidemic.

Lack of funding is not the only obstacle preventing LGBT homeless youth from receiving the services they need. In 2002, President George W. Bush issued an executive order permitting federal funding of faith–based organizations (FBOs) that provide social services.[60] While more and more FBOs are receiving federal funds, overall funding levels for homeless youth services have not increased in real terms. Consequently, there is a possibility that the impact of FBOs will not be to increase services to the homeless, but rather only to change *who* provides those services.

A number of faith–based providers oppose legal and social equality for LGBT people, which raises serious questions about whether LGBT homeless youth can access their services in a safe, nurturing environment. If an organization's core belief is that homosexuality is wrong, that organization (and its committed leaders and volunteers) may not respect a client's sexual orientation or gender identity and may expose LGBT youth to discriminatory treatment.[61]

---

58. Data compiled from the federally administered Runaway and Homeless Youth Management Information System (RHYMIS).

59. Cited in National Network for Youth. (2006, March 30). *Statement for the record of the National Network for Youth on FY 2007 Labor–HHS–Education–related agencies appropriations before the Subcommittee on Labor–Health and Human Services–Education–related agencies. Committee on Appropriations. U.S. House of Representatives.* Author. Retrieved September 11, 2006, from http:// appropriations.house.gov/_files/AnitaFriedmanTestimony.pdf#search=%22HHS%20capacity%20 of%20basic%20center%20program%22.

60. White House Office of Faith–Based and Community Initiatives. (2006). President Bush's faith–based and community initiative. Author. Retrieved August 31, 2006, from http://www. whitehouse.gov/government/fbci/mission.html.

61. BBC News. (2006, September 15). *Profile: Pope Benedict XVI.* Author. Retrieved October 12, 2006, from http://news.bbc.co.uk/2/hi/europe/4445279.stm.

For example, an internal Salvation Army document obtained by the *Washington Post* in 2001 confirmed that "...the White House had made a 'firm commitment' to issue a regulation protecting religious charities from state and city efforts to prevent discrimination against gays in hiring and providing benefits."[62] Public policy that exempts religious organizations providing social services from non-discrimination laws in hiring sets a dangerous precedent. If otherwise qualified employees can be fired simply because of their sexual orientation or gender identity/expression, what guarantee is there that clients, including vulnerable LGBT homeless youth, will be supported and treated fairly?

Experiences of LGBT Homeless Youth in the Shelter System

The majority of existing shelters and other care systems are not providing safe and effective services to LGBT homeless youth.[63] For example, in New York City, more than 60 percent of beds for homeless youth are provided by Covenant House, a facility where LGBT youth report that they have been threatened, belittled and abused by staff and other youth because of their sexual orientation or gender identity.[64]

At one residential placement facility in Michigan, LGBT teens, or those suspected of being LGBT, were forced to wear orange sweatshirts to alert staff and other residents. At another transitional housing placement, staff removed the bedroom door of an out gay youth, supposedly to ward off any homosexual behavior. The second bed in the room was left empty, and other residents were warned that if they misbehaved, they would have to share the room with the "gay kid."[65]

---

62. Allen, M. & Milbank, D. (2001, July 12). Rove heard charity plea on gay bias. *Washington Post.* Retrieved September 25, 2006, from http://www.washingtonpost.com/ac2/wp–dyn/A48279–2001Jul11?language=printer. p. 1.

63. Mallon, G. P. (1997). The delivery of child welfare services to gay and lesbian adolescents. In Central Toronto Youth Services, *Pride and Prejudice: Working with lesbian, gay, and bisexual youth.* Toronto: Central Toronto Youth Services.

64. Email communication between the author and the Empire State Coalition of Youth and Family Services. New York, NY. See also: Murphy, J. (2005). Wounded pride: LGBT kids say city–funded shelter for the homeless breaks its covenant. *Village Voice.* Retrieved September 10, 2006, from http://www.villagevoice.com/news/0517,murphy1,63374,5.html.

65. Both examples were confirmed in personal conversations between the author and social service agency staff who had worked at the offending agencies, or had worked with youth who had resided at those agencies.

LGBT homeless youth at the Home for Little Wanderers in Waltham, Massachusetts, have reported being kicked out of other agencies when they revealed their sexual orientation or gender identity. Many also said that the risks inherent to living in a space that was not protecting them made them think that they were better off having unsafe sex and contracting HIV because they would then be eligible for specific housing funds reserved for HIV–positive homeless people in need.[66]

Some Good News

The Home for Little Wanderers is just one of the service providers that is doing amazing work with homeless LGBT youth. These agencies set an example for their peers, either focusing explicitly on providing appropriate care to LGBT youth in need or ensuring that their agencies treat all clients with respect regardless of sexual orientation or gender identity, even though this imperative can sometimes be a challenge for the agency itself. Five such agencies contributed to our report, and these service providers represent the diverse range of agencies working with homeless LGBT youth, though they are by no means the only agencies doing great work. Along with the Home for Little Wanderers, Green Chimneys in New York City, the Ruth Ellis Center in Detroit and Ozone House in Ann Arbor, Michigan, represent the best of the best.

Policy Recommendations

In light of the tremendous challenges this community is facing, I offer eleven specific policy recommendations that may begin to alleviate this crisis.

> 1. *Reauthorize and increase appropriations for federal Runaway and Homeless Youth Act (RHYA) programs.* The release of our report served as a catalyst not just for the Task Force's lobbying efforts on this issue, but also as a critical tool to help with bringing on board partners who have previously focused on homelessness more broadly and who, in some cases, were not used to working on youth or LGBT aspects of the issue. The U.S. Department of Health and Human Services' figures (cited earlier) make clear that extra funding is needed. The numbers of turned–away youth can be equated to a capacity shortfall of at least eleven basic centers and at least fifteen transitional living projects.

---

66. As confirmed by Colby Berger, LGBT training manager at Waltham House.

2. Develop a national estimate of the incidence and prevalence of youth homelessness through gathering data that aids in the provision of appropriate services. Reasons to overcome the methodological and political barriers to obtaining a more accurate estimate of the population of homeless youth nationwide include:

- Obtaining a more accurate idea of how many youth, and with what experiences and needs, are experiencing homelessness;

- Aiding in the most efficient, appropriate allocation of scarce resources; and

- Providing crucial data that will teach us much about this community and provide direction for additional research to further inform decision–making in this area.

3. Authorize and appropriate federal funds for intervention programs targeted to LGBT youth. Drop–in centers, funded through current federal homeless youth programs and often connected to street outreach programs, are crucial to helping LGBT youth who have run away or who are experiencing homelessness for many reasons. The benefits include peer bonding, recreation, safety, public health and youth development. Such centers might work with housed youth as well as those experiencing homelessness.[67]

4. Broaden the U.S. Department of Housing and Urban Development's (HUD) definition of "homeless individual" to include living situations common to homeless youth. Inconsistencies and incompleteness in counts of homeless people contribute to the difficult task homeless advocates have in seeking more funds from the federal government and others. What constitutes "homeless" for one agency is merely "sleeping on a friend's couch" for another.

---

67. Many youth–specific and general LGBT community centers offer programming for LGBT youth, but the mechanics of funding such programs can be haphazard. For example, in Tucson, Arizona, the Eon youth program is a collaboration of Wingspan, Southern Arizona's LGBT Community Center, Pima County Health Department and the Southern Arizona AIDS Foundation. A single stream of federal funds that enabled groups like Eon to cover the basic operations of an LGBT youth center would make things far simpler.

HUD's definition of homeless individuals should be broadened to encompass the diverse living arrangements of people in homeless situations. The definition of "homeless individual" in the federal statute restricts the meaning of that term to persons living on the street, emergency shelters and other locations "not fit for human habitation." Excluded from this definition — and thus from federal homeless assistance — are individuals and families living in doubled–up arrangements, transitional housing, motels and hotels when there is no suitable alternative. The generosity of a friend providing a couch to sleep on should not constitute being adequately housed.

These are the very living arrangements commonly deployed by unaccompanied youth. Consequently, the exclusion of these living arrangements from the federal definition of homeless individuals renders HUD and other federal homeless assistance programs inaccessible to thousands of homeless youth and young adults.

5. *Establish funding streams to provide housing options for all homeless youth. Require that recipients of these funds are committed to the safe, appropriate treatment of LGBT homeless youth with penalties for noncompliance, including the loss of government funding. These funds would supplement federal appropriations.* In addition to funding allocated to them from federal programs, more than a dozen states have developed their own funding streams to provide runaway and homeless youth service providers with a pool of money for prevention, outreach, emergency shelter and transitional housing services. Some of the existing state programs are competitive, inviting agencies to apply for funds, while others are managed and distributed by the states in a non–competitive process. Since the needs of homeless youth exceed the funds from any one source, we strongly encourage all states to research the possibilities for creating state– and local–level funding complementary to RHYA funds.

For example, in Berkeley, California, the city council has set aside increased funding for programs to meet the needs of homeless youth specifically because, as a member of the city's homeless commission noted, "Young people often avoid adult shelters because they...don't want to be associated with the older homeless crowd."[68] In 2002, the city provided the Youth Emergency Assistance Hostel (YEAH!) program $5,000 of public funds towards a total budget of $22,000 to run a twenty–week winter shelter.[69] By 2004–2005, the city's contribution had risen to approximately $40,000 of an $119,000 annual operating budget, a clear sign of the city's commitment to helping an underserved population.[70]

Other cities have also made commitments to youth homeless programs. In New York City, the city council in 2006 approved $1.2 million of funding specifically for LGBT youth.[71] These funds were allocated to three agencies to secure the necessary licenses to expand the services they could offer to this population. Licensing is obviously a crucial requirement to ensure that all youth are being cared for in appropriate spaces by appropriately qualified staff. However, the process can be time–consuming and expensive, rendering it almost impossible for smaller agencies to qualify to receive funds that might enable them to increase their efforts working with LGBT or other homeless youth.

6. *Permit dedicated shelter space and housing for LGBT youth.* Theoretically, all shelter space should be safe for LGBT youth, but this is not the case. The absence of sufficient safe space for LGBT homeless youth has resulted in the creation of LGBT–only facilities to accommodate the immediate need for shelter housing options. If grant–making child welfare agencies were to approve funding for programs that specialize in serving LGBT runaway

68. Bhattacharjee, R. (2006, February 28). Program aims to remove homeless youth from the streets of Berkeley. *Berkeley Daily Planet.* Retrieved August 19, 2006, from http://www.yeah–berkeley. org/Berkeley_Daily_Planet_28Feb06.pdf.

69. Hoge, P. (2004, February 6). Home for the night: Alameda County's new shelters for young adults open many doors. *San Francisco Chronicle.* Retrieved August 19, 2006, from http://www. yeah–berkeley.org/SF_chronicle_6Feb04.pdf.

70. Youth Emergency Assistance Hostel. (2006). Our program. Author. Retrieved August 19, 2006, from http://www.yeah–berkeley.org/page2.php.

71. Siciliano, C. (2006, March 2). At long last, progress on homeless LGBT youth. *Gay City News.* Retrieved August 19, 2006, from http://www.gaycitynews.com/gcn_509/atlonglastprogress. html.

and homeless youth, it could make a tremendous difference to the lives of these young people.

It is important to acknowledge that LGBT–specific housing is not necessarily a useful or desired option for *all* LGBT youth. In fact, some youth may not want to live in a space that identifies them as LGBT. Further, the creation of LGBT–specific spaces is not intended to shift responsibility away from mainstream providers. The goal is for both mainstream and LGBT providers to have the capacity and knowledge to serve LGBT youth effectively and compassionately.

7. *Repeal existing laws and policies that prevent single and partnered LGBT individuals from serving as adoptive and foster parents.* The federal government has documented the vast number of children who are awaiting adoption: 119,000 as of 2003.[72] In addition, many youth are not formally in the child welfare system but would nevertheless benefit from a stable and "permanent, loving home."[73]

Same–sex couples and LGBT individuals should not be restricted from helping to meet this need solely because of their sexual orientation or gender identity. Unfortunately, six states restrict adoption and/or foster care by LGB people and/or same–sex couples.[74] Additionally, only 24 states and the District of Columbia permit second–parent adoption by a same–sex partner.[75] Many youth awaiting placement in foster or adoptive homes are older,

---

72. U.S. Children's Bureau. (2005). *The AFCARS report.* Washington, DC: Administration on Children, Youth and Families.

73. The Evan B. Donaldson Adoption Institute. (2006, March). *Expanding resources for children: Is adoption by gays and lesbians part of the answer for boys and girls who need homes?* New York, NY: The Evan B. Donaldson Adoption Institute.

74. See National Gay and Lesbian Task Force. (2006, July). Foster care regulations in U.S. Author. Retrieved September 13, 2006, from http://www.thetaskforce.org/downloads/FosteringMap_06.pdf and National Gay and Lesbian Task Force. (2006, July). Adoption laws in the U.S. Author. Retrieved September 13, 2006, from http://www.thetaskforce.org/downloads/adoption_laws_06.pdf.

75. National Gay and Lesbian Task Force. (2005, January). Second parent adoption in the U.S. Author. Retrieved September 13, 2006, from http://www.thetaskforce.org/downloads/secondparentadoptionmap.pdf.

ill or suffering from the consequences of physical or mental abuse. There is a growing body of evidence that LGBT people are adopting these children, who in their own best interests are often placed with LGBT families when social workers are determined to turn a blind eye to official regulations.[76]

There are already a great many children with one or more gay or lesbian parents, with estimates ranging from 1.6 million to 14 million.[77] Among the authors who have analyzed parenting by same–sex couples and LGBT individuals is Leslie Cooper of the ACLU's LGBT Rights Project. In her recently published, thorough review of academic literature, she finds nothing to suggest that LGBT people cannot be equally effective as parents as their non–LGBT counterparts,[78] a finding seconded by the nonpartisan, academically affiliated Evan B. Donaldson Adoption Institute whose staff also conducted a review of the existing literature on adoption by gay and lesbian parents.[79]

8. *Discourage the criminalization of homelessness and the activities inherent to the daily lives of people experiencing homelessness.* The National Coalition for the Homeless and the National Law Center on Homelessness and Poverty have reported the criminalization of many life–sustaining activities associated with homelessness nationwide.[80] Many cities and towns are being creative in their

76. Sullivan, R. T. (1994).

77. Patterson, C. J. & Freil, L. V. (2000). Sexual orientation and fertility. In Bentley, G. & Mascie–Taylor, N., *Infertility in the modern world: Biosocial perspectives.* Cambridge, England: Cambridge University Press.

78. Cooper, L. & Cates, P. (2006). *Too high a price: The case against restricting gay parenting.* (2nd ed.) New York, NY: American Civil Liberties Union Foundation. See also: The American Academy of Pediatrics (AAP), the American Academy of Family Physicians, the Child Welfare League of America, the National Association of Social Workers, and the American Psychological Association all recognize that gay and lesbian parents are just as good as heterosexual parents and that children thrive in gay– and lesbian–headed families. For example, see: Patterson, C. J. (1995). *Lesbian and gay parenting: A resource for psychologists.* Retrieved from http://www.apa.org/pi/parent.html.

79. The Evan B. Donaldson Adoption Institute. (2006, March). p. 10; Ryan, S. D. (2000). Examining social workers' placement recommendations of children with gay and lesbian adoptive parents. *Families in Society, 81*(5).

80. The National Coalition for the Homeless & The National Law Center on Homelessness and Poverty. (2006). *A dream denied: The criminalization of homelessness in U.S. cities.* Washington, DC:

efforts to force homeless people, including youth, out of the public eye. Criminalization efforts are directed at people experiencing homelessness via laws against sleeping, sitting or laying down under certain conditions in certain parts of a town or city, and more subtly, by permitting selective enforcement of other ordinances or even targeting people who feed the homeless in public spaces.[81] Pushing people away from downtown areas and into the suburbs takes them away from needed services and serves only to deny the existence of a critical social problem. Often, the result is involvement with the criminal justice system and ultimately being further away from escaping the streets altogether. These approaches do not address the problems that lead to homelessness, nor are they likely to achieve long–term success in moving everyone into safe, affordable housing.

9. Require all agencies that seek government funding and licensure to serve homeless youth to demonstrate awareness and cultural competency of LGBT issues and populations at the institutional level and to adopt nondiscrimination policies for LGBT youth. As part of the initial licensing process that any facility must go through and the renewal of that license in subsequent years, we recommend that state agencies regulating facilities that care for youth mandate the following:

- Private and nonprofit entities seeking a license to care for youth must demonstrate that administrators and staff have completed appropriate cultural competency training regarding the provision of safe spaces for LGBT youth prior to issuance of the license.

- Agencies must agree to adopt, post and enforce a state– mandated nondiscrimination policy including sexual orientation and gender identity / expression prior to being licensed to care for youth, with in–service training on the policy available annually. Training should be provided not

---

The National Coalition for the Homeless & The National Law Center on Homelessness and Poverty. See also, The National Coalition for the Homeless. (2004).

81. Ibid. p. 9.

only to staff but also to all prospective clients during the intake process.

Related to this provision in the licensing process, a non-discrimination performance standard should be established. Such a standard would ensure that ongoing measurement of each agency's performance would include consideration of their demonstrated capacity to provide fair, equal access for, and treatment of, LGBT youth.

10. *Mandate individual–level LGBT awareness training and demonstrated cultural competency as part of the professional licensing process of all health and social service professions.* Staff employed by organizations providing care and support to youth must meet certain educational and licensing standards. There is also an ethical aspect to this recommendation because "[t]he social work code of ethics mandates that social workers must not undertake a social service unless [they] have the competence or can acquire the competence to provide that service."[82] In many instances, the solution to this dilemma is to deny adequate service rather than to secure the necessary training.

States must ensure that LGBT homeless youth are accessing services not just in a space where their safety and equal treatment are directly related to the licensing process, but where individual staff cannot let personal biases translate into unfair treatment of any clients. Specifically, as part of licensing examinations, states should test a potential social worker or other counseling staff person's awareness of the specific needs of LGBT youth and the challenges they face in the social welfare system and beyond.

States must work with in–state education establishments that train the workers they hire to ensure that their relevant programs not only incorporate LGBT issues into the variety of classes that constitute an MSW program, for example, but also engage those programs in the development of coursework that is specific to the experiences of LGBT youth in the child welfare system. If schools know that their graduates will be tested on these issues as

---

82. Dame, L. (2004).

part of their licensing exams, then they will have an incentive to make any necessary curricular changes. Students will also know that ignorance of the issues will only hinder their performance on exams that ultimately dictate their ability to secure a job. Voluntary certification programs for "paraprofessional" youth workers should also include an LGBT awareness component.[83]

11. *Mandate LGBT cultural competency training for all state agency staff who work in child welfare or juvenile justice divisions.* Many state child welfare or juvenile justice staff are under–educated about the existence of LGBT clients and their particular issues. While potentially supportive of LGBT youth, many do not know how to raise or discuss LGBT issues with their clients. Cultural competency training is important to promote clear and open communication and to help staff recognize how to create a safe space for all the youth with whom they work.

Conclusion

Once implemented, these policy recommendations will help not only LGBT homeless youth but all youth abandoned by their families or forced to leave home. Research makes clear that despite the multitude of challenges they face day in and day out, many of these youth are remarkably resilient and have benefited from programs like those provided by Green Chimneys, Ozone House, the Ruth Ellis Center and the Waltham House at the Home for Little Wanderers.

The report by the Task Force and the National Coalition for the Homeless will continue to enlighten the service provider community to the scale of this epidemic and to bring renewed attention to an issue that has been inadequately addressed for far too long. While the stories in *Kicked Out* put a face on the research and the work such agencies already do, the policy recommendations in the report indicate that the government has a critical role to play in curbing this epidemic. Regardless of sexual orientation or gender identity, every young person deserves a safe, nurturing environment in which to grow and learn.

---

83. Paraprofessionals include youth outreach workers, youth developers, health education and risk reduction specialists and case managers.

Sylvia's Place Resident

Samantha Box

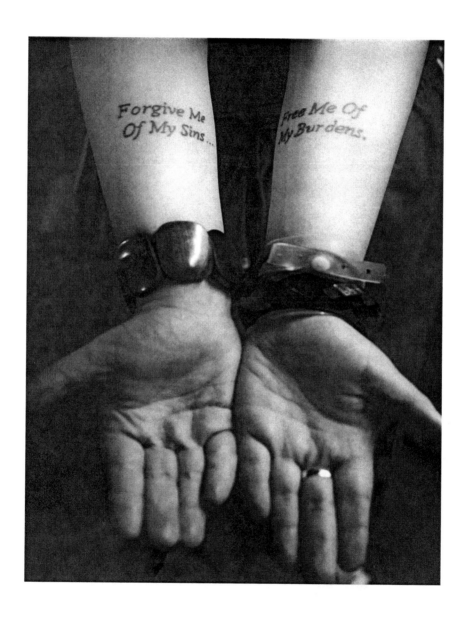

Afterword

Karen Staller, Ph.D.
Associate Professor, University of Michigan, School of Social Work

In case you haven't already noticed, this is a unique book.

I have been working with, and writing about, runaway and homeless youth for over twenty years, and never have I seen gathered in one place such a compelling chorus of voices from those who have experienced being "kicked out" of their family homes. The stories are at times heartrending as well as uplifting, and reflect both the pain and the resilience so often demonstrated by young people who find themselves severed prematurely from their biological family emotionally and physically.

Sadly the narratives also share a universal timelessness. For those of us who have worked among young people of similar ilk, they are all too familiar. Nonetheless, the power of putting them together in a single volume is palpable, and the lessons that can be drawn from them are many.

In the spirit of the personal narratives presented here, perhaps I should offer a word about my credentials (or lack thereof) at the beginning of this essay. If I were to tell my story to you simply, it would read in stark contrast from the ones laid out in the proceeding pages.

I grew up in a happy home in a small town. My father was a university professor, and my mother was a "domestic engineer" or "the minister of internal affairs" (as my parents joked about her full–time, round–the–clock job of mothering). I can't remember either of them ever raising a hand against me. They never yelled, and I can't recall a family argument. I never contemplated running away (and in fact was desperately homesick during short separations for summer camp). I never once worried where I would sleep at night. Hunger—to the extent I ever experienced it—was self–induced (better known as "dieting"). I loved attending school and did well. I never once questioned my sexual orientation nor wondered about my gender identity. In sum, I grew up in a position of privilege in all regards.

That said, all this dependency, comfort and security can come with its own set of small costs. At some point, I had to leave home and to strike out on my own, but for someone who had lived such a sheltered life, the weaning process was a bit bumpy. Immediately following my graduation from college, I married. The marriage was motivated, at least in part, by my fear of independence and insecurity about my ability to take care of myself. I soon learned that storybook marriages and happy endings are not a God–given right. In my mid–twenties, I unceremoniously, even irresponsibly, fled a marriage that made me unhappy, as I finally sought personal freedom and the space to figure out who I was.

What I discovered—when I went wandering—was a big exciting city and a runaway and homeless youth program. While employed at this shelter in New York City in the mid–1990s, I found young people not unlike the ones you have met on the pages of this book. They came from every area of the United States as well as from around the globe. They were of every race and ethnicity. They came from affluent homes as well as poor ones. They were straight, gay and bisexual; male, female and transgendered. Some had serious health problems, mental illnesses and substance abuse issues, but others did not. Some had been charged with crimes, and others had not. They were so diverse that no single label could capture the variety. What they tended to share, like the narratives of young people in this book, was the lack of a stable, loving home on which to rely.

These youth introduced me to decidedly different kinds of families than the one I had known. They introduced me to a variety of survival skills for negotiating life on their own, including the art of couch-surfing, street survival and intermittent shelter use. What astonished me at the time was that these young people seemed already to possess a set of skills that I was only beginning to develop for myself. I marveled at their ability to create families and the fierce loyalty and support they provided each other. They were independent, spunky, resilient and had gained great insight from living at the margins. They came to play Virgil to my Dante, and served as my constant guides in, around and of a netherworld I had never known existed.

My memories of these youth are like a colorful collage. Some of them came and went so quickly I never knew what ultimately happened to them. But early on, in an attempt to make sense of them, I tried to write down their stories. Some of these accounts have been published, but most have not.[1] But unlike the narratives reflected on the pages of this book, the ones I captured were filtered through my lens and perspective. Invariably they ended up being not so much about the youth in question, but rather my attempt at making sense of the lessons I had learned from them.

Some of my memories of these youth are of unadulterated joy, like that of the spontaneous song and dance performance of Madonna's then–popular "Vogue" by a small group of young men in my office. The lyrics of the song spoke directly to them: *"You try everything you can to escape the pain of life that you know/ You long to be something better than you are today,"* and then promised that there was a *"place you could get away"* called a *"dance floor."* The dance floor—for their complete reenactment of the music video—turned out to be the space in front of my office desk.

But there are other memories that are much darker. Two particularly haunt me. One involved the death of one of my all–time favorite clients, an exuberant young man with a mane of tangled blonde hair and the fervent desire to become a drummer in a rock band. We never learned the specific details surrounding his death—it had something to do with a cross–dressing, sexual hustling tryst gone terribly wrong—but what was clear was that he bled to death of a knife wound in the hallway of an abandoned tenement building in a seedy neighborhood a few blocks from the shelter. The second involved the solemn gathering of my staff around the hospital bed of young man dying of AIDS whose last wish was that his only worldly possession—a small portable TV—be given to his partner. It was a poignant and tragic moment at the same time.

Armed with these life experiences, I went back to school for my Ph.D. in social work. Today I teach at the University of Michigan School of Social Work, and I sit on the board of my community's runaway and homeless youth service provider, Ozone House.

These darker stories from my past are a reminder why some social scientists have dubbed "kicked out" youth as a "high–risk" or an "at–risk" population; in fact, scholars from many disciplines have studied these "at–risk" youth for decades. Frankly the picture that gets painted from their efforts is pretty gloomy. Academics have documented a long list of factors associated with running away

---

1. See: Staller, 1997.

and being homeless. They include acute and chronic health problems,[2] sexual risk factors and behaviors,[3] including pregnancy, HIV and AIDS,[4] crime and delinquency,[5] substance abuse,[6] and/or mental health problems.[7]

After four decades of research, you can get a more nuanced understanding of these factors by reading this book. For example, study after study has concluded that youth run away from home because of family conflict.[8] "Family conflict" is used as a sterile variable to measure predictors of homelessness. The proceeding pages of this book offer contextual understanding for what "family conflict" looks and feels like.

For years, social scientists have devised ingenious ways to count the population and to grapple with its size and basic characteristics. In the gold standard of these enumeration studies conducted by Hammer, Finkelhor & Sedlak, (2002), they concluded that in 1999, "1,682,900 youth had a runaway/thrownaway episode"—nearly 1.7 million a year—and of those, 71 percent (1,190,900) were considered "endangered during their runaway/throwaway episode." Again, through the pages of this book, you can attach some meaning to what "endangerment" is or what an "episode" might look like.

---

2. Council on Scientific Affairs, 1989; Deisher & Rogers, 1991; Ensign, 1998; Farrow, Deisher, Brown, Kulig, & Kipke, 1992; Sherman, 1992; Wright, 1991.

3. See: Clatts, Goldsamt, Yi, Gwadz, 2005; Forst, 1994; Greene, Ennett, & Ringwalt, 1999; Halcon & Lifson, 2004; Hotaling, Finkelhor, 1988; Kipke, Simon, Montgomery, Unger, & Johnson, 1997; Pennbridge, Freese, & MacKenzie, 1992; Tyler, Whitbeck, Hoyt, & Cauce, 2004; Zimet, Sobo, Zimmerman, Jackson, Mortimer, Yanda, & Lazebnik, 1995.

4. See: Allen, Lehman, Green, Lindegren, Onorato, Forrester, et. al., 1994; Athey, 1991; Clatts, 1998; English, 1991; Goulart & Mandover, 1991; Moon, McFarland, Kellogg, Baxter, Katz, MacKellar, & Valleroy, 2000; Rotheram–Borus & Koopman, 1991; Rotheram–Borus, Song, Gwadz, Lee, Van Rossem, & Koopman, 2003.

5. See: Baron & Hartnagel, 1998; Baron & Hartnagel, 1997; Chapple, Johnson, & Whitbeck, 2004; McCarthy & Hagan, 1995.

6. See: Baron, 1999; Booth, Zhang, & Kwiatkowski, 1999; Chen, Tyler, Whitbeck, & Hoyt, 2004; Forst, 1994; Greene, Ennett, & Ringwalt, 1997; Johnson, Whitbeck, & Hoyt, 2005; Kipke, Montgomery, Simon, & Iversen, 1997; Kipke, Simion, Montgomery, Unger, & Johnson, 1997.

7. See: Bao, Whitbeck, & Hoyt, 2000; Edelbrock, 1980; Feitel, Margetson, Chamas, Lipman, & Nathan, 1992; Grigsby, 1992; Slesnick & Prestopnik, 2005; Unger, Kipke, Simon, Montgomery, & Johnson, 1997; Whitbeck, Johnson, Hoyt, & Cauce, 2004.

8. See: Bass, 1992; Janus, 1987; Whitbeck & Hoyt, 1999; Crespi & Sabatelli, 1993; Garbarino, Wilson, & Garbarino 1986; Johnson & Carter, 1980; Mallet, Rosenthal, & Keys, 2005; Ringwalt, Greene, & Robertson, 1998; Whitbeck, Hoyt, & Ackley, 1997.

In these large, official government reports, the way we count things says something about the problem as we see it or at least conceptualize it. For example, social scientists fret over what labels to use to describe the population under investigation,[9] and we have experimented with terms such as *runaway, homeless, shoveouts, castaways, street youth, systems youth, throwaways* and *thrownaways*. But there is good reason why in the Hammer, Finkelhor & Sedlak (2002) study the once free-standing categories of "runaway" (those who voluntarily leave home) and "thrownaway youth" (those who have been "kicked out") have been collapsed into one category——runaway/thrownaway——separated only by a forward slash: it is virtually impossible to distinguish one group from the other. The researchers note that many "runaway" children have left home "as a result of intense family conflict or even physical, sexual, or psychological abuse. Children may leave to protect themselves or because they are no longer wanted in the home." These reasons will come as no surprise to the youth whose voices are reflected in this book. *Kicked Out* illustrates and transcends the slippery nature of these various labels.

In addition to estimating the overall number of youth, the Hammer, Finkelhor & Sedlak (2002) study attempts to make sense of the population's characteristics. For example, they collected information on the numbers of youth reported missing, the numbers of youth grouped by age, gender, race/ethnicity, the time of year they left home, the distance they ran, the duration of the episode, the dangers they faced, and the outcome of their "episode." Interestingly, nowhere in this study is there an attempt to determine the sexual orientation of the youth being counted. Nonetheless practitioners have repeatedly and consistently reported that disproportionately large numbers of gay, lesbian, queer and questioning youth are among the homeless street population. Until policymakers identify something as a concern or a potential area for investigation, social scientists don't collect the relevant data that helps to define the parameters of the problem. Again, you will find "data" about the lives of these "uncounted" youth on the pages of this volume.

In closing, I find myself ending with the same point that opened this essay: this book is special and offers extraordinary insight into the complicated lives of

---

9. See: Adams, 1980; Adams, Gullotta, & Clancy, 1985; DeMan, Dolan, Pelletier, & Reid, 1993; Duyan, 2005. Discussion of terminology included a distinction between the terms "throwaway" and "thrownaway." Early on in their work, the Finkelhor team switched the label from the former to the latter based on an argument that "throwaway" is too much about characterizing the youth as opposed to "thrownaway," which was about the action of the parent. In fact, "thrownaway" is closer to the idea of being "kicked out."

young people who have been "kicked out" of their family homes. Certainly, this book will speak to other similarly situated young people. Hopefully they all will find comfort and guidance here. *Kicked Out* will also speak to the dedicated practitioners, professionals and volunteers who work with these youth. In addition, I'm hoping that this volume will also find its way into the hands of one other audience of readers: the uninitiated.

My father once thanked me for the work I had done at the runaway shelter. Baffled, I asked why. He said because I had introduced him to a world and a population that he never knew existed. I am hoping that some of you, like my father, are learning about these young people for the first time. More importantly, however, I hope that these stories will compel you to take action no matter what your religious, political or personal persuasions might be. In battles for social justice, marginalized or disadvantaged groups need allies if they are to make progress. They need the legitimizing voices of the mainstream to join them and to share a sense of outrage. If this territory and these stories seem new and strange to you, please consider joining the efforts to help in any way you can. Practice tolerance; speak out against intolerance; intervene in the life of a young person you are concerned about; send a letter to a politician supporting policies mentioned on the preceding pages; write a check to the struggling runaway and homeless youth program or drop–in center in your community; volunteer to staff a crisis hotline; or donate needed items to a shelter.

The one thing I hope you won't do, after reading these compelling stories, is nothing.

References

Adams, G. R. (1980). Runaway youth projects: Comments on care programs for runaways and throwaways. *Journal of Adolescence*, 3, 321–334.

Adams, G. R., Gullotta, T., & Clancy, M. A. (1985). Homeless adolescents: A descriptive study of similarities and differences between runaways and throwaways. *Adolescence*, 20 (79), 715–724.

Allen, D. M., Lehman, J. S., Green, T. A., Lindegren, M. L., Onorato, I. M., Forrester, W., et. al. (1994). HIV infection among homeless adults and runaway youth, United States, 1989–1992. *AIDS*, 8 (11), 1593–1598.

Athey, J. L. (1991). HIV infection and homeless adolescents. *Child Welfare, 70,* 517–28.

Baron, S. W. (1999). Street youth and substance use: the role of background, street lifestyle, and economic factors. *Youth & Society,* 31 (1), 3–26.

Baron, S. W. & Hartnagel, T. F. (1998). Street youth and criminal violence. *Journal of Research in Crime and Delinquency,* 35 (2), 166–92.

Baron, S. W. & Hartnagel, T. F. (1997). Attributions, affect, and crime: street youths' reactions to unemployment. *Criminology,* 35 (3), 409–34.

Bass, D. (1992). *Helping vulnerable youth: Runaway & homeless adolescents in the United States.* Washington, D.C.: NASW Press.

Bao, W. N., Whitbeck, L. B., & Hoyt, D. R. (2000). Abuse, support, and depression among homeless and runaway adolescents. *Journal of Health and Social Behavior,* 41 (4), 408–420.

Booth, R. E., Zhang, Y., & Kwiatkowski, C. F. (1999). The challenge of changing drug and sex risk behaviors of runaway and homeless adolescents. *Child Abuse & Neglect,* 23 (12), 1295–1396.

Chapple, C. L., Johnson, K. D., & Whitbeck, L.B. (2004). Gender and arrest among homeless and runaway youth: An analysis of background, family, and situational factors. *Youth Violence and Juvenile Justice,* 2 (2), 129–147.

Chen, X., Tyler, K. A., Whitbeck, L. B., & Hoyt, D. R. (2004). Early sexual abuse, street adversity, and drug use among female homeless and runaway adolescents in the Midwest. *Journal of Drug Issues,* 34 (1), 1–21.

Clatts, M. C. (1998). Correlates and distribution of HIV risk behaviors among homeless youth in New York City: Implications for prevention and policy. *Child Welfare,* 77, 195–207.

Clatts, M., Goldsamt, L., Yi, H., & Gwadz, M. V. (2005). Homelessness and drug abuse among young men who have sex with men in New York City: A preliminary epidemiological trajectory. *Journal of Adolescence,* 28 (2), 201–214.

Council on Scientific Affairs, (1989). Health Care Needs of Homeless and runaway youth. *JAMA,* 262 (10), 1358–1361.

Crespi, T. D. & Sabatelli, R. M. (1993). Adolescent runaways and family strife: A conflict–induced differentiation framework. *Adolescence*, 28 (112), 867–878.

Deisher, R. & Rogers, W. M. (1991). The medical care of street youth. *Journal of Adolescent Health*, 12 (7), 500–503.

DeMan, A., Dolan, D., Pelletier, R., & Reid, P. C. (1993). Adolescent runaways: Familial and personal correlates. *Social Behavior and Personality*, 21, 163–168.

Duyan, V. (2005). Relationships between the sociodemographic and family characteristics, street life experiences and the hopelessness of street children. *Childhood: A global journal of child research*, 12 (4), 445–459.

Edelbrock, C. (1980). Running away from home: Incidence and correlates among children and youth referred for mental health services. *Journal of Family Issues*, 1 (2), 210–228.

English, A. (1991). Runaway and street youth at risk for HIV Infection: Legal and ethical issues in access to care. *Journal of Adolescent Health*, 12 (7), 504–510.

Ensign, J. (1998). Health issues of homeless youth. *Journal of social distress and the homeless*, 7 (3), 159–174.

Farrow, J. A., Deisher, R. W., Brown, R., Kulig, J. W., & Kipke, M. D. (1992). Health and health needs of homeless and runaway youth: A position paper of the Society for Adolescent Medicine. *Journal of Adolescent Health*, 13 (8), 717–726.

Feitel, B., Margetson, N., Chamas, J., & Lipman, C., (1992). Psychosocial background and behavioral and emotional disorders of homeless and runaway youth. *Hospital and Community Psychiatry*, 43 (2), 155–159.

Forst, M. L. (1994). A substance use profile of delinquent and homeless youths. *Journal of Drug Education*, 24 (3), 219–31.

Forst, M. L. (1994). Sexual risk profiles of delinquent and homeless youths. *Journal of Community Health*, 19 (2), 101–14.

Garbarino, J., Wilson, J., & Garbarino, A. (1986). The Adolescent runaway. In J. Garbarino, C. J. Schellenbach, & J. M. Sebes (Ed.), *Troubled Youth, Troubled Families*. NY: Aldine Publishers.

Greene, J. M., Ennett, S. T., & Ringwalt, C. L. (1999). Prevalence and correlates of survival sex among runaway and homeless youth. *American Journal of Public Health* 89 (9), 1406–1409.

Greene, J. M., Ennett, S. T., & Ringwalt, C. L. (1997). Substance use among runaway and homeless youth in three national samples. *American Journal of Public Health*, 87 (2), 229–235.

Goulart, M. & Mandover, S. (1991). An AIDS prevention program for homeless youth. *Journal of Adolescent Health*, 12 (7), 573–575.

Grigsby, R. K. (1992). Mental health consultation at a youth shelter: An ethnographic approach. *Child and Youth Care Forum*, 21 (4), 247–261.

Halcon, L. L. & Lifson, A. R. (2004). Prevalence and predictors of sexual risks among homeless youth. *Journal of Youth and Adolescence*, 33 (1), 71–80.

Hammer, H., Finkelhor, D., & Sedlak, A. J. (2002, October). NISMART–2 Second National Incidence Studies of Missing, Abducted, Runaway and Thrownaway Children. *Office of Juvenile Justice and Delinquency Prevention*.

Janus, M. D. (1987). *Adolescent runaways: Causes and consequences*. Lexington: Lexington Books.

Johnson, K. D., Whitbeck, L. B., & Hoyt, D. R. (2005). Substance abuse disorders among homeless and runaway adolescents. *Journal of Drug Issues*, 35 (4), 799–816.

Johnson, R. & Carter, M. M. (1980). Flight of the young: Why children run away from their homes. *Adolescence*, 15 (58), 483–489.

Kipke, M. D., Montgomery, S., Simon, T. R., Unger, J. B., & Johnson, C. L. (1997). Homeless youth: drug use patterns and HIV risk profiles according to peer group affiliation. *AIDS and Behavior*, 1 (4), 247–59.

Kipke, M. D., Montgomery, S. B., Simon, T. R., & Iversen, E. F. (1997). "Substance abuse" disorders among runaway and homeless youth. *Substance Use & Misuse*, 32 (7/8), 969–989.

Mallet, S., Rosenthal, D., & Keys, D. (2005). Young people, drug use and family conflict: Pathways into homelessness. *Journal of Adolescence*, 28 (2), 185–199.

McCarthy, B. & Hagan, J. (1995). Getting into street crime: the structure and process of criminal embeddedness. *Social Science Research*, 24, 63–95.

Moon, M. W., McFarland, W., Kellogg, T., Baxter, M., Katz, M. H., MacKellar, D., & Valleroy, L. A. (2000). HIV risk behavior of runaway youth in San Francisco: Age of onset and relation to sexual orientation. *Youth & Society*, 32, 2, 184–201.

Pennbridge, J. N., Freese, T. E., & MacKenzie, R. G. (1992). High–risk behaviors among male street youth in Hollywood, California. *AIDS Education and Prevention*, Fall Supplement, 24–33.

Ringwalt, C. L., Greene, J. M., & Robertson, M. J. (1998). Familial backgrounds and risk behaviors of youth with thrownaway experiences. *Journal of Adolescence*, 21 (3), 241–252.

Rotheram–Borus, M. J. & Koopman, C. (1991). Sexual risk behaviors, AIDS knowledge, and beliefs about AIDS among runaways. *American Journal of Public Health*, 81 (2), 208–210.

Rotheram–Borus, M. J., Song, J., Gwadz, M., Lee, M., Van Rossem, R., & Koopman, C. (2003). Reductions in HIV risk among runaway youth. *Prevention Science*, 4 (3), 173–187.

Sherman, D. J. (1992). The neglected health care needs of street youth. *Public Health Reports*, 107 (4), 433–453.

Slesnick, N. & Prestopnik, J. (2005). Dual and multiple diagnosis among substance using runaway youth. *American Journal of Drug and Alcohol Abuse*, 31 (1), 179–201.

Staller, K. M. (1997). Changing directions: Practicing—The bear–Zoe's turn. *Reflections: Narratives of Professional Helping*, 3 (3), 6–26.

Tyler, K. A., Whitbeck, L. B., Hoyt, D. R., & Cauce, A.M., (2004). Risk factors for sexual victimization among male and female homeless and runaway youth. *Journal of Interpersonal Violence*, 19 (5), 503–520.

Unger, J. B., Kipke, M. D., Simon, T. R., Montgomery, S. B., & Johnson, C. J., (1997). Homeless youths and young adults in Los Angeles: prevalence of mental health problems and the relationship between mental health and substance abuse disorders. *American Journal of Community Psychology*, 25 (3), 371–94.

Whitbeck, L. B. & Hoyt, D. R. (1999). *Nowhere to grow: Homeless and runaway adolescents and their families*. NY: Aldine de Gruyter.

Whitbeck, L. B., Hoyt, D. R., & Ackley, K. A. (1997). Families of homeless and runaway adolescents: A comparison of parent/caretaker and adolescent perspectives on parenting, family violence, and adolescent conduct. *Child Abuse and Neglect*, 21 (6), 517–28.

Whitbeck, L. B., Johnson, K. D., Hoyt, D. R., & Cauce, A. M. (2004). Mental disorder and comorbidity among runaway and homeless adolescents. *Journal of Adolescent Health*, 35 (2), 132–140.

Wright, J. D. (1991). Health and homeless teenager: Evidence from the national health care for the homeless program. *Journal of Health & Social Policy*, 2 (4), 15–35.

Zimet, G. D., Sobo, E. J., Zimmerman, T., Jackson, J., Mortimer, J., Yanda, C. P., & Lazebnik, R. (1995). Sexual behavior, drug use, and AIDS knowledge among Midwestern runaways. *Youth and Society*, 26 (4), 450–462.

Angie Guerra. In 2001, Angie graduated from the University of Wisconsin–Milwaukee with a Bachelor of Arts degree in Mass Communication and Journalism. Through her work with Visit Milwaukee, Milwaukee's convention and visitors bureau, and as a member of their LGBT Advisory Team, Angie soon discovered her passion for working within the LGBT community. This passion led her to seek a career working full–time for the Milwaukee LGBT Community Center. There she served in a number of different roles. As the first Director of Development, the Center grew, as did its staff. Angie then became the Director of Development and Marketing and eventually the Director of Communications. Angie has volunteered for various organizations promoting community, including the Women's Fund of Greater Milwaukee (as co–chair of the Lesbian Fund), the Hispanic Professionals of Milwaukee and the 41/26 Venture Committee, which recognizes LGBT leaders. As part of the Committee, Angie developed the "Gay Neighbor Billboard Campaign" to address job discrimination, adoption, parenting issues, marriage rights and violence against LGBT people. Angie serves on the Sedona Pride Association as secretary.

Anne Giedinghagen. I hate labels and other attempts to affix static meaning, yet I feel compelled to try to pin the world down with words. Hence, the labels I'd staple to myself, if forced to choose: lesbian, writer, student, seeker, androgynously femme. I was born and raised in what most Americans consider fly–over country: Kansas City. I write manifestos but am inherently distrustful of them; I seek definitions only in order to deconstruct them. I overuse parentheses and semicolons, and someday this poor stylistic habit will spiral out of control; I will write an entire essay composed of a single sentence (and associated parentheticals). Ultimately my goal is to give and receive the maximum amount of love and to accumulate the fewest possible moldering regrets. Besides the biological basics—nourishment and air—I can't survive without a steady stream of art supplies, fresh notebooks, touch and caffeine. I thank my chosen family for the support and encouragement that has sustained me all these years.

Anthony. For most of his life, Anthony has been advocating for the rights of marginalized people. As a product of the foster care and social services systems, he has overcome many struggles and has succeeded when people told him he would fail. He has been involved with many LGBTQ advocacy groups over the years. He was active in lobbying efforts as well as speaking on panels, facilitating GSA groups in high schools and performing with the troupe, Language of Paradox, with Kate Bornstein. He was one of the organizers for the first Oregon Queer Youth Conference. Anthony has been working with homeless youth for over five years. In his current position, he is working with homeless youth as an alcohol and drug counselor while he also attends school part–time to finish a bachelor's degree in social work. When Anthony has free time, he enjoys playing with his dog, spending time with friends, writing and creating mail art and collages.

Booh Edouardo received a BFA and MFA from the California Institute of the Arts. His artwork has been featured at many private and public venues. He currently studies as an MA candidate at San Francisco State University and volunteers as a tutor with Project Read at City College of San Francisco. More of his writing will be featured in the anthology, *Why Are Faggots So Afraid of Faggots*, edited by Mattilda (a.k.a. Matt Bernstein Sycamore).

E. F. Schraeder's creative work has appeared in *Blue Collar Review* and *New Verse News*. Since completing a doctoral program (ethics and social justice), she has worked and volunteered with community projects ranging from urban art programming to LGBTQ political organizing and has facilitated writing workshops and other programs for LGBTQ youth groups. A former college prof, she now works as Research Director for a health and wellness organization. When she isn't working or writing, she's with her dogs or gardening (or gardening with her dogs). When she isn't doing any of those things, and sometimes while she is, she is thinking about writing, dogs and gardening.

Jenn Cohen has worked as a professional circus performer and coach for over fifteen years. Her training includes: The Circus Space in London, Dell'Arte International School of Physical Theatre, sacred clown and buffoon work with Sue Morrison and Chinese acrobatics with Master Lu Yi at the San Francisco Circus Center. Jenn has performed extensively in ensemble theaters throughout the United States and as a solo aerial artist in Europe. She has coached children and adults in aerial and acrobatic work, from very beginners to advanced and professional students. In addition, she has worked as a choreography consultant for companies including Teatro ZinZanni (San Francisco) and UMO Ensemble (Seattle). Jenn was a tenured instructor at the San Francisco Circus Center from 2001 to 2004. Upon moving to Portland, Jenn worked with both Do Jump! and Pendulum Aerial Dance. She graduated *summa cum laude* with a BS in psychology from Portland State University and recently received her MA in Process Oriented Psychology from the Process Work Institute in Portland. In addition to her work with The Circus Project, Jenn offers workshops in aerial improvisation and Process Oriented Psychology across the globe.

Karen M. Staller is an Associate Professor at the University of Michigan School of Social Work in Ann Arbor, Michigan. She is the author of *Runaways: How the Sixties Counterculture Shaped Today's Practices and Policies*.

kay ulanday barrett is a performer, poet, educator and martial artist. Kay connects life as a pin@y–amerikan trans/queer navigating struggle, resistance and laughter in the u.s. In Mango Tribe and in solo work, kay has been featured in colleges, cafes and stages internationally. Honors include: *Venus Zine's* featured reader, LGBTQ 30 under 30 awards, Crossroads Fund's individual activist award, finalist in The Gwendolyn Brooks Open–Mic Award and a feature in the documentary film *BAKLA/TOMBOY: Filipino Gay & Lesbians in the U.S.* For kay's online swerve see: kaybarrett.net.

Kestryl Cael is a performer, activist, culture–maker and gender revolutionary. When forced to choose a label, he identifies as a transgender butch. Cael has appeared at conferences, colleges, festivals and local theatres across North America. Whether on–stage or behind a podium, he considers it his artistic duty to engage his audiences in provocative dialogue without letting them take him (or themselves) too seriously. Kestryl was a member of "The Language of Paradox," a performance ensemble founded and directed by Kate Bornstein. His writing appears in anthologies, and he is half of the performance duo, PoMo Freakshow. His one–queer show, *XY(T)*, has been described as "provocative," "brave," "appealingly wry," "heartfelt," "profound" and "essential."

Born in the USSR, **KJP** grew up in the Bensonhurst section of Brooklyn (back when it was pretty much all Sicilian). After getting kicked out at the beginning of his senior year in high school, KJP discovered a terminal inability to shut up, which led to years of advocacy for the rights of LGBT youth. Having recently graduated from Hunter College (CUNY), he is back in Bensonhurst, trying to get into law school, and he still can't shut up.

L. Wolf. I am a twenty–year–old genderqueer transboy who lives in Philadelphia. When I'm not writing, I spend my time in parks, reading and playing the guitar. I go to college for Liberal Arts, though I'm not sure what I want to do with my life. I own one cat and live with three others, plus a Russian tortoise and an amazing roommate. I love animals. I also struggle with depression, and I hope to someday put that behind me.

At twenty-seven years old, **Lucky S. Michaels** has experienced more than most people twice his age. Born in Ohio but raised in Detroit, Michigan, Lucky grew up with his three brothers and his single mother in a poverty–riddled environment, surrounded by people who were abusive and involved in drugs, all of which left his family homeless and struggling to survive. In the spring of 2003, Reverend Pat Bumgardner of Metropolitan Community Church of New York invited Lucky to help open Sylvia's Place, New York's first emergency shelter for LGBTQ youth and young adults; he began working as an overnight counselor. Lucky has been instrumental in the creation of the new Marsha P. Johnson Center, a drop–in center for LGBTQ youth and young adults that never closes. He continues to work full–time as the program's outreach director. Lucky is the author of *Shelter*, published by Trolley Books, which features his photographs of the residents.

Mx. Mirage. I am a radically queer trannyboi with a big mouth. I flip–flop between being femme and not being femme. I don't think I could ever live without my writing. It doesn't matter if other people hear me, or if I lose my sight; my words are always with me. I write and perform slam poetry and stories. The queer community has given me so much strength, I once thought I was invincible. I no longer believe so. When you catch a group of us together, we are one, and we are a force to be reckoned with. I believe in the abilities of queer youth and all queers, really. The possibilities are endless, and now's the time to stand for something. Much love and solidarity.

Nat Roslin. I'm a genderqueer, female–presenting lesbian who chooses words over fists. I can be in femme mode one minute and boi mode the next, finding my place as one of the boys at work or a so–called fag hag with a lot of gay male friends. I'm as happy surrounded by drag queens with feather boas and sequinned dresses as I am sitting on the beach, reading and not being amidst the attention. If there's one thing I've learned, it's that family is what you make it.

Sometimes your friends are the only family you can rely on. Thankfully I have a fair few in the queer community and several outside of the queer community who have helped me through some difficult times. I've always been encouraged to write, to let my feelings out in a way that makes me feel comfortable. Poetry, prose, anything that enables me to get my message out. I've learned the hard way that words have power. I believe that if we want to change the world, we have to fight for what we believe and to share our experiences with others. It's only by sharing our knowledge that we'll get to where we want to be.

Nick Ray took an absurdly circuitous route to the once–in–a–lifetime opportunity to serve as lead author for the National Gay and Lesbian Task Force's report on the epidemic of homelessness among LGBT youth. Born in England, he traversed the Rainbow Bridge at Niagara Falls and entered the United States for the first time at eighteen. Overwhelmed by the sheer bravado of Mario Cuomo placing a picture of himself on a billboard above the bridge, he determined then and there that he would, one day, return to these United States and make them his home. After completing a Diploma in Accounting and a BA in Politics and History at Oxford Brookes University, Nick moved to the United States for graduate school. Master's degrees in Political Science (University of Rhode Island) and Higher Education (University of Arizona) followed, interspersed with various (all short!) spells of usually gainful employment. In 2005, he joined the Task Force's Policy Institute and immediately began work on a project that became his signature piece of work. He has traveled the country discussing this work with LGBTQ youth, their families, their advocates and social service professionals who really DO want to do a better job of working with this underserved population. Nick currently serves as the Executive Director of 1n10. Nothing in his life to date, and it's been nearly four decades, has impacted or inspired him as much as the young homeless LGBT youth he's met in the course of this work. If you want to know where he is today, please look him up on Facebook!

Philip J. Reeves was born in Minnesota and grew up in a small town in North Dakota. After coming out as a gay man and losing his family, he found a new family, and they moved to Buffalo, New York, together. He finished his BA in English in May 2009, and is now pursuing a career in the law. Phil enjoys helping people and wants to use his experiences to make a difference.

Richard Hooks Wayman is the Senior Youth Policy Analyst for the National Alliance to End Homelessness. Formerly the Public Policy Campaign Director for the Minnesota Youth Service Association, Rich authored the Minnesota

Runaway and Homeless Youth Act and the Minnesota Youth Advancement Act. Rich received his Juris Doctor degree from the University of Iowa College of Law in 1992 and worked as a public interest litigator for the Legal Aid Society of Minneapolis for eight years, primarily focused on disability civil rights, housing and family law. Rich left Legal Aid to serve as the Collaborative Director of StreetWorks for six years. The StreetWorks Collaborative is comprised of ten youth–serving agencies providing street–based outreach to homeless and runaway youth in the Twin Cities metropolitan area. While at StreetWorks, Rich coauthored a national training manual, *StreetWorks: Best Practices and Standards in Outreach Methodology to Homeless Youth*. Rich also represents abused and neglected youth in juvenile court on a pro bono basis and has been a foster parent.

In third grade, **Sabine T. Vasco** won her school's creative writing contest with whimsical tales of her desire to grow up, move to Asia and shoot tigers—with her camera. The following summer, her grandmother destroyed her Wham! *Make It Big* cassette by launching it into a nearby construction site, which she attempted to recoup by enlisting the aid of her cousins. It was never recovered. At the age of nineteen, finding herself far from Asia, she wondered if perhaps photographing people could be just as fascinating as photographing tigers. She devoted herself to documenting the quixotic characters she encountered in her travels throughout the United States, Amsterdam, Colombia, Costa Rica and Mexico with her trusted 35 mm camera. Sabine has since worked in television and documentary productions for CNBC, PBS and the Sundance Foundation, hunting for the perfect shots as a photo and film archivist. She continues on her quest for tigers and the meaning of "growing up," but lives each day gloriously fueled by the words of Tom Robbins, "It's never too late to have a happy childhood."

Samantha Box, a photographer based in New York City, was born in Kingston, Jamaica in 1977. Having worked for many years in the media—first at the *New York Post*, a daily newspaper, and later at Contact Press Images, an international photojournalism agency—she decided in 2005 to attend the International Center of Photography, where she pursued a certificate in Photojournalism and Documentary Studies. Dedicated to photography that results in social change, she has spent the past four years photographing homeless lesbian, gay, bisexual and transgendered (LGBT) youth in New York City.

Stephanie Mannis is a full–time writer and part–time activist who lives in Philadelphia, where she has been heavily involved in GLBT organizations, such as The Attic Youth Center and Sapphire Fund. When not interviewing D–list celebrities or advocating for women, queers and animals, she spends much of her time wondering why she got an MBA and how she can get into a gender studies Ph.D. program despite it. She hopes to one day be quotable, if not footnotable.

Tenzin Chodron (born Jeanne Norris) is a transgender Buddhist monk who was homeless on the streets of San Francisco, Santa Rosa, Placer County, in the Oakland hills and on beaches in the Santa Cruz area of California intermittently between the ages of thirteen and twenty–one during the 1980s and 1990s. He was an exceedingly strange child who exhibited spiritual predilections and had aspirations to become a Fransican monk or a Jedi like Obi Wan Kenobi. He is a former AIDS caregiver and activist and is currently a proud parent, a transgender activist, a member of the Interfaith Dialogue group of Eugene, Oregon and a member of the Religious Response Network, a group that seeks to counter religious–based discrimination against queer people. He graduated *summa cum laude* from the University of Oregon Religious Studies department in 2007 after numerous interruptions in his education throughout years in foster care and while living on the streets. He is in the process of hormonal and surgical morphological gender reassignment and practices Drikung Kagyu and Nyingma Tibetan Buddhism and the teachings of the gender–bending Buddhist saint Ksitigarbha.

Tommi Avicolli Mecca is an out queer, southern Italian–American radical whose published works include *Between Little Rock and a Hard Place, Hey Paesan: Writings by Lesbians and Gay Men of Italian Descent* and *Avanti Popolo: Italian Writers Sail Beyond Columbus*. His current project is *Smash the Church, Smash the State: The Early Years of Gay Liberation*, a collection of articles on the post–Stonewall queer movement that has just been released by City Lights Books. His music (which he performs with The Peaceniks) is featured at youtube.com/avimecca, and his articles regularly appear at beyondchron.org. He lives in San Francisco.

About Homofactus Press

Thank you for purchasing a Homofactus Press book. Your purchase enables us to keep doing what we love to do: make great writing available to all people, regardless of income or ability. Learn more about our business practices at homofactuspress.com. You can also find us at twitter.com/homofactuspress as well as Facebook.

The mission of Homofactus Press is to publish books that discuss our complicated relationships to our bodies and identities, with all the complexities and contradictions such an endeavor entails.

If you enjoyed this book, please consider other Homofactus Press titles:

Self-Organizing Men, edited by Jay Sennett
The Marrow's Telling, by Eli Clare
Two Truths and a Lie, by Scott Turner Schofield
Cripple Poetics, by Petra Kuppers and Neil Marcus
Visible: A Femmethology, Volume 1, edited by Jennifer Clare Burke
Visible: A Femmethology, Volume 2, edited by Jennifer Clare Burke

When I was abused, the animal cops took me to safety. When my human came out as gay to his family, they abused him. But the people cops just sent him back until he ran away.

2009 © Jay Sennett.